Marx

Also available:

Durkheim
A Critical Introduction
Kieran Allen and Brian O'Boyle

Weber
Sociologist of Empire
Kieran Allen

MARX
THE ALTERNATIVE TO CAPITALISM

Kieran Allen

First published 2011 as *Marx and the Alternative to Capitalism*
by Pluto Press
345 Archway Road, London N6 5AA

This edition published 2017

www.plutobooks.com

British Library Cataloguing in Publication Data
A catalogue record for this book is available from the British Library

ISBN   978 0 7453 3742 5   Paperback
ISBN   978 1 7868 0201 9   PDF eBook
ISBN   978 1 7868 0203 3   Kindle eBook
ISBN   978 1 7868 0202 6   EPUB eBook

This book is printed on paper suitable for recycling and made from fully managed
and sustained forest sources. Logging, pulping and manufacturing processes are
expected to conform to the environmental standards of the country of origin.

Typeset by Stanford DTP Services, Northampton, England

Simultaneously printed in the United Kingdom and United States of America

Contents

Preface

We live in an era of tremendous inequality with 71 per cent of the world's population owning less than 3 per cent of the global wealth. Yet despite the evident failures of capitalism, there is a brazen flaunting of privilege in the eyes of the poor. Sometimes this is justified by reference to market forces which, apparently, obey a cold logic that takes no account of human sentiment. On other occasions, plain duplicity is used. Before his election, Donald Trump, talked about 'draining the swamp' yet afterwards he stuffed his cabinet with billionaires whose combined wealth is greater than many countries.

If sociology has any value, it must surely inquire into causes of inequality. It should not descend into such a level of abstraction that it does not connect with the world we live in. Nor should it adopt a ponderous tone by using academic jargon to show how clever its writers are. We need explanations for why a society which has the capacity to eradicate famine and poverty continues to create both.

This short book provides an introduction to the writings of Karl Marx. Its aim is to demonstrate the relevance of his theories to the modern world. It is addressed to students and workers who are critical of our current social relations and who wish to understand their dynamics in order to change them.

In Marx's time, there were a number of writers who spent considerable energy in describing a future utopian society. Marx thought *that this neglected the question of agency – of who or how* such a better society might be brought about. His writings on the specific ways an alternative society might be organised were therefore more limited. However, throughout his writings there is an implied alternative based on democratic participation. His notion of both economic and political democracy was on a scale barely imaginable to those who think that 'Western democracy' is the highpoint of human achievement. This alternative had nothing to do with the tyrannies that took the name of 'communism'. It was based on the possibility that human beings could collectively control the productive forces in order to enhance their own freedom.

This book is written from an agreement with that perspective.

Acknowledgements

This book has benefited considerably from comments, discussion and criticism that were provided to me.

I would like to thank Marnie Holborow, John Molyneaux, Margaret O'Regan, James O'Toole, Theresa Urbainczyk Gabriela Weberova, and Ruth Willats.

I would also like to thank Kulwant Gill for her constant support, encouragement and questioning.

Finally, this book is dedicated to my mother, Maura Allen, with whom I learnt to argue politics. I suspect she would not agree with much of the book's contents but it was her astute mind that forced me to clarify my ideas many years ago.

Introduction

As long as there is class division and social inequality, Karl Marx will be the most relevant social thinker of the twenty-first century. Consider the opulence of Dubai. Originally a tiny port for pearl fishermen, it has become a fantasy playground for the wealthy.[1] The Palm Island project contains 2,000 villas, 40 luxury hotels and shopping malls, which are supposedly visible from the moon. The ocean bed had to be dredged to create artificial islands, which mirrored the intricate shape of a palm tree. Coincidently, this also solved the 'beach shortage' problem[2] by creating private inlets for the super-wealthy. Another construction project, The World, was designed as a vast concrete map of the planet where individual 'countries' could be owned by consortia of property speculators. There is also an indoor ski resort with real snow in the middle of the desert and a special Tiger Woods Golf Course which consumes over four million gallons of water every day. The water supply for these projects came from desalination plants powered by burning gas. The demand was so high that the electrical grid, which also relied on gas, began to falter and Dubai turned to its US ally for help in building a nuclear power plant. At 145 million gallons of water a day, the rich of Dubai were so opulent that they needed a nuclear power plant just to meet their needs.

Dubai is just one extreme symbol of an uneven, class-divided world. According to UNICEF, about 26,000 children die each day in some of the poorest villages on earth.[3] One of the causes of their deaths is diarrhoea, for 1.1 billion people, or one in six people in the world, do not have adequate access to water.[4] Millions of women spend several hours every day in back-breaking toil, collecting water or finding the means to cook. Some 2.5 billion people rely on firewood, charcoal or making animal dung patties by hand to cook their meals.[5] Despite the vast technological capacities of the twenty-first century, a quarter of humanity lives without electricity[6] while 80 per cent lives on less than €70 a week.[7]

Marx was not the first person to write of class conflict but he was unique in suggesting that it was a driving force for how societies change. His vision directs our attention constantly to social class and this has become even more important in a world of soothing

1

images, which invite escapist fantasies. The magazine sections of many Sunday newspapers run features on Dubai's Burj Khalifa, the world's largest tower block. The reader is invited to ogle at a hotel interior decorated by Georgio Armani or the Atmosphere restaurant located on the 122nd floor and to imagine staying in one of its bedrooms as a VIP. By contrast, the Indian peasant woman gathering cow dung by hand is rendered invisible. The names, images and short biographies of children whose lives are struck short by diarrhoea are erased from existence by a culture in pursuit of the latest tittle-tattle on celebrities.

More than 150 years ago, Marx wrote that:

> It is true that labour produces wonderful things for the rich – but for the worker it produces privation. It produces palaces – but for the worker, hovels. It produces beauty – but for the worker, deformity. It replaces labour by machines, but it throws one section of the workers back into barbarous types of labour and it turns the other section into a machine. It produces intelligence – but for the worker, stupidity, cretinism.[8]

His words cut across a comforting escapism to ask: who were the builders of playgrounds like Dubai? Under what conditions did they work? How was the wealth created to fund these fantasy constructions? Answering Marx's questions means discovering, for example, that the opulence of Dubai rests on work undertaken by 600,000 workers who were recruited from Pakistan, India, Sri Lanka and Bangladesh. Often crammed seven to a room, in facilities located near open sewers, they live in labour camps out of sight of the wealthy. Despite claims about the new freedoms brought on by globalisation, their passports are often withheld to force them to work in blistering heat of over 100 degrees Fahrenheit.[9] However, as Marx predicted, these workers are not just victims, but also rebels and fighters. Despite threats of deportation, they have marched, rioted and gone on strike against their inhuman conditions in Dubai. Siding with, and celebrating, that resistance is also part of the vision of Marx.

Playgrounds like Dubai are only possible because the top 2 per cent of humanity hold 50 per cent of all personal wealth.[10] Numbered among them is Microsoft boss Bill Gates, who owns €40 billion, and the arch-speculator Warren Buffet, who owns €37 billion.[11] Which begs an obvious question: what possible reason could justify one person having €40 billion of the world's resources while a quarter of people do not even have electricity? In past centuries, people believed that huge inequalities of wealth were the result of God's design. God was supposed to have selected one family from the mass of humanity to be his representatives on earth and one of their number was given the honour of being a king or queen. Around them were formed concentric circles of nobles, courtiers, barons, knights and, somewhere in the dark periphery, the peasantry. These fables were shattered by Enlightenment writers of seventeenth- and eighteenth-century Europe, who thought that society originated in a 'social contract' to which people gave their consent. In the far distant past, they suggested, people came together and agreed to give up some of their individual freedom to found a state with a monarch at its head. In other words, inequality resulted from human action rather than God's design and so could be changed again in a more enlightened age. More radical figures, such as Rousseau went further in his *Discourse on the Origin of Inequality among Men* and argued that 'it is obviously contrary to the law of nature, however it may be defined ... for a handful of people to gorge themselves on superfluities, while the starving multitude lacks necessities of life.'[12]

These attacks on inequality were directed at a pre-modern society and its claims about blood and family lines. But what about modern society, where wealth arises from the normal workings of 'the market'? How do vast inequalities arise in a society where people are 'free to choose' whether to sell their labour or 'take a risk' and establish businesses? In a world where there is no compulsion to stay on the land, where people can buy and sell commodities, it is often suggested that wealth arises from initiative, innovation or simply excess human energy

Marx is the key thinker who cut through the rhetoric about market 'choice' to explain how class relations arise. He argued that behind the appearance of freedom a greater robbery is taking place than in any previous society. While a figure such as Bill Gates may see himself as a philanthropist, his ability to *be* a philanthropist rests on robbery and exploitation. The fact that no armed force is used or that no special privileges are claimed by him is irrelevant to Marx. His aim was to show how capitalist robbery arises automatically through the workings of the free market itself.

Marx's writings also resonate with a moral outrage against the system. When silk manufacturers employed children for ten hours a day, Marx coolly claimed that 'The children were quite simply slaughtered for the sake of their delicate fingers, just as horned cattle are slaughtered in southern Russia for their hides and fat.'[13] He denounced capital as 'vampire like, [it] lives only by sucking living labour, and lives the more, the more labour it sucks.'[14] But alongside this outrage, there is something more devastating at work – Marx aimed to provide a strategy for change.

Exposing injustices can be valuable but, strangely, it can also leave the moral critic passive or even embittered. If one believes that terrible wrongs are occurring but thinks that the majority of people simply accept them, one can easily dismiss one's fellow men and women. The 'brainwashed masses', it may be suggested, do not see or want to see the injustices all around them and so have become complicit in its operation. This moralism can lead to a cynical passivity or even acceptance of the present order because one thinks that only small reforms are possible. Marx provides an important starting point for breaking out of this negative mode of thinking by showing how change is possible.

Running through his writings is a vision that capitalism contains the seeds of its own demise. It has its own self-destruct button that needs to be pushed and so an end to capitalism is a real possibility. If he is right about this claim, then the critic of capitalism may not just be engaging in moral denunciation but may, through their practical activity, contribute to changing the world. This type of criticism is, of course, revolutionary and that is why universities face a difficulty in teaching Marx.

In modern universities the student is often treated as a consumer who can peruse alternative 'theories'. Just as one chooses between brands of washing detergent in a supermarket, the university also displays its intellectual wares. Standard summaries of ideas are made available for essay writing and the 'brighter' student will be encouraged to find critical points for evaluation. Armed with these intellectual goods, the student can decide between Marx's theory of social class and Weber's theory of stratification. They can 'compare and contrast' Durkheim's theory of anomie to Marx's theory of alienation. But the notion that one might actually act on any of these theories is tacitly discouraged. Yet Marx's whole vision is summed up in his aphorism, 'The philosophers have only interpreted the world in various ways; the point is to change it.'[15]

This book therefore differs from many sociological books which cut off discussion on Marx's ideas when it comes to revolution and the alternative to capitalism. The implicit assumption is that the student should contemplate the world through Marx's writings rather than engaging in a debate about how to change it. This, unfortunately, helps to deprive the reader of the liberating realisation that 'Another world is possible'. The present book is written in a language that is, hopefully, accessible to a new generation who are being radicalised by the failure of twenty-first-century capitalism. To achieve this, it avoids many of the arcane debates that have arisen among Marxists in the academy. While some genuinely help our understanding of Marx, many read like the works of medieval scholastics who have different interpretations of the Bible. *Marx and the Alternative to Capitalism* provides an introductory summary of Marx's ideas but tries to relate them to the world of contemporary capitalism. This sometimes means preserving the sense of Marx's message while drawing on examples and conflicts from the current era. While this may be unsatisfactory to those who only want to use Marx's exact words, it may nevertheless help those who are more familiar with iPods and computers than how cotton and linen is manufactured.

On the 25 November 2009, when the Muslim festival of Eid coincided with the traditional US holiday of Thanksgiving, a shocking announcement was made: Dubai World, the company behind the fantasy building project, would not pay interest to international bondholders for at least six months. This thunderbolt helped to bridge a supposed 'clash of civilisations' by uniting all who worshipped at the altar of Mammon. From New York to Riyadh, worried news presenters spoke of sharp falls on the FTSE and Nikkei indices.

A symbol, perhaps, that the arrogance of wealth was beginning to disintegrate.

1
Rebel with a Cause

Karl Marx was born in 1818 in Trier, an old city on the banks of the River Moselle. His father was a lawyer who had converted from Judaism to Protestantism in 1824 to avoid anti-Semitic laws that prevented Jews having a public career. Marx's initial love was not politics but poetry. However, as he developed as a literary critic he found that his own creations were not up to his standards.[1] In his teenage years he moved to Berlin to study philosophy, completing a doctorate on two ancient Greek philosophers, Democritus and Epicurus.

From an early age Marx came up against a deeply repressive society. After a rally for free speech in a nearby town, the police raided his school and removed seditious literature. Two years later, the mathematics and Hebrew teachers were arrested and charged with the crimes of 'atheism' and 'materialism'.[2] This repression produced in Marx a burning desire to rebel and debunk authority. His doctorate on two Greek classical philosophers might seem like a dry-as-dust subject, but Marx's opening page displayed an unusual passion.

> As long as a single drop of blood pulses in her world-conquering and totally free heart, philosophy will continually shout at her opponents the cry of Epicurus: 'Impiety does not consist of destroying the gods of the crowd but rather in ascribing to the gods the ideas of the crowd'. Philosophy makes no secret of it. The proclamation of Prometheus – 'In one word, I hate all gods' – is her profession, her own slogan against all gods in heaven and earth who do not recognize man's self consciousness as the highest divinity. There shall be none other beside it.[3]

This sentiment was directed not just against the gods but against all those who oppressed the masses to promote their own greatness. He stuck with it for the rest of his life.

The Confederation of Germany in which Marx grew up was a loose association of 39 states, dominated by Prussia and Austria.

Its towns were tiny and bounded by walls and gates that were closed at night. Just eight years before Marx was born, serfdom – the obligation to provide free labour to aristocrats – was formally abolished but, as a concession, the aristocrats were allowed take more common land as their private property.[4] This old imperial nobility had special privileges and sometimes their landed estates effectively amounted to states within states. In Prussia, there was no constitution and the king could rule as he pleased. The only concession to wider representation throughout Germany were provincial parliaments where seats were reserved for the Church and the aristocracy. The property qualification for voting was so high that only 70 people qualified in the duchy of Nassau.[5] Censorship, bans on political discussion and adherence to the official religion of Christianity were the order of the day.[6]

In this extremely repressive society, philosophy was one of the few areas where there was no regulation and standing at its pinnacle was the towering figure of Georg Wilhelm Friedrich Hegel, who had died in 1831. In his youth, he supported the French Revolution and privately welcomed Napoleon's invasion of Germany, hoping it would bring greater liberty.[7] By liberty he did not mean freedom for the individual against society but rather 'a recovery of society where men are free and undivided … in which public life is a common expression of the citizens rather than being imposed by unchallengeable authorities on subjects'.[8] This was a more radical vision than that held by other Enlightenment writers who saw society as a collection of independent, atomised individuals. The defeat of the French Revolution and the restoration of absolute monarchy in Germany formed the backdrop to Hegel's philosophy.

Although it was extremely complex, a brief summary is necessary to understand Marx's own development. The radical aspect of Hegel's outlook was that change, process and development were at the heart of human experience. These did not occur randomly and history was not a story of disparate battles, betrayals and individual foibles. With some justice, Hegel argued that things could not be seen in isolation but must be viewed in their relationships. Everything that was had to be produced – it did not appear from nowhere. The state, cultural practices, political ideas had all emerged from somewhere and were in a process of birth and eventual decay. Change, however, could only occur because of division and contradiction. There was first a unity, then a split and finally a reconciliation at a higher unity. Through these mechanisms there was a pattern in history – it was a march towards freedom. 'The history of the world,' Hegel wrote, 'is none other than the progress of the consciousness of freedom'.[9]

While there was a revolutionary kernel to this outlook, the weakness of the progressive forces in Germany meant that Hegel saw history as a mystical process. Philosophy has traditionally divided on the question: What exists? For a *materialist* matter exists and all forms of consciousness must be rooted in the life process of the brain or the wider social community from which we derive language and culture.[10] For an *idealist* it is Spirit (or God or Thought) that really exists and human society is but an expression of it. The most radical idealism was Plato's philosophy where men were imagined to live in caves, watching shadows on a wall that were faint traces of a higher Spirit that lay outside, shining through one of the cracks.

In his idealist outlook, Hegel was not far removed from Plato because he thought Spirit (*Geist*) was at the origin of all existence. This Spirit had become alienated from the world it created and so had to 'go through a cycle, a drama, a division in order to return to unity'.[11] This sounds like a retelling of the Christian story of the division between God and the world but with one important difference. Whereas in traditional religion God stood alone in the heavens in all his perfection, Hegel had the temerity to suggest that 'Without the world, God is not God'.[12] The Spirit has to make the journey back to an identity with the world and so man became 'the vehicle for *Geist*'s spiritual journey'.[13] Or to put it more scandalously, history is the autobiography of God.[14]

The progress of the Spirit towards the world, or in Hegel's language, self-awareness, was manifested in the unfolding of human history. Hegel had a brilliant, encyclopedic mind and drew on examples from religion, art, law and politics to show that there was a certain unity in the culture of any particular society. This unity was an expression of the journey of the Spirit at a particular stage. However, the 'mole of history' only moved through great contradictions and clashes before it could advance to a new stage. Its end point was a universal state that rose above all the divisions of civil society and offered freedom to all its citizens. The state was, for Hegel, the embodiment of reason and bestowed on man whatever value he had. Civil society was just 'society as a human herd'[15] where each individual treated everyone else as a means to an end.

After Prussia's defeat by Napoleon in 1806, the monarch, Frederick William III, was forced to embark on an era of reform and appoint liberal ministers such as Baron Von Stein and Baron

Altenstein. Economic tariffs between the provinces were lifted, Jews given some civil rights and the political interests of the middle class championed.[16] As part of the liberalisation, Hegel was given the post of university professor in the newly established Berlin university where he championed the reforming administration. But he went further and argued the reformed Prussian state was the final reconciliation of the Spirit with the world, the end of human history. Which is why, not surprisingly, he was proclaimed Germany's official philosopher.

This was clearly a conservative and absurd conclusion. Even before his death in 1831, the reactionary clique around Frederick William III undermined the reforms and restored the absolute monarchy. A young left Hegelian movement emerged using a radical version of the philosophy to attack the state. They focused on Hegel's method rather than his wider system because this allowed them to make connections between different aspects of culture, thinking of them as a 'totality'. So religion, philosophy and art all had a certain unity as an expression of a particular society. But each totality was made up of the unity of opposites and would undergo change through great clashes. No society would persist for more than a limited time and would eventually be surpassed as History continued its march towards freedom.

One typical Hegelian approach was to argue that ideas and social practices were not wrong but that the need for them had been surpassed. David Strauss's book *The Life of Jesus*, published in 1835, provides a good example of this. This treated the Gospels as another text and showed, through its inconsistencies, that they were an expression of the collective consciousness of early Christian communities. By ignoring the debate about whether or not the Gospels were true, Strauss's book was even more devastating because it treated them merely as a cultural expression that had been surpassed.

The radical implications of this method were particularly dangerous. If history was a journey towards Reason and Freedom, then the existing society could be criticised as falling short and all social institutions could be measured against the possibility of a society where 'the rational was real and the real was rational'.[17] Viewed from this standpoint, monarchy and aristocratic privileges were soon-to-be relics that should be swept aside to speed up the march of history. Even if the older Hegel shrank from these conclusions, his Young Hegelian followers were determined to press the point home.

When Marx first began to study philosophy in Berlin in 1836, he rejected 'the harsh, grotesque, melody' of Hegel's philosophy[18] but later he joined the Doctors' Club, a group of Young Hegelians who took the radical content of Hegel's doctrine seriously. They accepted Hegel's view of history as moving towards an ideal state but did not think that the Prussian state had reached that stage. In particular, they believed that its development had been stifled by the links between the state and the Church. The task of philosophy, they believed, was to liberate the state from religion and to promote 'Critical Criticism'.[19] By this they meant free thought in a free society.

Initially, the Young Hegelians had high hopes in Friedrich Wilhelm IV who ascended to the throne in 1840, but the new king proved to be as reactionary as the old. He suppressed the Young Hegelian journal, the *Hallische Jahrbucher*, and appointed Hegel's arch-enemy, Friedrich Schelling, as Professor of Philosophy at Berlin, with instructions to root out the 'dragon seed of Hegelianism'.[20] In 1842, Bruno Bauer, the leader of the Young Hegelians, was sacked from his academic post for promoting atheism after which Marx gave up all hope of being appointed a lecturer.

The philosophers who were driven out of the lecture halls then sought positions in the editorial offices of newspapers. Fortunately, the *Rheinische Zeitung*, which had been founded by liberal businessmen in Cologne who distrusted Prussian domination, began to employ a number of the Young Hegelians. One of their number was Karl Marx and in October 1842 he became the paper's editor. Marx's first published article was a vociferous attack on censorship of the press and, in a sign of things to come, he also attacked the half-hearted liberals who did not wage a strong enough fight. He suggested that 'the absence of freedom of the press makes all other freedoms illusory. One form of freedom governs another, just as one limb of the body does another.'[21] His opposition to censorship and his contempt for the bureaucratic Prussian state turned him into an extreme democrat who despised all suggestions that the people had to be guided by their superiors. Rule by the people might bring all sorts of mistakes but Marx replied to paternalistic arguments for restricting freedom:

> For [the advocate of paternalism] true education consists in keeping a person swaddled in a cradle all his life, for as soon as he learns to walk he also learns to fall, and it is only through falling that he learns to walk. But if we all remain children in swaddling

clothes, who is to swaddle us? If we all lie in a cradle, who is to cradle us? If we are all in jail, who is to be the jail warden?[22]

Marx displayed an equal passion in opposing state bureaucracy. He rejected Hegel's celebration of the Prussian state and denounced the pretension of all bureaucracy to represent the common good of society:

> The bureaucracy is a magic circle from which no one can escape. Its hierarchy is the hierarchy of knowledge … . [It] degenerates into ... passive obedience, the worship of authority, the mechanism of a fixed, formal action, of rigid principles, views and traditions. As for the individual bureaucrat, the purpose of the state becomes his private purpose, *a hunt for promotion and careerism*.[23]

When some suggested that the problem of bureaucracy could be solved with better leaders, he wrote that 'hierarchical organisation is itself the principal abuse and the few personal sins of officials are as nothing compared to their necessary hierarchical sins'.[24]

All of this put Marx far in advance of classic liberal writers who advocated more freedom but instinctively distrusted 'the mob' who might interfere with the rights of property. The founders of the Western liberal democratic tradition typically sought to restrict popular franchise through a House of Lords or a more elite second chamber or a powerful Supreme Court that could overrule the popular will. Marx, however, advocated unrestricted democracy with no censorship or bureaucratic power and this democratic instinct makes a mockery of claims that his ideas were responsible for Stalinist tyranny. No thinker can be responsible for those who claim adherence to their ideas, especially after they are dead, and so it makes as much sense to claim that Jesus Christ was responsible for the Spanish Inquisition as to argue that Marx was to blame for Russian communism.

Ironically, Marx's editorship of the *Rheinische Zeitung* led to a break with his former philosophical friends. The main reason was, as he later explained, that he had experienced 'for the first time the embarrassment of having to take part in discussions on so-called material interests'.[25] One of these discussions concerned a wood theft law that was being debated in the Rhine provincial parliament. For centuries, peasants had enjoyed a customary right to gather wood in forests for fuel but as legislation to protect private property expanded, this was defined as theft and subject to harsh penalties.

Marx's sympathy with the peasants was instinctive and their struggle led him to explore the economic issues that lay behind the laws on private property. By contrast, the other Young Hegelians, who were now calling themselves The Free, were moving to more verbally radical attacks on religion and had started to denounce 'the masses' as the true enemy of Mind.

On 1 April 1843 Marx's paper was banned and he decided to leave Germany for Paris along with another Young Hegelian, Arnold Ruge, to found a new *Deutsch–Französische Jahrbücher*. However, only one issue of the journal appeared because the two fell out over Marx's growing interest in the struggles of the downtrodden and his support for the revolt of the Silesian weavers in 1844. These handloom workers had gone into battle with a song which told how 'one fine day, the money of the rich will disappear like butter in the sun'[26] and had fought bravely before being suppressed by armed soldiers. Ruge belittled their revolt and called for a political party that would seek reform within the state. Marx, however, celebrated the revolt, declaring that while the 'burning desire of the entire liberal bourgeoisie for freedom of the press could be suppressed without the aid of a single soldier', the weavers fought with immense courage.[27] Far from looking only for reforms within the state, Marx argued that 'the existence of the state is inseparable from the existence of slavery' because it had to rest on 'the cutthroat world of modern business'.[28]

Marx remained in Paris until he was expelled in February 1845 when he left for Brussels. During his stay, he gained from two experiences that informed him for the rest of his life. First, he made contact with a number of workmen's clubs and communist secret societies, including the 1,000-strong League of the Just.[29] He was deeply impressed by the courage and nobility of these artisan fighters and decided to join them. The League, however, tended to concentrate solely on the 'social question' and to ignore political struggles for democracy. Yet as soon as he joined, Marx took the opposite approach and advocated full involvement in the struggle for parliamentary rule in Germany.

He also began his longstanding relationship with Friedrich Engels, who had already begun research on economic questions and had made contacts with the Chartist Movement in Britain during the course of writing his *Condition of the Working Class of England*. The Chartists were a working-class movement that campaigned for the vote and for parliament to be elected on an annual basis so that they could be subject to democratic pressure.[30] Engels was the son of a millowner who had been sent to Manchester to learn the family business. There he met, and became a partner with, Mary Burns, an Irish working-class woman who introduced him to parts of the city a respectable bourgeois would never have visited. Engels had come to similar political conclusions to Marx's and their meeting in Paris led to a friendship which, in the words of Lenin, 'surpassed the most moving friendship among the ancients'.[31] Later, Engels funded Marx's family and promoted their joint ideas in more popular forms.

After their experience of the Chartists, the Silesian weavers' revolt and the Paris workingmen's clubs, Marx and Engels came to a radical new conclusion. Whereas previously they thought that philosophy could seize hold of, and inspire, the working class, now they they began to think of workers as agents of their own liberation. They were no longer simply victims of capitalism but had the capacity to become its gravediggers. Instead of small sects of 'educators' providing a vision of a new society, real change would come from the political development of the working-class movement. Marx and Engels' turn was expressed in two books, *The Holy Family* and the *German Ideology*, which marked their final break with the remnants of Hegelianism. Marx described their new approach to change as follows:

> We do not confront the world in a doctrinaire way with a new principle: Here is the truth, kneel down before it! We develop new principles for the world out of the world's own principles. We do not say to the world: Cease your struggles, they are foolish; we will give you the true slogan of struggle.
>
> We merely show the world what it is really fighting for and consciousness is something that it *has* to acquire, even if it does not want to.[32]

As Marx and Engels became more involved with the League of the Just, they also took up a number of arguments with others on the left. They opposed a style of conspiratorial politics that had arisen from secret societies. This was a tradition which stretched back to François-Noel Babeuf and the Conspiracy of Equals who had been active during the later stages of the French Revolution. Their methods influenced many of the early workers' clubs, which often saw themselves as tight groups of revolutionaries operating behind the scenes and waiting for the opportune moment to give a signal for insurrection. This involved a degree of political elitism as initiative and direction of the movement were assigned to a secret

Directorate within the secret societies. One of the key figures in the clubs, Wilhelm Weitling, also suggested that if the insurrection was a success, a communist dictator would later be needed to guide society.[33] Marx, however, rejected this top-down approach in favour of an open politics and the participation of workers in their own liberation.

Opposition to conspiratorial methods, however, also came from moderates who argued for 'moral persuasion' and education for both the rulers and the ruled in order to create a better society. They often appealed to justice and truth to encourage elites to reform. This suggested that poverty and exploitation resulted from individual wickedness rather than the workings of the system. Marx and Engels, however, equally rejected this non-revolutionary approach because the problem was that, as Hal Draper put it, 'everybody "believes in" truth, justice and morality, provided they can implement their own versions'.[34] In other words, abstract calls to morality did not supersede class interests.

Finally, Marx argued against Pierre-Joseph Proudhon's programme of establishing mutual credit societies and 'fair labour exchanges' where workers could receive the full value of their labour. Despite being hailed as one of the fathers of anarchism, Proudhon hankered after an older world of craft independence. He thought that strikes were evil and women's rights an abomination. His opposition to politics did not prevent him taking state support for his credit societies and the French dictator Louis Bonaparte was later to exploit this desire to help tame the workers' movement. Marx argued that it was an illusion to assume that the market could be made fair through a return to more local conditions. All schemes for mutual aid would eventually be made subject to the laws of the market and could not undermine them. Against this older 'petty bourgeois' radicalism, Marx argued that workers had to take control of the modern economy and replace the domination of the market with conscious planning of the economy.

By 1847, Marx and Engels had won considerable support for these new revolutionary methods and were asked to write a manifesto for the Communist League, as the renamed League of the Just was known. The pamphlet they produced, *The Communist Manifesto*, appeared at a particularly fortuitous time and became one of the most famous books of all times, because of its brilliant rhetorical style and its bold claim that 'the history of all hitherto existing society is the history of class struggles'.[35] When it appeared in 1848, revolutions were sweeping across France, Germany, Austria,

Ireland and Czechoslovakia. These revolutions were primarily about establishing democracy, though in the course of the struggle, social issues also arose. French workers, for example, demanded the creation of national workshops to alleviate the problem of unemployment and, for a period, forced the republican democrats reluctantly to provide them.

When the German revolt broke out, Marx immediately returned to his home country and took over the editorship of the *Neue Rheinische Zeitung*, which was subtitled, the 'Organ of Democracy'.[36] This was a popular paper with many activists and made him one of the key figures in the radical wing of the democratic movement. He also drafted a short leaflet outlining the political programme of the Communist League which included demands for a German republic, arming of the people, an end to legal fees, abolition of all feudal obligations, a state bank, public ownership of transport and free transport for the poor, free education and a guarantee of the right to work.[37] His aim was to push the democratic movement in a left direction through an alliance of workers, peasants and the lower middle class.

The revolutions of 1848 were defeated, however, mainly because the liberal bourgeois leaderships were too timid and too worried about the growing radicalism below them to launch a serious fight. In June, the French workers had risen up against the planned closure of the national workshops they had won months previously. The republican leaders of the democratic movement massacred 1,500 of them and deported another 15,000 political prisoners to Algeria. These conflicts were a signal to liberals across Europe that it was time to bring their revolt to a close. In Germany, the elected Frankfurt Assembly did not take any decisive measures against the monarchy, but confined itself to passing resolutions about a new constitution until it was eventually dissolved in 1849.

Summing up the experience of the 1848 democratic revolts, Marx argued in his *March Address* that workers had to organise independently of even the most radical-sounding middle-class politicians. If there were to be a new attempt at revolution, they should try

> to make the revolution permanent until all the more or less propertied classes have been driven from their ruling positions, until the proletariat has conquered state power and until the association of the proletarians has progressed sufficiently far – not only in one country but in all the leading countries of the world.[38]

Unfortunately far from a renewed attempt at revolution, reaction set in after 1850 and Marx became an asylum-seeker in London. For most of the next decade until the outbreak of the American civil war, he was the London correspondent of the *New York Tribune* and wrote many articles on contemporary subjects. Although an ardent advocate of political activism up to this point, Marx now retreated to his economic studies in the British Museum. In April 1851 he told Engels, 'I have got so far that I could be finished with the whole economic shit in five weeks'.[39] His major work, *Capital*, was, however, not published until 1867 and even then vast quantities of it remained. The second and third volumes, which were edited by Engels, only appeared after his death, in 1885 and 1894 respectively.

Marx's life as a political refugee was dominated by poverty and wretched living conditions. When his daughter, Franziska, died in 1852, his wife, Jenny, had to borrow money from a French émigré to pay for the coffin. Later in the same year, Marx told a correspondent that he could not leave the house because he had pawned his coat and shoes.[40] Ten years later, he noted that 'every day my wife tells me she wished she was dead. And I really cannot argue with her.'[41] The fact that *Capital* was written under these terrible conditions is an amazing feat. Yet even while writing the three-volume masterpiece, Marx found time to resume political activism when the workers' movement revived. In 1864, the Workingmen's International Association, commonly known as the First International, arose out of an international gathering of French and British trade unionists in St Martin's Hall, London, in solidarity with Polish independence. This brought together many of the different trends of political opinion in the international labour movement and included French supporters of Proudhon, Italian followers of the radical nationalist Giuseppe Mazzini, British trade unionists and a host of anarchists.

Marx quickly became one of the key figures within the First International and was repeatedly elected to its 50-strong General Council where he represented the German delegation, alongside five others who were all members of the Communist League. He wrote the Inaugural Address for the organisation in which he celebrated internationalism and argued that the conquest of political power had become the great duty of the working class. He also drafted its Provisional Rules which opened with the line: 'The emancipation of the working class must be the act of the working classes themselves'.[42] While active in the First International, Marx drafted a message of solidarity to Abraham Lincoln in his fight against slavery. He pressed for support for Polish independence, despite some objections that this was too political. He sprang to the defence of the Irish Fenians who were being branded as common criminals rather than political fighters against an empire. He supported the formation of the Reform League which advocated universal suffrage. This mobilised tens of thousands on the streets and was a major factor in bringing pressure on the British elite to open up the vote to working-class males in the 1867 Reform Act.[43]

However, the key text he wrote for the First International was *The Civil War in France*, which was a bold defence of the Paris Commune. This was a workers' uprising in defiance of the French government's attempt to hand over the city to the victorious Prussian armies. For two months in 1871, workers ran Paris in their own interest and instituted a form of direct democracy that terrified the wealthy across Europe. When French right-wing forces re-took the city they imposed a reign of terror on its population, executing about 20,000 Communards and exiling another 7,500 to places like New Caledonia. More people may have died than during Robespierre's Reign of Terror but while every schoolchild has heard about this 'Terror', few are told about the class terror meted out on Paris workers in 1871. Marx's defence of the Commune brought considerable notoriety and repression against the First International. He was depicted as the 'Red terror doctor' and his life was threatened several times, but far from being cowed, he wrote jubilantly to Engels, 'It is doing me good after twenty long years of idyllic isolation like a frog in a swamp'.[44] However, there was a drawback to notoriety because many of the more moderate British trade unionists were frightened away by the witch-hunt. Even before this, the First International had been weakened by a split fomented by anarchists. The first attempt to create a global organisation of workers was effectively dead.

Marx spent the last ten years of his life largely aloof from public agitation but in 1875 he intervened in a debate on the formation of the German Social Democratic Party to write *A Critique of the Gotha Programme*. The SPD was to become the first mass Marxist party in the world but even at this early stage Marx detected a softness in its politics and called for a more radical approach. He also engaged in an extensive correspondence with Russian revolutionaries after studying the Russian language and statistics. But that was as far as he went. For the rest of his life he retired to private study and coping with continual illness. On 2 December 1881 his wife died; his eldest daughter, Jenny, died on 11 January 1883 and then, on 14 March of the same year, Marx too passed away quietly seated in his armchair. At his funeral oration, Engels said,

> Marx was before all else a revolutionist. His real mission in life was to contribute, in one way or another, to the overthrow of capitalist society... And he fought with a passion, a tenacity and a success such as few could rival.[45]

Engels' prediction that 'his name will endure through the ages and so will his work' has certainly proved true.

2
A for Profit Society

Let's take a journey to the heart of twenty-first-century capitalism. The Carlyle group is valued at €84.5 billion and employs 415,000 people worldwide. That makes it wealthier than many middle-sized countries such as Croatia, Serbia or Lithuania. But what does it do?

This is a difficult question to answer. It has acquired a host of companies such as Dunkin' Donuts and car component makers such as Allison Transmission and Metaldyne. But it is not concerned about any particular product or service as it is a private equity investment company. This means that it moves capital in and out of other companies, seeking the highest rate of return. It prides itself on being fluid and fast, not tied to fixed investment in machinery or building, but searching everywhere for the 'bottom line'.

William Conway Jr. is one of its principal owners and features on the US 'rich list' of billionaires. He has collected a trophy set of former politicians for his board of directors, among them the former British Prime Minister John Major and the former US President George Bush Sr. Each of these individuals receives a considerable amount of money for gracing Carlyle's 'shadow cabinet' with their presence. But none of them – neither Conway nor the ex-politicians – make or create anything. At most, Carlyle uses 500 'investment professionals' to spot opportunities for profit-seeking missions. Actual production is carried out by complex networks of workers over many continents.

So what gives the shareholders of Carlyle the right to draw millions of dollars in profit to enrich themselves?

In a previous society, the equivalents of Carlyle's owners would have used the threat of violence to extract wealth from the peasantry and it would have been clear when the robbery took place. For part of the week, the peasants worked for themselves on small plots of land. For the rest of the week they worked directly on the *corvée* system where they gave unpaid labour to their lord or provided him with some of the fruits of their work. Under capitalism there is no such clear division between working for yourself and working for the boss. Profit appears to be generated in normal, clean ways with no recourse to violence. How does it happen? When and how did this society emerge?

Capitalism is a comparatively recent development in human history and needs 'free' workers and employers to forge a relationship. Employers gain control of factories, offices and workplaces and employ workers who are free in a double sense. First, there are no ties of personal dependence and this allows both parties to enter into a contractual arrangement with no sentimentality or traditional bonds. It is purely an economic relationship whose only link is cash and the relationship lasts only as long as the worker is useful to the employer. Second, workers must also be free in the sense that they are 'free from, or unencumbered by, any means of production of their own'.[1] They must own nothing beyond personal property.

Despite modern rhetoric about freedom of choice, there is a profound inequality here. By its very nature capital is fungible – it can morph and change form. The employer can close workplaces to move money out of production and into banks or other financial institutions. Production facilities can be relocated to the other side of the world while workers are constrained by immigration rules. Carlyle represents the purest form of this freedom as its capital is constantly changing form. The worker, however, is only free to choose between individual capitalists but must hire him- or herself to at least one capitalist. There is, therefore, compulsion for one and real freedom for the other.

How did this relationship come about? One myth is that the early capitalists lived frugally and saved up to buy factories and machinery. In reality, the early accumulation of capital was built on violence and skulduggery. Monasteries, which had large estates, were grabbed by supporters of the new rich. Slavery, and what Marx called 'the conversion of Africa into a preserve for the commercial hunting of black skins',[2] created the early wealth of cities like Liverpool and Bristol. Merchants in companies like the East India Company won a monopoly of trade in tea, salt and opium to accumulate vast hordes of money. Far from arising through the efforts of 'innovative', rugged individuals, the early capitalists used the power of the state to accelerate the transition from a feudal society.

A long process then brought about change from commercial capital to gaining control over labour. At first, merchants used differences in time and place to insert themselves between buyers and sellers, skimming off both by buying cheap and selling dear. The goods were often produced by craft workers who were organised into guilds, which enforced strict rules on the number of apprentices and traditional ways of working. But at a certain point, the merchants or the wealthier master craftsmen of the guilds broke free of these restrictions and took control of production. Sometimes they established their domination over the guilds and changed the rules. At other times, they moved to new rural towns where guilds had less control. Instead of buying finished products, they established a 'putting out' system whereby the merchant capitalist loaned out raw materials and machinery in return for a guarantee of finished products. Still later, they centralised this new system of production into workshops and factories where they imposed their own division of labour. Modern capitalism only came into existence when labour could be bought and controlled in these new workplaces.

Where did the workers – the forerunners of most people in modern society – come from?

The vast majority did not want to work in factories and preferred clean air and open spaces. They had to be stripped of their own property to force them. One of the great myths is that modern society is built on a respect for 'private property' but, as Marx pointed out, the modern workforce could not develop unless people were deprived of property that allowed them to work for themselves. There had to be a transformation of 'the dwarf like property of the many into the giant property of the few'.[3] To illustrate, Marx told the story of a Mr Peel who bought land in Australia and took 3,000 people with him to settle there. But Peel forgot that the land on the new continent was freely available and, to his shock, found his settlers scattered as soon as they discovered this. The hapless Mr Peel was left 'without a servant to make his bed or fetch him water from the river'.[4] To overcome this labour supply problem, a variety of methods have been used.

One of the most crucial ways was depriving people of access to common land. In England, this took place in the fifteenth and sixteenth centuries through enclosures which transformed arable land into sheep walks to produce wool. 'Enclosures make the herds fat and the poor people thin' is how one contemporary put it.[5] In the US and Australia, where there was an abundance of space, workers were sent as indentured servants or convict labour and forced to work for their masters for a number of years. In Africa, the colonial powers introduced poll taxes that had to be paid in money to force workers off the land in order to earn a wage. One governor, Sir Perry Girouard, put the matter succinctly, 'We consider taxation is the only possible method of compelling the native to leave his reserve for the purpose of work'.[6] But even when people were separated from their original means of production, they still had to be moulded into accepting the 'work ethic'.

This took place through a mixture of repression and religion. Laws against begging and vagrancy were used to compel the 'idle poor' to sell their labour. The original idea of 'Three strikes and you're out' came in the reign of Queen Elizabeth I in 1572 when it was decreed that beggars were to be branded on the left ear for the first offence, taken into service for the second offence and executed if caught a third time. To this day nomadic people who wander without selling their labour are anathema to capitalist society. Irish travellers, Australia aborigines, Native Americans and English New Age travellers are all targets of vilification because they have not embraced the work ethic. In 2005, for example, 24,359 people in the US were convicted of vagrancy offences.[7]

Alongside overt repression, the new rulers used religious doctrine to denounce idleness and gain acceptance for the disciplines of industrial capitalism. People's relationship with the rhythms of the seasons had to be replaced with a work regime that served capitalism. One way this occurred was through the 'triumph of the Sabbath' over the ancient saints' days of pre-modern Christian society.[8] Sunday replaced a vast number of local and regional saints' days; longer carnival celebrations died out and the traditional 'Saint Monday', when people recovered from their weekend drinking, was abolished. Religion, particularly Methodism in the case of Britain, was used to denounce idleness as evil. In John Wesley's tract on *The Duty and Advantage of Early Rising*, for example, he warned that 'By soaking ... so long between warm sheets, the flesh is, at it were, parboiled and becomes soft and flabby. The nerves, in the meantime, are quite unstrung.'[9] Once at work, workers had to be 'taught' that what they produced no longer belonged to them but to the capitalist who hired them. A 'judicial onslaught' of hangings and transportation was launched in eighteenth-century London to show those coming off the land that they could not take what belonged to their masters.[10]

Through all this long and complicated historical process, two classes came to dominate modern capitalist society: a minority of people who owned and controlled the means of production, and a vast majority who were compelled to sell their labour. The owners of Carlyle can now appoint managers to boss workers, but their right of command has nothing to do with personal qualities – they are neither better people nor more intelligent. Their right to command is derived solely from their control of capital.

COMMODITY PRODUCTION

One other condition was necessary for modern capitalism – commodity production had to become the norm. Commodities are produced for exchange rather than for oneself or one's master and have a double aspect. As *use value*, they have to be a specific thing or service which can satisfy human needs 'whether from the stomach or the imagination makes no difference'.[11] But they also must have a common value – an *exchange value* – which allows them to be swapped with each other. Commodity production normally begins when a tribal group have a surplus beyond their own needs which they exchange with others. Over a long period there is a shift from commodities being produced as an accidental or surplus element to their becoming the main purpose of production. If technology and organisation permit, this can expand further so that the bulk of production is geared towards exchange. When this occurs on a large scale, a number of related changes take place.

First, labour itself eventually becomes a commodity. Because production is not tied to specific use values which a particular social group need, there is a possibility of continual expansion. For a period there may be, what Engels termed, simple commodity production where independent, self-employed producers engage in exchange.[12] But as possibilities for expansion grow – not least because some are forced out of business – additional labour will be required. Theoretically, this labour could come from slavery and the American cotton plantations offer an example. But slavery cannot be adjusted to the fluctuations of the market and slaves have to be physically maintained even when they are not producing. The great advantage of workers is that they can be sacked when there is no production of goods for exchange.

Second, commodity production changes the way the division of labour is organised. All societies, from hunter-gatherer society to modern capitalism, divide tasks according to different occupations and this is usually referred to as the division of labour. Or, to put it differently, the collective work effort has to be allocated to different branches of production. In a tribal society, a village chief would simply decide who is to engage in food production, metalwork or hunting. In a modern factory, the boss decides on the division of labour between workers. Outside the factory, however, the mechanism for allocating the wider social effort under capitalism is through the exchange of commodities.

The classical economist, Adam Smith, argued that a division of labour was necessary for all societies but assumed this was based on a natural tendency to 'truck and barter and exchange'. This led him to conclude that commodity production was rooted in human nature and that the study of economics could only be the science of commodity production.[13] However, Marx pointed out that the

> division of labour is a necessary condition for the production of commodities, although the converse does not hold; commodity production is not a necessary condition for the division of labour.[14]

Commodity production evolved from an earlier form of social organisation and changed the nature of those societies in fundamental ways.

For one thing, we become ever more dependent on each other. Few people in modern Western society can receive even a fraction of the food we need without the help of others. Getting a cup of coffee in a works canteen requires the collective effort of Ethiopian farmers, clerical workers in a New York trading exchange, sailors on Greek-owned ships, retail assistants, truckers and waiters. In fact, commodity production leads to greater social dependency than in any previous human society. Yet there is no mechanism by which we can organise our dependence on one another. We relate to our cooperative social labour solely through the exchange of commodities. These things or services, and the measurement of them in 'the markets', assume a life of their own. They conceal the social relationship which we forge with each other and create the conditions in which our productive life becomes a power over us rather than a means to satisfy our needs.

Third, a major shift occurs in the nature of money. Initially, money emerges as a more efficient system of exchange than barter. Marx summarised the pattern of simple commodity circulation as C-M-C, where C stands for a particular commodity and M for money. At this point, money is simply a mechanism to exchange one object for another. But, as commodity production expands, a new dynamic sets in which is summarised as M-C-M1. Here the owner of money starts with money, which then enters a cycle by producing commodities in order to gain more money. In the first case, the aim is to sell in order to buy and then consume. In the second case, however, the self-expansion of money becomes an end in itself.

Capitalists who engage in this activity are not trying to satisfy a particular need or even make a onetime gain. Their aim is none other than a restless, never-ending search for more profit and here they share a motivation with the miser. Both are driven by a fanatical desire for an abstract object, money, which is not related to their physical needs. But there is a difference between the two: the miser withdraws money from circulation in order to hoard it while the capitalist returns it again and again to make ever more profit. As Marx summarised it, 'this boundless greed after riches [is] common to the capitalist and the miser; but while the miser is merely a capitalist gone mad, the capitalist is a rational miser.'[15]

Fourth, commodification spreads like a virus through society. If the objective of production is not to satisfy a particular need but the self-expansion of capital, then it matters little what commodity serves this purpose. Early nineteenth-century capitalism started by turning clothing into a commodity rather than it being produced at home. The cotton mill became the symbol of a new age and it was quickly followed by the production of new machinery to facilitate the mass marketing of clothing. But soon many new arenas open up and there is a relentless drive to commodify every aspect of human life. In the twenty-first century there is barely an area of human life that is not commodified.

Sex is a natural human activity, but today the 'sex industry' has become a vast network which distorts our desires in order to sell fantasy and pleasure. Water was once a simple drink drawn from rivers or lakes but today 17 million barrels of oil are needed for the plastic containers that hold America's bottled water. Football was once a village game where people jostled and kicked a leather ball around a field but today football players and their associated brands are marketed as commodities. Art was once intrinsically connected with wider social activities where craft workers poured their creativity into mundane objects such as chairs or into special decorative objects for festivities. Today art students are taught courses on entrepreneurship and the 'art market' stands aghast at Jeff Koon's achievement in selling his magenta Hanging Heart for €23.6 million. One of the most disturbing trends is the commodification of childhood itself. Today the average American child views 40,000 commercials annually and makes 3,000 requests for products and services.[16] There is virtually nothing that capitalism has not turned into a commodity.

To understand this strange system, we have to get at its inner dynamics. Marx starts this inquiry by asking an extraordinarily simple question. On what basis do commodities exchange?

THE LABOUR THEORY OF VALUE

The price of a toy such as Playmobil Grand Mansion will fluctuate, according to the laws of supply and demand. If there is a shortage of supply at Christmas the price will go up and, conversely, if more parents become unemployed and there is less demand, the price will go down. But these fluctuations oscillate around a particular axis point or value and we hardly expect that the price of this toy will overtake that of a laptop or a car. What, therefore, establishes the value relationship between these items?

It cannot be any physical qualities inherent in a commodity because so many diverse items are exchanged with each other. If I exchange a computer for a toy house, there is no property in terms of colour, weight or shape that is common to both. The only common element is human labour. If a toy house requires much less labour to produce than a computer, it will have less value. The reason a loaf of bread sells for €1, while a shirt sells for €20 and a car for €10,000 is, in the final analysis, that it takes 10,000 times as many hours of labour (with current levels of technology) to make a car, and 20 times as many to make a shirt as it does to make a loaf of bread. The labour in each case consists of a small fraction of past labour in the form of machinery, which is used up in the production process materials, and a much greater portion of living labour, which is added on. This elementary *labour theory of value* was accepted by the classical economists Adam Smith and David Ricardo. Smith, for example, asserted that:

> It was not by gold or by silver, but by labour, that all wealth of the world was originally purchased; and its value to those who possess it, and who want to exchange it for some new production, is precisely equal to the quantity of labour it can enable them to purchase or command.[17]

Marx, however, took the matter further by introducing a number of qualifications.

First, the labour involved is *abstract labour*. The eternal condition of human life is that we have to interact with nature to meet our daily needs and this interaction often involves specific skills that transform the objects we extract from nature. The skills of a carpenter are on display in furniture whereas those of a tailor appear in clothes. Marx refers to this as *concrete labour*. *Abstract labour,* however, refers to quantitative measurement of human labour for the purposes of exchange. It is viewed as general, human labour that is not marked by any specific features and can be reduced to a common denominator so that units of labour can be compared to one another.[18] It reflects the fact that in a capitalist society labour is bought and sold. Labour is also highly mobile in this society, constantly moving between different branches of production. This abstract labour can also be viewed as a part of the overall social labour force and so each commodity can be measured by how much social labour it contains.

The reason why a suit of clothes now exchanges with a chair in a certain proportion is that both contain a distinct quantity of abstract labour. Another way of putting this is to say that the different types of skilled labour have become transformed into multiples of simple labour. Of course, there is no agency or individual that draws up tables or charts for each specific type of labour. It happens behind our backs through 'the market'. The constant talk of 'labour costs' and the 'benchmarking' of 'unit costs' of one workplace against another is a reflection of this process.

Second, the labour involved must be *socially necessary*. If I am a useless carpenter and I take ten times as long to make a chair than a skilled carpenter, my commodity can hardly become more valuable. If two commodities exchange in equal measure, they must both contain the same amount of labour that is of the average skill and productivity for that given society. If one capitalist is producing goods at a low level of productivity, rivals will undercut their prices and so the goods may remain unsold.

Socially necessary labour also implies that I must engage in types of work designated as economically useful by my society. Under capitalism, work is designated as economically useful if I am producing for a profit and so other types of work are defined as private labour and considered to have no value. Although I spend hours looking after an elderly parent or caring for my children, this is not labour undertaken for the purpose of making commodities for exchange. Under capitalism, only labour that is devoted to commodities which are exchanged produces value.[19]

Once again, socially necessary labour time is not determined by a conscious agency that draws up detailed figures for these averages. When production starts, the factory owners or 'service providers' have no idea if their products are based on socially necessary labour time or not. Rather, the chaotic, unconscious process of market competition establishes the average level of productivity and does so after the event – so there is a huge possibility of waste as individual owners get calculations wrong. The *law of value*, as Marx called this process, operates behind the scene and is a little like the law of gravity. No one has ever seen, touched or felt gravity, but it governs how much of the natural world behaves. Unlike gravity, however, the law of value develops in a particular class society and does not exist in all societies. It is the mechanism by which a capitalist society allocates its distribution of labour time and is, in effect, a vote of no confidence in the human capacity consciously to plan this allocation.

This process is linked to the mystification and dominance of money in our lives. Money sometimes appears as a social force whose power is derived from a mysterious object called gold. In reality, money is simply the medium with which we exchange commodities. Instead of expressing the value of a chair as the equivalent of so many shirts, and then later so many footballs, and still later, so many pens, a universal equivalent evolves to express its value. It is similar to using scales. To find the weight of any item, we have to measure it in terms of something else but eventually standard weights or a universal equivalent emerge in which all weights can be expressed as a magnitude.

However, if money functions as a 'universal equivalent', this is only because it is an expression of value generated by collective human labour. When I sell a commodity, I am exchanging one item that contains socially necessary labour for a euro coin or dollar bill that represents a portion of society's labour time. As Marx put it, with money 'the individual carries his social power, as well as his bond with society, in his pocket'.[20] This helps to explain the joke made by the Russian revolutionary Lenin when he suggested that in a socialist society the toilets would be paved with gold. He was not, as some right-wing writers claimed, making a utopian promise that the workers of Russia would enjoy the gold-plated luxury of Dubai's bathrooms. Rather, he was seeking to demystify the precious object and explain that it was simply frozen human labour – there would be no need to hide that fact in a socialist society.

PROFIT

But we run ahead of ourselves. Having established some of the inner dynamics of how commodities exchange, Marx asked where profit comes from. Answering this means cutting through other myths.

One is that profit is made by 'risk-taking'. Risk-takers are supposed to gamble all to find new ways of producing a good or providing a service and they will only do this, it is argued, because society offers them a reward in the form of profit. However, this explains very little. Even if some people took an initial risk in founding a company and got a large reward, it does not explain how they or their offspring continue to receive rewards for decades. Nor does it explain why many workers such as fire-fighters or ambulance drivers also take risks which benefit society and are not substantially rewarded. Moreover, the mythology of the capitalist risk-taker was decisively shattered after the financial crash of 2008. The great giants of global capitalism, such as Goldman Sachs, General Motors, Chrysler, American Express and JP Morgan Chase, received billions in state bailouts. Far from being risk-takers, the largest capitalists survive on corporate welfare.

Another myth is that profit represents a return for capital invested or even for the work undertaken by the owners of a large corporation. Capital, however, in the sense of machinery or buildings cannot add value by itself and a factory that stands idle at night after workers have left produces no new value. Machinery stores the past value produced by the workers and an element of this capital will enter production as depreciation when used by living workers. Account books for the firm will normally show a charge for this 'depreciation allowance' that is distinct from profit. Nor does the reward theory explain the activities of firms like Carlyle or the enormous profits that accrue to Bill Gates. Carlyle works as a corporate raider that raises its capital by selling off parts of the companies it seizes control of – in other words, it adds very little. And there is no way that Gates' work rate – or the capital he initially put into his company – could make him worth €40 billion! This theory only pushes back the original question: if the profit is simply a return for capital, how did the capitalist make enough profit to be able to accumulate capital?

Given the inconsistencies in these stories, there is a tendency to revert to an older theory of profit, namely, that some individuals buy parts cheap and sell them dear. This was a theory that could explain the profits of merchant capital but not modern capital where differences of time and space have become more compressed in a global marketplace. It suggests that profit arises from bending the rules of 'fair exchange' or even outright fraud. The problem, however, is that while this might explain how one firm made a profit at the expense of another, it cannot explain how additional profit is made for all the capitalists in society. It is like the game of 'pass the parcel', but it cannot explain how the parcel got bigger at the end of the round.

Marx's theory of surplus value gets round many of these problems. His starting point is that profit cannot arise from the sphere of circulation where goods and services are exchanged on an equal basis. This arena is supposed, as Marx remarks, to be the 'very Eden of the innate rights of man – the exclusive realm of Freedom, Equality, Property and Bentham'.[21] In this sphere, everyone enters contracts of their own free will; they exchange commodities that are of equal value; they dispose of their own property; and, as Jeremy Bentham in the nineteenth century put it, their motives are pure self-interest. To see how profit is really made, Marx argues, you have to leave this noisy realm where everything takes place on the surface and go into 'the hidden abode of production on whose threshold hangs the notice "No admittance except on business".'[22]

The workplace is the arena where the key relationship in modern society is forged. The worker arrives with a commodity to sell – his or her own labour – and in return receives a wage in an apparently fair exchange. It is all perfectly legal and free – both parties are treated as free commodity owners. However, there is a problem.

Even though economic theory suggests that the labour–wages transaction is just another commodity exchange, there is a major difference: the worker is a human being and his or her labour is not a thing or a service that can be traded like any other. What is being sold is something that is inseparable from basic humanity – it is their physical and mental energy that is sold to the capitalist for a definitive period. Rather than seeing labour as a definite, specific thing, it is more correct to refer to it as *labour power*. What is being exchanged, therefore, is something indefinite – the ability of workers to use their energy for something limited, which is a set amount of money.

You can see how this works if you try an experiment. According to the rules of the market, you are allowed to bargain over your wages before the contract with your employer is signed. (Most, of course, do not because they are desperate for a job but, theoretically, you can.) Let's say, however, you try to bargain over your work commitment. You could try a line like 'I will give you 80 per cent commitment or work effort if you give me €400 a week.' Your prospective employer would quite literally consider you mad. They want your total work energy and creativity made available to them while you are employed, even though they are giving you a fixed wage. In other words, they want to establish their property rights in your *full* labour power during a particular time-frame. The reason is that this most unusual commodity can create more value than it receives in a 'fair exchange' of wages.

To see why this occurs let us ask what happens when the worker goes through the factory or office door. Their employer has, according to the laws of the market, paid the exchange value for this commodity. This exchange value – the wage – is determined by the amount of labour time socially necessary to produce it, i.e. to rear, feed, clothe and educate the worker so that he or she is able to work. In other words, the wage will have to cover the costs of food, shelter and all the cultural necessities that a modern worker expects as the average requirement for living in their society.

But once the owner has taken possession of the commodity, they are entitled to its full use value like any other and the worker is put to work under the control of the capitalist to whom their labour now belongs. The basis of the wage labour system is that workers can make no claim on the goods or services they create because these belong to the capitalist. The capitalist will employ the most modern managerial techniques to get the maximum possible labour out of the worker. They will remind the workers repeatedly that 'time is money' and that not a minute can be wasted because 'they are not on their own time'.

This occurs because labour power has the capacity to produce more value than the price it was bought at. The workers will produce enough goods or services in the first few hours of the working day to cover the cost of their wages and for the rest of the day will be working for free for the capitalist. The working day is, therefore, divided between paid labour time and unpaid labour time. Workers create *surplus value* because there is a difference between the cost of their wages and the value that their labour produces.

Behind the appearance of a fair and equal exchange there is, therefore, an unequal exchange. When someone is forced to give something for nothing, we can reasonably call this *exploitation*. Profit arises from this exploitation of workers and this in turn explains why there is a conflict of interest between employers and workers. It also explains why every effort to improve wages meets with resistance from employers and why they constantly seek to squeeze extra effort out of workers to boost their profits. They know that the working day can be divided into two periods: *necessary labour time*, when workers produce enough value to cover their wages, and *surplus labour time*, when they are working for free to make profits. If they can cover the cost of wages quicker by squeezing more effort from workers and then selling the goods, more surplus value will be created.

So far we have used a model of an individual corporation and its workforce to show how surplus value is created, but Marx's concern was how society as a whole functioned. He therefore sees surplus being extracted from the collective mass of workers in different corporations, which then creates a general pool of surplus value. Different capitalists fight it out between each other until eventually there is a broad equalisation of the rate of profit across society. One way this occurs is through capital shifting out of areas with lower rates of profit and into sectors with higher rates. When this occurs, there is less pressure on the remaining capitalists and they can win greater market share and thus help drive up their rate of profit. Through these flows of investment between one sector and another an equilibrium point is established, which is the average rate of profit.

Much of the surplus value returns to the capitalist who originally hired the workers in the form of profit. But different slices of the total surplus value are also reallocated according to the conflicts between individual capitalists. Microsoft, for example, demands a licensing fee based on the use of its software. This means that it claims a slice of the surplus value produced by other corporations as well as its own workforce. Similarly, banks demand interest payments as the price for lending money. Still other capitalists specialise in accelerating the turnover time in which goods are sold, and they too demand an extra share of the surplus value created from goods imported from, say, China. Finally, other capitalists in heavy machine-producing industries charge high prices and so demand a greater share of the surplus value of others to compensate for their higher capital investments.

The whole system is driven by competition. No matter how successful each capitalist is in exploiting their workforce, they can always be eliminated by their rivals. This explains the restless, fanatical and ultimately irrational element of how the economy is organised. Although Microsoft or Carlyle may make vast profits, they still face constant challenges from rivals. They are, therefore, compelled to reinvest a proportion of those profits in order to find new ways of making more profit. They also face a contradictory pressure as shareholders press for ever-higher dividend payments, threatening to sell out to rival firms if they do not get a 15 per cent or 20 per cent return on their investment each year. The result is that capitalism is driven by a mad, relentless drive to accumulate, to realise its essential mission – the self-expansion of capital.

These pressures mean that it is both an extremely dynamic and also a chaotic system. In its early phases, it laid the conditions for liberating people from low levels of productivity. In the *Communist Manifesto* Marx and Engels noted that 'the bourgeoisie, during its scarce one hundred years, have created more massive and more colossal productive forces than all the preceding generations put together'.[23] They readily acknowledged this, even while attacking the system for producing poverty and exploitation. But as the system matures, the irrationality that lies behind its essential drive to accumulate comes ever more to the fore. In *Capital*, Marx describes the main dynamic of modern capitalism as

> Frantically bent on making value expand itself, he (the capitalist) ruthlessly forces the human race to produce for production sake. Accumulate, accumulate! That is the Moses and the prophets ... Therefore save, save i.e. reconvert the greatest proportion of surplus value or surplus product into capital. Accumulation for the sake of accumulation, production for production's sake: this was the formula in which classical economists expressed the historical mission of the bourgeoisie in the period of its domination.[24]

This is a different dynamic from that in all previous societies. In a pre-modern society, the walls of the lord's stomach set limits on the exploitation of the peasantry. The lord could only consume so much, enjoy so many feasts, live in so many castles – and was not bound to compete with rivals except through occasional military encounters. The lords treated their peasants dreadfully – but they were not driven by the same pressure to keep on accumulating. Yet modern society is fundamentally different. Bill Gates may be wealthier than any aristocrat of the past, but his 'tragedy' is that he cannot rest. He cannot consume all his wealth or relax and take it easy – he is a driven man who has to compel his workforce to produce for production sake. This leads to a strange hybrid of rationality and irrationality.

The most scientific methods are employed to squeeze more out of workers, to invent new techniques of production, to delve into human psychology in order to manipulate people to buy. There is no room for superstition or sentimentality – the culture is built on a cold, calculating rationality, but at a different level it is fundamentally irrational. The whole economy has been disconnected from the needs of people and its sole purpose is the self-expansion of capital.

The result is a society that is out of control and, as we shall see, one that is subject to ever more crisis.

3
Alienation

In the United States 26 per cent of adults have experienced mental illness in the past year and almost a quarter of these episodes have been severe. Over their whole lifetime, half the population will suffer.[1]

How can this amazing social phenomenon be explained? Research on the Human Genome Project has led some scientists to seek a gene for every behavioural problem and so there is supposed to be a gene for aggression, alcoholism or mental depression. This trend has led to a denial of social problems and a focus on the genetic defects of individuals yet this explanation can hardly apply to the US figures. Depending on the particular studies, Americans are between three and ten times more likely to suffer depression today than in the 1950s.[2] The genetic profile of the US population could hardly have changed that quickly to account for these changes.

The belief that emotional distress is primarily caused by maladjusted individuals leads to two main solutions.

The first is to change your image and look positive. There is huge focus on appearance in modern Western culture with its implicit motto: 'I appear, therefore I will be'. The message is that your dress, image and skin texture can transform your relationships and empower you. Conversely, if you have a poorly paid job or are suffering loneliness in unfulfilled relationships, you only have yourself to blame. You should instead choose to 'look good' and with this 'positive' attitude you can succeed. Reality, however, contradicts this at almost every turn. The beauty myth industry, as Naomi Wolf called it, provokes 'cycles of self-hatred' through the constant promotion of images of 'goddesses' who have little in common with the lives of normal women.[3] Meanwhile the multi-billion diet industry grows ever larger on failure as up to 95 per cent of people regain the weight they lose. The 'change your image' message leads only to further dissatisfaction for many.

The second solution is consumerism. Instead of *being* fully human, *having* is the way to express our humanity. We are supposed to surround ourselves with products that identify who we are instead of forging relationships that enrich our lives. Through the mystical power of these products, we can get in touch with a deeper part of our souls. Use aromatherapy soap and you will dispel your morning blues and develop a mystical communion with the Yawanawa people of the Brazilian rainforest.[4] Spend your weekend in a DIY shop and you will create an idealised home that is your refuge from a cruel world. Yet mass consumerism is based on an endless cycle of buy–satisfy–dissatisfy–buy. The products that are supposed to change our lives resume their mundane status very quickly and our dissatisfaction can only be relieved by new products.

Marx wrote in a different era and did not offer ready-made, individual solutions to the malaise of modern culture but his theory of alienation offers astonishing insights into the current dehumanising of humanity.

FROM FEUERBACH TO HUMAN NATURE

Marx was not the first to use the term alienation but he gave it a radical meaning. Alienation was a concept used originally in Christian theology to denote being cast out from the grace of God into a state of outer darkness. In legal theory, it referred to a right to sell property in contrast to the 'inalienable' ties that existed in feudal society. In Hegel, Absolute Spirit was said to 'alienate' itself in nature in order to progress to self-consciousness. Marx's particular use of the term alienation was, however, derived from Ludwig Feuerbach, who had broken with religion after studying under Hegel. In 1830, he wrote his first book entitled *Thoughts on Death and Immortality* where he argued that belief in a personal God and one's own immortality was an expression of egotism. Against such egotism, Feuerbach advocated a philosophy of love and defended the value of sexual love. These beliefs led to persecution as his book was confiscated and he was dismissed from his university post. Facing such a hostile reception, he retired to Bavaria, as Engels put it, to 'rusticate and grow sour in a little village',[5] but was still subjected to raids by the police.

In 1841, he published *The Essence of Christianity*, which received an enthusiastic reception from Marx. Here Feuerbach declared his break with the speculative philosophy of Hegel, stating that:

> I unconditionally repudiate absolute, immaterial, self-sufficing speculation ... I differ ... from those philosophers who pluck out their eyes so that they may see better; for my thought I require

the senses, especially sight; I found my ideas on materials which can be appropriated only through the senses.[6]

This attack reflected Feuerbach's adherence to materialism – a standpoint that sees the material world as the sole foundation for human consciousness. In accordance with this, Feuerbach argued that real knowledge derived from our senses rather than speculation and denounced Hegel's abstract philosophical system as just another form of religion. The most subversive element of his argument, however, concerned God.

Here he turned philosophy upside down by claiming that God did not create man, but rather man created God. Arguments about whether or not God exists were subverted by the claim that the 'divine' was simply a projection of human traits. If God was all-loving, it was because human beings had an immense capacity to love. If God was infinitely wise, it was only because humans had wonderfully creative minds. If God was a creator, it was only because making and changing the world were distinct human characteristics. What man adored in God were, therefore, his own 'divine' qualities and so the basis of religion was none other than human characteristics projected onto an alien being that took on a life of its own.

The act of creating a God, however, demeaned humanity because the more that God appeared as beautiful and good, the more human beings appeared as sinful and selfish. The more empty life is, Feuerbach wrote, the fuller and more concrete is God. 'The impoverishing of the real world and the enriching of God is one act. Only the poor man has a rich God'.[7] In order to create the Virgin Mary, for example, believers had to deny their own sexuality:

> The monks made a vow of chastity to God; they mortified the sexual passion in themselves, but, therefore, they had in Heaven, in the Virgin Mary, the image of women – an image of love. They could the more easily dispense with real women, in proportion as the ideal woman was an object of love for them [8]

Alienation was, therefore, like the story of Frankenstein's monster – our own creations rose to become a power that oppressed us. Feuerbach summarised his solution as follows:

> The necessary turning-point of history is, therefore, the open confession, that the consciousness of God is nothing else than

the consciousness of the species ... that there is no other essence which man can think, dream of, imagine, feel, believe in, wish for, love and adore as the *absolute,* than the essence of human nature itself.[9]

Marx took Feuerbach's use of the term alienation and defined it as a pattern whereby our own creations become a power over us. He was in agreement with Feuerbach's sentiments but he raised a number of problems with the argument. Feuerbach never explained why people created gods or why they hid this from themselves. But if creating gods was not an inevitable or natural activity, why did people do it? Why did they demean themselves by giving their own creations such a power over them? Feuerbach had also assumed that alienation could be solved by an 'open confession'. But if this were the case, why had people not already made the confession? Why had they remained blind to their own creation? Was it simply a matter of waiting to be awoken by a philosopher who had seen the truth?

In his short, highly compressed *Theses on Feuerbach*, Marx challenged this by arguing that the roots of alienation went much deeper than mere illusion. The creation of a god could only have arisen from a real need in people who must experience something in their daily lives in order to need an alienated god. One of the great images of the Christian religion, for example, is of the Holy Family who reside in heaven. In order to discover why this image was so powerful you had to look for the secret, Marx argued, in 'the earthly family'.[10] People often wanted a haven from a heartless world and desperately hoped that their family could provide the security and fulfilment they could not get from the wider society. The Holy Family, therefore, was an idealised image of a family that people wished for but could never attain. More generally, Marx argued, the roots of religion had to be sought in the 'cleavages and self-contradictions within this secular basis'.[11]

Feuerbach had partially recognised some of these dynamics, but he wrote constantly about man in general rather than men and women in a specific, historic society. He had resolved the mystery of religion by showing how it mirrored human essence, but this 'humane essence' was an abstract individual with no history of society. Individuals, however, are part of an 'ensemble of social relations' and these real, concrete relations had a decisive impact on how they thought and acted.[12] By closing off an inquiry into these specific relations and speaking of 'Man', Feuerbach had fallen back into the type of speculation he accused Hegel of. He had not examined the social conditions that gave rise to alienation. Instead of asking why 'Man' had created God, Marx thought it was necessary to look at specific societies to see what gave rise to a need for a god and, more crucially, why other forms of alienated activity also occurred.

In the *Economic and Philosophical Manuscripts* of 1844, Marx produced a short but brilliant outline of his own theory of alienation and many of its themes would re-appear throughout his later writings. To understand his argument, we need to look at how he answered the question: what was different about human beings?

WHAT IS A HUMAN?

Following Plato, many philosophers argued that Mind or Soul formed the core definition of what it means to be human. Man was supposed to live in the lofty world of the Soul and his body was simply a temporary backdrop for his wider spiritual journey. The natural world that man inhabited was driven by base animal instincts and so philosophers established a dualism that divided him into body and soul, spiritual and material. Marx, however, held the opposing materialist view and asserted that there could be no 'pure' consciousness because it was always tied to matter and could not exist independently of it. Even the contents of our consciousness had to be expressed in the material form of language.

> From the start the 'spirit' is afflicted with the curse of being 'burdened' with matter, which here makes its appearance in the form of agitated layers of air, sounds, in short, of language. Language is as old as consciousness, language is practical consciousness that exists also for other men and for that reason alone it really exists for me personally as well.[13]

To inquire into the nature of humanity one therefore had to start by looking at how human individuals establish a relationship with nature. People must first look after their real bodily needs before they can have a spiritual life. We must eat, create shelter, maintain body warmth before we can philosophise, compose music, paint sublime beauty. Marx and Engels, therefore, wrote in the *German Ideology*:

> In direct contrast to German philosophy which descends from heaven to earth, here we ascend from earth to heaven. That is to say, we do not set out from what men say, imagine, conceive, nor from men as narrated, thought of, imagined, conceived, in

order to arrive at men in the flesh. We set out from real, active men, and on the basis of their real life-process we demonstrate the development of the ideological reflexes and echoes of this life-process.[14]

This embrace of materialism, however, did not mean that Marx thought that humans were simply passive products of their environment, as some of the Enlightenment writers had suggested. They had propounded a mechanical materialism whereby human beings were determined by climate, geography or even their social conditions. They wanted to argue that if the conditions changed, humans would change automatically. Marx, however, rejected this approach because it ignored the active relationship that people forged with their environment. The old materialism had neglected 'sensuous human activity' and so 'the *active* side was developed abstractly by idealism'.[15] While we are part of the natural world, we are not simply identical with it or simply shaped by it. We are not just naked apes whose behaviour can be explained by mating rituals or animal drives, but have a unique, active relationship with nature. The nature of this relationship is what will define us as human beings.

A cursory glance at the human body shows that we do not have a well-developed defence system for survival. Our evolutionary history means that our bodies are not covered in fur to keep us warm; we do not have sharp claws or strong jaws to ward off attacks; we are not particularly fast or agile; our hearing range is comparatively low compared to other animals. With these significant disadvantages, we are easy prey to the many wild beasts seeking tasty and tender meat. Fortunately, we have other attributes that compensate for these weaknesses.

Our evolutionary history has produced a thin skull which allows the brain to expand in proportion to our body mass. Binocular vision and a short snout allows for more accurate and in-depth vision. Our early ancestors lost the habit of using their knuckles to balance while walking and adopted a more erect post which left their hands free. They also had an opposable or prehensile thumb that allowed for fine motor skills. The humble hand was, therefore, free to play a huge role in human evolution as we learnt to make tools in order to fashion the world around us. But the more we used our hands to make tools, the more we learnt to use this physical organ differently.[16] Human labour became the key to human survival and this made us a unique species in a host of ways.

First, the act of transforming nature helped to bring individuals together in mutual support and so we became super-social animals.

An animal survives by adapting to a particular environment through biological organs which result from natural selection and cannot be replaced. Oystercatchers with long fine beaks, for example, fit in with an environment where small worms can be unearthed from sand but if this source of food vanishes, the oystercatcher must either move on or die out. Only those with a different type of beak that is suitable for other types of food will survive. Similarly, dark-coloured moths are more likely than pale-coloured moths to survive in an industrial environment marked by soot and grime because they have a better camouflage.

Humans, however, learn to work cooperatively to change their environment rather than simply adapting to it because we use tools that are replaceable rather than relying on our biological organs. Over a period people learn to judge how efficient these instruments are for their purposes and these judgements create new conditions for human communication. As Fischer put it:

> Animals have little to communicate with each other. Their language is instinctive; a rudimentary system of signs for danger, mating etc. Only in work and through work do living beings have much to say to each other. Language came into being with tools.[17]

Second, human labour dramatically changes the natural world. Today many ecologists such as Bill McKibben argue that 'original nature' has largely disappeared and imply that human intervention is necessarily bad.[18] Yet once people started using tools to produce for their needs, this change was inevitable. Animals, of course, also change the natural world by building nests, webs and dwellings, but their production is 'one-sided'.[19] They produce for their own direct physical needs or those of their young and they stick with the normal behaviour of their species. By contrast, humans produce even when they are free from physical need and, additionally, can copy the activities of all other species. Human activity is, therefore, far more 'universal' because it can make all of nature an object of human gratification. In other words, human intervention gives nature a history.

Third, by changing the world around us, we change ourselves and become historical beings in a way that no other species have. A lion alive in 2011, for example, acts no differently from its ancestors of thousands of years ago. The human being, however, has not only moved from a technology based on the stone age axe to one that uses wireless broadband on computers but has also changed his or her sensuous nature. We start with basic primitive needs but to meet them we create a social organisation of labour that in turn generates other non-physical or 'spiritual' needs. As well as food and shelter, we need different forms of companionship, intellectual and emotional stimulation, a sexuality that reflects changing social mores and new modes of art and communication. Even our basic senses of seeing, hearing, feeling, tasting and smelling are changed through society. The human ear learns to appreciate different types of music, and food no longer becomes just a stomach-filler but is linked to cultural practices that evoke memories and images of particular communities. What we think of as natural changes profoundly over the course of human history.

All of this means that there is no fixed human nature which can explain social behaviour in all societies. Instead of acknowledging the really dynamic ways in which people change, advocates of this argument take a snapshot of behaviour under the present society and claim that it has deep roots in human history. Humans do not, however, compete against each other because of their genetic make-up or a 'natural propensity'. We do so only at a particular point in history because these practices grew out of a specific way of organising our relationship with nature. At different points in history, people forged different relationships and developed different sensibilities. Instead of static qualities that are implanted in people from all time, humans are free, within certain limits, to make and remake ourselves, through our interaction with nature.

This leads to the crux of Marx's understanding of the human species. In order to be fully human, we need to participate in a free and active way in changing the world around us. We need to recognise ourselves in the world we have made, and come to know ourselves through the eyes of other human beings with whom we cooperate.

This imperative is barely captured by the word 'production' because this has been so distorted by our experiences under capitalism. A claim that 'production' is central to humanity will sound as if you are advocating a labour camp with the words 'Work Makes You Free' emblazoned over the entrance gates. However, this difficulty in meaning only arises from the real distortions of our present world. Marx put labour at the centre of his analysis of alienation only because he wanted to contrast a really human life with the distortions imposed on us. He did not want people to work harder or spend more time in factories or extol the virtues of the model worker who could move 102 tons of coal in less than six hours. Rather, as Meszaros puts it, 'the central theme of Marx's moral theory is: how to realize human freedom'.[20] Real freedom, however, could not arise from a rejection of the world though a flight into high-sounding intellectualism or spirituality. You are not 'mentally free' if your body is imprisoned by a distorted form of labour. Freedom can only be based on an affirmation of what distinguishes us as humans.

In *Capital*, Marx summarised how labour means objectifying our ideas in nature and how this distinguishes us as human beings:

> A spider conducts operations that resemble those of a weaver, and a bee would put many a human architect to shame by the construction of its honeycomb cells. But what distinguishes the worst architect from the best of bees is that the architect builds the cell in his mind before he constructs in wax. At the end of every labour process, a result emerges which had already been conceived by the worker at the beginning ...[21]

Productive activity or, more precisely, our active relationship with nature, is therefore not just work; it is actually 'life engendering life'.[22] People will only be really free when nature becomes our work and we can recognise ourselves in a world we have already made.[23]

Under capitalism this cannot happen because we produce commodities that exert great power over us. Here an interesting parallel arises with the mechanisms Feuerbach suggested were at play when humans created a god. The adoration of a god arises because believers think that that god has created them rather than that they have created him. But the same inversion occurs with capital because workers believe 'it provides them with jobs'. The markets – the name commonly given to flows of capital – appear as a tempestuous and unpredictable power that has to be obeyed. Just as there are priests who claim special access to God, so too there are expert economists who claim special access to the higher power of the market. As Marx put it:

> Just as in religion the spontaneous activity of the human imagination, of the human brain and the human heart, operates on the individual independently of him – that is, operates as an alien, divine or diabolical activity – so is the worker's activity

not his spontaneous activity. It belongs to another; it is loss of his self.[24]

The alienation that developed under capitalism has four main aspects.

ALIENATION IN THE LABOUR PROCESS

Human labour should, according to Marx, be a life-affirming activity that unleashes our creativity. Even to this day, a link between 'creativity' and 'work' survives in a small number of instances. The writing of free Linux programs, for example, is undertaken for pleasure because software engineers enjoy problem-solving. In the past, the construction of elaborate furniture by artisans involved both work and artistic expression. Other forms of work involve more drudgery and few would suggest that maintaining sewers or picking fruit is a form of creative expression. But there is no necessary reason why one group of individuals should perform drudgery all their lives while another does all the more pleasurable activity. It is possible to mix different skill sets to give an overall opportunity for creative expression.

Marx argued that this does not happen under capitalism because work is entirely external to the worker. Workers have no say in what is produced or how it is produced – the activity does not arise from their needs or desires and is entirely alien to them. As a result, work does not support the life energy of the worker but leaves him or her stunted. When working,

> He does not affirm himself but denies himself, does not feel content but unhappy, does not develop freely his physical and mental energy but mortifies his body and ruins his mind. The worker, therefore, only feels himself outside of work, and in his work feels outside of himself. He feels at home when he is not working and when he is working he does not feel at home.[25]

Once a worker passes through the office or factory door, his or her 'labour is no longer voluntary, but coerced, it is forced labour'.[26] Workers have to do what they are told by management and so their work has no element of spontaneous creativity. As soon as there is no compulsion, work is shunned because it has literally become a type of self-sacrifice. This explains why people think of the weekend and holidays as their 'free time' and why work is only a means to an end. In an almost prophetic description of modern life, Marx claimed that the worker

> no longer feels himself to be freely active in any but his animal functions – eating, drinking, procreating, or at most in his dwelling and in dressing-up, etc.; and in his human functions he no longer feels himself to be anything but an animal. What is animal becomes human and what is human becomes animal.
>
> Certainly eating, drinking, procreating, etc., are also genuine human functions. But in the abstraction which separates them from the sphere of all other human activity and turns them into sole and ultimate ends, they are animal function.[27]

Since Marx's day, alienation of the labour process has been intensified as work is broken into minute parts that form part of a detailed division of labour. The individuals deployed to work on these tiny parts have often no idea how it all fits together and certainly have little say in how it is organised. Call-centre workers, for example, are put through periods of excruciating boredom, selling the same products in a telesales department. So alienating has the job become that the very words they use in customer support units are scripted.[28] This detailed division of labour is based on a separation of conception and planning from routine operations.

One of the key innovations of capitalism was the assembly line which was invented by Henry Ford as a way to control the pace of work and even the body movement of workers. Instead of acknowledging that this work system deprived workers of the use of their intelligence, Ford argued that workers were naturally stupid and so fitted for his systems:

> Repetitive labour ... is a terrifying prospect to a certain kind of mind. It is terrifying to me. I could not possibly do the same thing day in and day out, but to other minds, perhaps I might say to the majority of minds it holds no terror. In fact to some kinds of mind thought is absolutely appalling ... the average worker, I am sorry to say, wants a job in which he does not have to think.[29]

In his classic study *Labor and Monopoly Capital*, the American Marxist Harry Braverman argued that Taylorism has become the dominant philosophy of work in modern capitalism. Frederick Taylor was the founder of a school of 'scientific management' that purported to use 'science' to establish greater managerial control over the labour process. Braverman summarised its three principles as follows:

> The first principle is the gathering together and development of knowledge of the labor process, and the second is the concentration of this knowledge as the exclusive preserve of management – together with its converse, the absence of such knowledge among workers – then the third step is the use of this monopoly of knowledge to control each step of the labour process and its mode of execution.[30]

After management takes workers' knowledge about how to do a job, they codify, measure and benchmark it against other methods. They establish written procedures that conform to their way of planning work and provide great detail of how work should be organised. Very little is left to chance and the space for decision-making by workers is constantly whittled down. In his early experiments on work organisation (which involved lifting pig iron) Taylor also revealed his inherent contempt for workers who were subject to his 'time and motion' methods. He wrote:

> Now one of the very first requirements for a man who is fit to handle pig iron as a regular occupation is that he shall be so stupid and so phlegmatic that he more nearly resembles in his mental make up the ox than any other type. The man who is mentally alert and intelligent is for this very reason entirely unsuited to what would, for him, be grinding monotony of work of this character.[31]

Managerial control over work has reached a new pitch with a further development known as Toyotaism or lean production. This aims to intensify work effort by measuring it not over the working day or hour, but in seconds. The Toyota standard for work performed each minute is 57 seconds. In other words, just three seconds downtime in every minute. Instead of more humane rhythms where natural breaks occur in the pace of work, the ideal, according to Taiichi Ohno, is to have '100 per cent value added work'.[32] This can only occur through total managerial control over labour process. The pattern of intensification of work is not, however, confined to the car industry but is evident throughout the global economy. A study undertaken by Francis Green noted that one of the paradoxes of modern work is that it has come 'under increased and unwelcome control from above, leaving individual employees with less influence over their daily lives and correspondingly a less fulfilling experience than before'.[33] It was an accurate summary of Marx's prediction.

ALIENATION FROM PRODUCTS

The estranging of the worker from his or her own productive activity is at the core of alienation. From this it follows that the products or services will also be alienated from the worker. The separation of products from their producers reaches a new pitch under capitalism.

In feudal society, people had not developed the means to control the natural world and so famines were a frequent occurrence. Between 1600 and 1800, for example, France recorded 26 major famines, while in Florence one harvest in every four years was insufficient for needs.[34] Control over land was the key to the economy and people were defined in relation to the land, being assigned a rank or estate established by their blood-line. This form of domination was, however, double-edged. Freedom was denied to peasants who were tied to the land, but this also meant that the land was tied to the people. As serfdom was abolished, tenant farmers controlled small plots of land and grew produce for their own subsistence. The lords took a proportion of their produce – in the Hurepoix region near Paris in the seventeenth century, for example, the lords took up to 50 per cent of the produce[35] – but the peasantry had control of the rest and could dispose of it as they saw fit. In the cities, the artisan guilds were able to impose restrictions on what was produced and how it was produced.

Capitalism changed all this by severing the links between the producer and his products so that people no longer had the right to dispose of what they produced. A building worker might construct houses but be deprived of ownership of a home. A toy factory worker in Thailand might produce for the global market but be unable to give her own children toys. No matter how desperate their needs, workers no longer had a right to use what they made. Workers have no control of what becomes of their produce – it becomes entirely alien to them.

Marx argued that products were not just independent and alien to the workers but had also become real power over them. This is most obvious in the case of machinery which, although a human creation, is often used to dehumanise the worker. Instead of being an extension of the skills and knowledge of workers it is used to eliminate their skills. It imposes unskilled, auto-monotonous activity on workers so that their ability to command a precious skill is minimised. David Noble's study of the design of computerised numerical control machinery, for example, showed how deliberate choices were made to reduce a reliance on skilled, unionised workers.[36] More generally, Marx argued:

> The means of production are at once changed into means for the absorption of the labour of others. It is now no longer the worker who employs the means of production, but the means of production that employ the labourer.
>
> Instead of being consumed by him as material elements of his productive activity, they consume him as the ferment necessary to their own life-process ...
>
> Furnaces and workshops that stand idle by night, and absorb no living labour, are 'a mere loss' to the capitalist. Hence, furnaces and workshops constitute 'lawful claims upon the night labour' of the work-people.[37]

Products also become a power over us in another, even more fundamental sense. The more workers create, the stronger capital grows in enslaving them as living commodities. The greater productivity they give, the more will be taken from them as surplus labour and transferred to capital. As Marx put it, 'labour brings about the accumulation of capital and with this increasing prosperity of society, it renders the worker ever more dependent on the capitalist'.[38] As workers are forced into ever more specialised tasks, the worker becomes ever more dependent on selling his 'one-sided, machine-like labour':[39]

> Just as he is thus depressed spiritually and physically to the condition of a machine and from being a man becomes an abstract activity and a belly, so he also becomes more dependent on every fluctuation in market price, on the application of capital, and on the whim of the rich.[40]

In brief, the more the worker spends himself, the more powerful becomes the alien world of objects which he creates over and against himself. In previous societies, if you worked harder you might consume more, even if it were only bigger crumbs. Under capitalism it is the opposite. The harder you work, the greater the likelihood that there are too many goods produced and your value as a labour commodity lessens.

ALIENATION FROM OTHERS

Alienation in the workplace has major implications for our relations with other people. One obvious and immediate consequence is the division of society into classes. If the product of labour does not belong to the worker, it must belong to someone else. As Marx remarked, 'Not the gods, not nature, but only man himself can be this alien power over man'.[41]

Antagonistic relationships pervade and poison society so that seemingly neutral, technical operations are implicated in the conflict. Behind an abstract rhetoric about citizenship, society is torn apart by class division. Access to education, the treatment of illness, even engineering projects are organised against a background of class privilege. One piece of research, for example, suggested that civil engineers often deny there is any general public interest in the large projects they are constructing. Instead they see it as part of their job to manage forms of 'stakeholder consultation' that enable corporate interests to hold sway.[42]

Alienation from other people, however, means more than simply class antagonism because the social nature of human beings is linked to productive activity. If the relationships in production are distorted, people seek solace through a retreat into the private sphere. Society is then conceived as made up of competing individual interests where each person sees others only as means to their own ends. Individualism, therefore, becomes the dominant cultural outlook in modern society because it promises spurious freedom in these private worlds.

The original meaning of the word 'individual' was an object or person that could not be cut or divided, and the word 'individuality' only assumed its modern meaning in the course of a rebellion against the suffocating ties of feudal society.[43] However, as capitalism developed, this evolved into the idea that there was an opposition between the individual and society. The aristocratic liberal Alexis de Tocqueville detected this trend when he visited America in the 1830s:

Individualism is a word recently coined to express a new idea. Our fathers only knew about egotism. Egotism is a passionate and exaggerated love of self, which leads a man to think of all things in terms of himself and to prefer himself to all. Individualism is a calm and considered feeling, which disposes each citizen to isolate himself from the mass of his fellows and withdraw into a circle of family and friends; with this little society formed to his taste, he gladly leaves the greater society to look after itself.[44]

De Tocqueville thought such a withdrawal from society was dangerous but neo-liberals subsequently turned it into a cause of celebration. According to the founder of this doctrine, Friedrich Hayek, there could be no talk of common social interests because only individuals existed. In the words of his follower Margaret Thatcher, 'There is no such thing as society'. Her aim was to break up every form of social solidarity in favour of personal responsibility and individualism. To that end she undertook a programme of privatisation to create more shareholders, but as she explained, 'Economics are the method but the object is to change the human soul'.[45]

Marx was very much for individual development and against suffocating ties of dependence but he challenged the idea that there was an opposition of the individual and society and the illusion that freedom arose from cutting social bonds. 'The individual', he argued, 'is *the social being*'[46] because we need other people to be fully human. He added that, 'man's relationship to himself becomes for him *objective* and *actual* through his relations to the other man'.[47] In *Capital*, he put it even more starkly emphasising how we can only know who we are through our relationships with other people:

Since he comes into the world neither with a looking glass in his hand, nor as a Fichtean philosopher, to whom 'I am I' is sufficient, man first sees and recognises himself in other men. Peter only establishes his own identity as a man by first comparing himself with Paul as being of like kind. And thereby Paul, just as he stands in his Pauline personality, becomes to Peter the type of the *genus homo*.[48]

Alienation under capitalism, however, leads to a fake individuality, akin to the notion that 'the Englishman's home is his castle'. There is a promise that lack of fulfilment and boredom in the public world can be magically blown away by a private relationship. Individuals are not only supposed to provide love and comfort to each other but to unearth the 'real' hidden self who can only blossom in a private relationship. Yet the higher the expectations of fulfilment, the more strains that are put on relationships. People are encouraged to think of themselves as atoms that are self-sufficient with no real social bonds, living in a society that is only held together by the power of the state. This atomised existence, however, is imaginary and spurious. Marx parodied it as follows:

> The egoistic individual in civil society may in his non-sensuous imagination and lifeless abstraction inflate himself into an atom, i.e. into an unrelated, self-sufficient, wantless, *absolutely full*, blessed being.
>
> [But] every activity and property of his being, every one of his vital urges, becomes a need, a necessity, which his self-seeking transforms into seeking for other things and human beings outside himself.[49]

The more we imagine that we are disconnected from each other, the easier it is to turn us into market targets. Corporations try to reduce the many, complex aspects of the human personality to the one dominant feeling of *having*. Their messages are similar: 'Wear Levi jeans and you will get a lover' or 'Wash with Dove soap and you will stay young forever'. Even washing detergents can help your emotional well-being, according to Kevin Roberts, CEO of Saatchi & Saatchi: 'Tide is not a laundry detergent. It's an enabler. It's moved from the heart of the laundry to the heart of the family.'[50]

The great irony is that the promise of uniqueness and individuality in the private sphere is suffocated by brands that produce a deep, repressive conformity. Each brand promises transcendence from conformity, but the brand itself creates the most conformist transcendence of conformity. Nike promises transcendence through sport, but Nike runners have become a must-have for every teenager. Starbucks offers a special 'third place' that is neither work nor home – but is the same dreary place in every part of the world. Capitalism tries to break the real bonds of solidarity and replace them with artificial, corporate ones. Genuine connections between people are replaced with loyalty to 'an abstracted corporate parent'.[51]

In a damning indictment of how corporations try to insert themselves in the lives of atomised individuals, Marx wrote prophetically:

> no eunuch flatters his despot more basely or uses more despicable means to stimulate his dulled capacity for pleasure in order to sneak a favour for himself than does the industrial eunuch.

He puts himself at the service of the other's most depraved fancies, plays the pimp between him and his need, excites in him morbid appetites, lies in wait for each of his weaknesses – all so that he can then demand the cash for this service of love.

Every product is a bait with which to seduce away the other's very being, his money; every real and possible need is a weakness which will lead the fly to the glue-pot.[52]

ALIENATION FROM OUR HUMANITY

In *Economic and Philosophical Manuscripts*, Marx argued that we had also become alienated from our 'species being'. By this he meant those potentialities which mark us off from other living creatures.[53] The greatest of those potentials is our ability to remake ourselves and our society. This capacity is primarily what we call the goal of freedom because it implies that we do not have to be confined within the boundaries of any one society. When a socialist society is established, people will be able to look back at the tremendous achievement of not just overcoming capitalism but also starting to create a new humanity.

For the socialist man, the *entire so-called history of the world* is nothing but the creation of man through human labour, nothing but the emergence of nature for man, so he has visible, irrefutable proof of his birth through himself, of his genesis.[54]

This fantastically optimistic vision challenged doctrines that emphasised a natural badness or evil that can restrict human potential. This assertion of human weakness became the foundation stone of most conservative philosophies that hark back to Edmund Burke's argument that people are prey to their passions and so need guidance. Authority, Burke argued, will always be necessary so 'the inclinations of men should be frequently thwarted … and their passions brought into subjection'.[55] Without this authority, humans are weak and directionless, bobbing about like corks on the ocean waves.

Marx did not believe in Burke's idea of innate human evil that seizes us through passion. Far from humans being blemished by an original fault-line, their tremendous potential was thwarted by capitalism and this led to all manner of evil. The system tore people away from their creative powers so that these only become a means to an end. Instead of work being an expression of human *essence*, it is no more than a means to supporting an individual *existence*. Meanwhile the social world that is left behind becomes dominated by the very things we have created.

Marx refers to this as commodity fetishism. 'Fetishism', contrary to its modern sexual overtones, originally came from the Portuguese word *feiticio* and was used by early merchants to describe a religious practice which venerated objects, thought to be animated by spirits. Marx used the word to describe a world where 'the definite social relations between men themselves … assume for them the fantastic form of a relation between things'[56]. The commodities we produce appear to us to have a life of their own and to be able to subjugate human beings to *their* rules. Instead of seeing how real people make decisions, the movement of these commodities – whether in the form of price movement or, by extension, flows of investment – appear to have a life of their own and to subject human beings to their needs.

To illustrate Marx's point, let us take a typical statement from recent times: 'Bondholders are concerned about sovereign debt in Greece.' Here people with no names are defined as the personification of things called bonds. These bonds – pieces of paper – have feelings of 'concern' which are articulated by their holders. The focus of that concern is another thing called the 'sovereign debt of Greece'. All reference to the social relations through which bankers borrowed money from other rich people has been obliterated. Throughout this discourse, the assumption is that there is no alternative – the 'concern' of the bondholders *must* be addressed because this is how markets work.

Another expression of commodity fetishism is the way money becomes 'the alienated ability of mankind'.[57] Dollar bills and euro coins arise from human activity but become an independent power over us, a 'truly creative power'[58] as Marx called it. Money stands for the congealed abstract labour of humanity. Possession of money determines what is real and what is fantasy, the differences between doing and thinking, 'between what exists within me merely as an idea and the idea which exists as a real object outside of me'.[59] If I have no money to travel, I have no effective need to travel. But if I am a Richard Garriot, a multi-millionaire videogame developer, I can travel into space on a twelve-day trip because I can spend $30 million to turn my desire into reality.

I am bad, dishonest, unscrupulous, stupid; but money is honoured, and hence its possessor.

Money is the supreme good, therefore its possessor is good. Money, besides, saves me the trouble of being dishonest: I am therefore presumed honest ... Do not I, who thanks to money am capable of *all* that the human heart longs for, possess all human capacities? Does not my money, therefore, transform all my incapacities into their contrary?[60]

This alienation of human powers cannot, however, be dismissed as a mere illusion because commodities actually do have a power over us. The real practical overthrow of capitalism is necessary, therefore, to realise human potential. Marx acknowledged that capitalists too experience alienation, but they suffer in a theoretical rather than practical way. They feel 'at ease and strengthened in this self-estrangement' and recognise it as a reflection of their own power.[61] Moreover, they have a direct class interest in perpetuating present-day society. Only 'the emancipation of the workers contains universal human emancipation'.[62] In other words, the goal of socialism is not just the victory of one class over another but the abolition of classes in a free, non-alienated society.

4
Social Class

Ever since the birth of capitalism attempts have been made to deny the reality of class conflict. Strikes and workers' protests were said to be caused by 'outside agitators' who led a mindless rabble. Today, however, the fear of class struggle has been replaced by a confidence among elites that it is all over. In Paul Kingston's *The Classless Society* it is claimed that today 'all the 'losers' of capitalism pose a lesser political threat to the fundamental tenets of the system.[1] Today's underdogs have given up on change and the wealthy, it would seem, can rest easily in their beds.

These comments however appear somewhat premature because growing inequality provides ample reason for conflict. In the US, the top 1 per cent of households have 35 per cent of all privately owned wealth.[2] According to Emmanuel Saez, the gap between the rich and the poor is at 'a level higher than any other year since 1917 and even surpasses 1928, the peak of the stock market bubble in the "roaring" 1920s'.[3] A *New York Times* survey showed that for every additional dollar earned by the bottom 90 per cent, those in the top 0.01 per cent earned an additional $162 in the period 1970–90. Yet from 1990 to 2002, the same tiny minority earned an extra $18,000.[4] This enormous concentration of wealth in modern capitalism has profound effects on social life.

On average, the richer you are the longer you live and the gap in life expectancy is increasing. While the studies vary in detail, the pattern is consistent. In Britain, the difference in life expectancy between the lowest and highest income groups was 7.3 years for men and 7 years for women.[5] In the US, those in the least deprived categories live an average of 4.5 years longer than those in the most deprived category yet in the early 1980s it was only 2.8 years longer.[6] Social class is also linked to illness and poor health. It is often assumed that stress and heart attacks, for example, are an occupational hazard for busy, high-flying executives, but a comprehensive series of health studies on Whitehall civil servants found the opposite to be the case: the lower the job status, the greater the risk of heart disease, some cancers, gastrointestinal disease, depression and suicide.[7]

So even if the tempo and pace of class struggles vary, the notion that social class is dead makes little sense. But what exactly do we mean by social class? Three broad approaches to thinking about social class are evident.

The first sees classes as rungs on a social ladder. This 'gradational view' divides society into categories that are 'above' or 'below' one another, based on income, status or a combination of the two. Status means a measure of respect or social esteem bestowed by other members of society. This view of class denies any fundamental conflict between them and sees classes as 'functional' for society because they motivate people to strive harder.[8] This view of class underlines the British Registrar General classification system which began in 1913 and has been modified several times since then.

The second view of class comes from the writings of the German sociologist Max Weber, and takes a 'relational view' of class because it recognises that there is a conflict relationship between classes based on antagonistic interests. Social classes were formed after individuals brought their different resources, such as various forms of property or educational credentials, to the market. This led to a wide variety of classes identified as having common resources. The classes engaged in constant conflict with each other as some tried to close off opportunities for lower classes to advance, while others tried to jump over the barriers erected by higher social classes. Through this market-based competition, both the working class and the capitalist class were fragmented. As Parkin suggested, there 'is a Hobbesian war of all against all as each group fights its own corner in the anarchy of the market place'.[9]

The third view of social class comes from Marx, who defined the relation between classes as being based on exploitation. It is not simply that different groups have different resources to sell in the market, but that the wealth and its attendant advantages – such as access to education or cultural capital – of one class are dependent on the exploitation of another. As Geoffrey de Ste Croix put it, Marx's theory suggests that class is the 'collective expression of the fact of exploitation, the way exploitation is embedded in the social structure'.[10] Formally, Ste Croix defined class as:

> A group of persons in a community identified by their position in the whole system of social production, defined above all according to their relationship (primarily in terms of the degree of ownership

or control) to the conditions of production (that is to say, the means and labour of production) and to other classes …

The individuals constituting a given class may or may not be wholly or partially conscious of their own identity and common interests as a class, and they may or may not feel antagonism towards members of other classes as such.[11]

Ste Croix's definition is a useful starting point because Marx did not provide such a precise definition and his discussion at the end of *Capital*, Volume 3 on classes ends abruptly as the manuscript breaks off. The above definition of social class will, therefore, be elaborated on in this chapter.

WHERE DID CLASS COME FROM?

In the *Communist Manifesto*, Marx famously argued that 'The history of all hitherto existing society is the history of class struggle'.[12] The reference here is to *written* 'history' because, as Engels later suggested, there was a long period of 'prehistory' before classes emerged.[13] In other words, there has not always been a 'them' and 'us'.

The human species is between 100,000 and 150,000 years old and for 90 per cent of that time there were no social classes. People lived as hunter-gatherers, foraging for food – wild animals or fish, fruits and nuts – and moving about in bands of between 30 and 40 people. Engels argued that these societies were mainly linked through lineage, which claimed descent from a common ancestor and that a form of primitive communism existed. 'Production was essentially collective', he argued, and 'consumption proceeded by direct distribution of the products within larger or smaller communistic communities'.[14] Reviewing anthropological evidence about the Iroquois Native Americans, he noted:

No soldiers, no gendarmes or police, no nobles, kings, regents, prefects or judges, no prisons, or lawsuit – and everything takes its orderly course … . There can be no poor and needy – the communal household and the gens (lineage) know their responsibilities toward the old, the sick and those disabled in war. All are free and equal – the women included. There is no place yet for slaves nor, as a rule, for the subjugation of other tribes.[15]

Engels' description appears very positive, but support for his overall argument has come from anthropologists such as Richard Lee, who claimed that 'This principle of generalised reciprocity has been reported of hunter gatherers in every continent and in every kind of environment'.[16]

The main reason for the culture of sharing was that these societies could only survive through cooperation. A hunt, for example, required that people work together to trap and make a kill, but as hunting was not always successful, the hunters had to rely on the generosity of the mainly female gatherers. The relatively precarious nature of the food supply meant that it was typically not consumed by individual families but was shared among the group. There was also no obsession with private property because goods had to be carried when the nomadic bands moved on when food supplies ran out. There were also few storage facilities and so an accumulation of wealth was not possible. The only items individuals owned were a few spears, axes or a bow and arrow. Lee sums up the pattern:

> Before the rise of the state and the entrenchment of social inequality, people lived for millennia in small scale kin based social groups in which the core institutions of economic life included collective or common ownership of land and resources, generalised reciprocity in the distribution of food, and relatively egalitarian political relations.[17]

This began to change after the Neolithic revolution – the shift from foraging to agriculture.

New forms of social relations developed as people began to live in village settlements based on a number of small households. Classes, however, only formed when these farming societies produced a surplus beyond their immediate needs. The very precariousness of existence put a premium on innovation and a number of developments in technology hastened this process. One was the discovery of the plough which was far more effective in breaking soil than the hand-held hoe. Another was the development of irrigation techniques by building dams or channelling waters to otherwise infertile land. In different parts of the world, people also learnt to dig wells, terrace hillsides or drain marshes.

However, this shift was double-edged. On the one hand, the existence of a social surplus was beneficial because food could be stored and so the uncertainty of existence could be mitigated. Storage of food was typically in temples and so the guardians of these temples were released from manual work and given an opportunity to study the movement of the skies and develop early recording techniques. This in turn led to further cultural advance and the discovery of more labour-saving techniques, but it also laid the basis for the division of society into social classes. For the first time, a small elite was freed from work and could live on the labour of others. Their original purpose was to coordinate and safeguard the wider community by ensuring that stored food was not all consumed, but when times were hard, this function also rapidly turned into ruling over others. Under conditions of scarcity, the new rulers had to ration food or coerce hungry people to complete the physical work of building dams or irrigation systems. Soon the good of the community came to be identified with the private power an emerging elite.

The first signs of a ruling class appear to date from about 6000–5000 BC in Egypt, Iran and China. The ties that bound tribal chiefs to their clans were loosened and they were allowed to own property and pass it on to their offspring. To enforce their rule, priests, warrior elites and kings established an entitlement to mete out physical punishments to others. Soon the road was opened to a new history based on states and class division. Marx and Engels saw the development of an upper class as a dialectical process. They argued that hierarchy or class division was not part of the natural order and showed that it arose at a specific historic moment. But they did not denounce this development and romanticise the surviving hunter-gatherer societies for their egalitarianism. Instead they saw the breakaway of a new ruling class from the wider social group as necessary for creating a greater social surplus because it created the conditions for even greater social advance. But simultaneously, they recognised that the new upper class appropriated more of the social surplus for themselves. They would put their private appropriation above the interests of the wider society and were, therefore, at some point also capable of hindering its development.

MODERN CLASS SOCIETY

Marx's view on the role of classes in modern society can be summarised under five main headlines.

Two Main Classes

In modern society, there are two main classes: workers and capitalists.

Capitalists are defined as the group who control the surplus labour of other people and who live from their exploitation. At its core belong the dominant shareholders of major corporations, boards of directors and chief executive officers. As the system has developed, these have surrounded themselves with an outer ring that organises the exploitation of workers and the sale of products and services. In return, they receive a portion of the surplus labour of others. In this category belong the top managerial elite who are bound into the capitalist class by large 'share options' and through their role in intensifying exploitation. Together, these groups constitute a corporate elite who exercise tremendous power over modern society. They are linked by tight networks to those who control the state hierarchy. Often there is a revolving door whereby former state officials join boards of corporations but even when this does not occur, private capitalists and top state officials share a similar outlook and a common political project. Together they constitute the core of the ruling class. Beyond this powerful core are smaller capitalists who employ fewer workers, receive less of a surplus and may be driven out of business by the large corporations.

Control over society's surplus gives the capitalist class four main forms of direct power. First, they have control over the flow of investment and over what is produced. They can decide to open or close factories, to expand or relocate production, to produce genuinely necessary goods and services or useless, wasteful items. Second, they have control over how the goods and services are produced. They can decide how much machinery is employed, what type of machinery is used and whether this machinery will add to or diminish the skills of workers. Third, they have disciplinary control over their employees. Not only can they fire or suspend workers, they can also impose dictatorial control within the workplace. Despite talk of free speech and the right to assembly, capitalists can ban unions from their workplaces, stop the distribution of left-wing leaflets and victimise anyone who tries to organise a union. Fourth, control over economic resources gives this class a huge influence over wider political decision-making in society. They can use their wealth to bribe or lobby politicians or blackmail or pressurise governments to accede to their demands with threats that they will relocate their business.

This level of control has enormous implications for society as the case of the pharmaceutical industry illustrates. Ten pharmaceutical companies – Pfizer, Johnson and Johnson, GlaxoSmithKline, Sanofi-Avensis, Novartis, Hoffman La Roche, Merck, Astra Zenica, Abbot

Laboratories and Bristol Myers Quibb – account for the production of half of all legal drugs. The largest corporation, Pfizer, controls one eighth of the drugs market and currently has 15 people on its board of directors, with an average age of 69. They are overwhelmingly white, American and male as is the twelve-person 'executive team' who run the day-to-day operations of the corporation. If we assume that Pfizer is typical in its hierarchical structure, then the industry as a whole is effectively controlled by 270 people. This tiny minority make decisions about what drugs are produced and how they should be made and marketed.

They have decided not to create drugs to deal with tropical illnesses even though these are the main killers of the world's population. Of the 1,393 drugs that reached the world market between 1975 and 1997, only 16 were for tropical diseases or tuberculosis.[18] They have also decided that their production systems should be mainly geared to producing 'me too' drugs, those that are based on minor chemical modifications of branded drugs whose 20-year patents have expired. Through this system, the pharmaceutical corporations prevent the emergence of cheaper, generic drugs. They have also decided to spend a high proportion of the income on 'marketing' rather than on research. The top ten companies spent 31 per cent of their revenue on marketing and administration in 2002 compared to only 13 per cent on research.[19] The decisions of the tiny corporate elite are hardly beneficial for the wider society.

The opposing class are workers who have grown in numbers as markets expand. Workers are defined as those obliged to sell their labour which is controlled by others. On this definition, it matters little whether one is working in manufacturing or services, or whether you are a blue- or white-collar worker.

This large class of people are shaped through their relation with capital. They are employed to serve capital and can therefore never assume a permanent security in wages, salaries or conditions. A high-earning building worker or office worker with an apparently secure pension can lose everything if the market changes and they no longer create profits. Similarly, job satisfaction is limited by the desire of capitalists to control the labour process. At certain times, key groups, such as software engineers in the computer industry, may enjoy considerable autonomy in decision-making and may temporarily benefit from high wages. Companies, however, try to erode these skills through further developments in technology in order to reduce their reliance on workers. Instead of being dependent on software engineers, for example, the computer industry will buy ready-made software packages which only have to be 'localised' for individual production systems.

Harry Braverman called this process 'proletarianisation' to indicate how work, which was not previously directly subject to capitalist control, is brought more firmly under its auspices.[20] It means that ever larger numbers of white-collar occupations are subsumed into the broader category of workers. Whereas at one stage they might have had a high level of autonomy or control over their work, this tends to be eroded over time. In the past, teachers and lecturers were barely supervised and were assumed to be professionals who could manage themselves. But in many countries, this has changed and they are subject to constant monitoring, targets and performance management. This is one reason why social class is a dynamic category and is not easy to delineate according to neat divisions. Marx noted that in his day England was the most industrialised society but 'even here the stratification of classes does not appear in its pure form'.[21] This was because 'Middle and intermediate strata even here obliterate lines of demarcation everywhere (although incomparably less in rural districts than in the cities)'.[22] These strata, however, could not escape from the logic of capital accumulation and so many of them are constantly being drawn into the working class.

While workers and capitalists constitute the two main classes, they are by no means the only ones in modern society. Contrary to some myths, Marx never held a 'two-class model' and throughout his writings discussed other social classes. He simply argued that there were two *main* classes which could shape the direction of society.

Landlords constituted a distinct class because they drew their income from rent rather than profit or wages. There was also a *petty bourgeois* who made a living by working with their own means of production, such as tools, or property, such as shops. To this category belong many of the self-employed – publicans, small shopkeepers, solicitors and a host of other occupations not controlled by large corporations. They may draw on the labour of their own families but if they become successful and start living off the efforts of other workers, they shade into the category of small capitalists. Technically, many of the peasantry are petty bourgeois as they work with their own property. However, it is best to treat them separately as there are often complex differences within them. The *peasantry* are still the largest class in the world and survive either as subsistence farmers producing food for themselves or cash crops for the global economy.

There is one other class that modern Marxists refer to even though it did not feature in Marx's own writings. The *new middle class* receive a salary from an employer but exercise a high level of control over the nature of their work. They therefore combine two contradictory elements: like other employees they sell their labour but they also exercise such a high level of autonomy over their labour – and others people's as well – that they belong to a different class from workers.

Finally, Marx made reference to the *lumpenproletariat* but this is less relevant to modern society as it primarily refers to those 'who fall out, or drop out, of the existing social structure so that they are no longer functionally an integral part of the society'.[23] In Marx's period, it referred to declassed elements of society who were often mobilised by the aristocracy to attack progressive causes. The *lazzaroni* in Naples, for example, who lived off crime, were easily bought off to become a 'church and king mob'.[24] Marx did not use the term *lumpenproletariat* to refer to workers who were thrown out of work regularly by the fluctuations in the economic system and who formed 'a reserve army of labour'. The current term 'underclass' has nothing to do with a Marxist analysis but has become a pejorative category used by right-wing social commentators who attack vulnerable groups such as single parents because of their supposed 'culture of poverty' and 'welfare dependency'.[25]

Nor should the term *lumpenproletariat* be applied to the vast numbers of people who leave the countryside to become underemployed in the mega-cities of the developing world. Mike Davis has argued convincingly that 'informal workers', who make up 40 per cent of the economically active population of the developing world may be underemployed but they still work or seek to work for someone else. They have 'informal' employment contracts which lead to super-exploitation; they are forced to display total 'flexibility' in adapting to the rhythms of either big or small capitalist firms; and they suffer from the fragmentation of work and income due to extensive outsourcing.[26]

Formed in Production

A social class refers to positions that people occupy in a system of production, in the broadest sense of both making objects for sale and providing services.

Within the sphere of production people form relationships and one's social class depends on one's position within those relationships. The dividing line between classes is primarily determined by answering two questions: Do I sell or buy labour? Is my work controlled by myself or by another? If my labour is bought and controlled by another, then I belong to the broader class category of worker. If my means of livelihood rests of the purchase of another's labour and I am controlling that labour to make a profit, then I belong to the capitalist or the petty bourgeois class.

This is a baseline definition but there are some complexities. Marx adopted from Adam Smith a distinction between productive and unproductive labour. Writing at the start of the system, Smith distinguished between labour which served capital accumulation and unproductive labour which absorbed resources. Into the latter category belonged, for example, domestic servants who performed personal services for the rich. Marx's distinction between productive and unproductive labour was also 'derived not from its content or its result, but from its particular social form'.[27] An actor or a clown could be productive if he or she helped to create profit for the capitalist, but a tailor could be unproductive if he or she patched the capitalist's trousers at their home. It was not the nature of the work but its role in capital accumulation that mattered.

Writers such as Nicos Poulanzas took this distinction to mean that only manual, nonsupervisory workers who directly produce profits should be considered part of the working class and that all white-collar employees are part of a 'new petty bourgeoisie'.[28] However, this makes little sense because capitalism today is not based on isolated factories which produce goods. It is an integrated system whereby a collective labour force produces surplus value, which is then distributed among the various capitalists through market mechanisms. This system needs the supply of an educated, healthy workforce whose 'socially necessary labour' – labour at the average skill and literacy level of the twenty-first century – allows for the continual expansion of capital. In Marx's day, the system did not organise for the supply of labour because it simply drew former peasants into factories. Today, however, the state educates the next generation of workers; keeps them relatively content though a welfare system; and ensures they remain healthy through its hospitals and clinics. Those who contribute to this 'reproduction' of the working class help to raise the productivity of labour, and this in turn adds to the surplus value available to the capitalist. The abstract labour that is contained in commodities is no longer just the result of the direct workers' efforts but has been made 'socially necessary' through the way the state organises this reproduction. State workers have the same interests as private sector workers in increasing their own wages or eventually doing away with the capitalist system. In that sense, therefore, state employees who sell their labour and whose labour is controlled by 'state capitalists' are part of the working class.

At the core of Marx's definition of workers lies the category of exploitation. Most conventional sociology, however, is influenced by Weber's argument that class is formed in the marketplace and ignores Marx's claim about exploitation. Even those sociologists that recognise that class conflict exists ignore the issue of exploitation. Instead they focus on the divisions within the modern workforce because they assume there is no common interest in resisting exploitation. Marx's approach, however, sees social class being formed in production where the key issue is the appropriation of a surplus and its control by a tiny minority.

An Objective Membership

Working-class life is often stereotyped by television and Hollywood. Programmes like *Shameless* on British television present crude images of hard drinking and bawdy sexuality. To be working-class according to this imagery is to live on a large council estate, to talk with a distinct accent and to frequent pubs and chip shops. Against this image many white- and blue-collar workers define themselves as 'middle-class'.

Marx's approach to social class is not, however, based on an association with a particular lifestyle. One can therefore be working-class and not conform to the upper-class stereotypes of working-class culture. So a baker who spends his time playing guitar music to a virtual cyberspace 'community' in Japan is as much a worker as someone who follows Chelsea and drinks heavily every time they play. A white-collar, graduate employee who is employed by a large capitalist corporation, where there are regular 'headcounts' for who will be fired, is as much a worker as a steelworker.

In the twenty-first century there has been a far greater diversity of lifestyle than at any point in history and it would, therefore, be foolish to claim that there is one lifestyle associated with being working-class. The modern working class is more coloured, more female and more white-collar than the traditional imagery of middle-aged men in overalls. It would be equally wrong to assume that all capitalists are overweight, cigar-smoking men in suits who talk with posh accents. In fact, the cultural shifts in modern society indicate that they are more likely to be fit and to embrace a more populist image where they are pictured in open-necked shirts and jeans just like everyone else – or so they would like us to believe.

Nor is Marx's approach reliant on personal definitions of one class position. People may define themselves as workers when, in fact, their work consists of organising the exploitation of others. Conversely, individual dockers or firefighters can claim they are middle-class because they have moved out of large council estates. The self-definition of one's social situation can be mistaken, delusional or more likely subject to interpretations promoted by others. Marx's analysis, therefore, starts from what people do rather than what they think they are.

The Fundamental Division

Class is not the only social division. Society is also divided by gender, ethnicity, nationality and a host of other categories.

However, class remains the fundamental divide in two senses. First, racism or sexism is experienced differently according to class. While all women can be subject to sexist abuse, wealthy women do not experience the daily sexual harassment that faces some working women. Capitalist society assumes that childcare is 'unproductive' work and often takes no social responsibility for raising children before school age. The burden of child-minding, therefore, falls predominantly on women, but upper-class women can more easily escape that burden by employing other women as nannies. Similarly, the experience of racism in the US is mediated through class. The arrest of black Harvard professor Henry Louis Gates is a classic example of racial profiling – wrong skin colour, wrong place. The US President, Barack Obama, expressed his indignation. But when black youths with hoodies are picked up for being on the wrong side of town it is barely noticed. The importance of these class divisions within the black 'community' was recognised explicitly by Lawrence Otis Graham, the author of *Our Kind of People: Inside America's Black Upper Class*. He told an interviewer that the reason why his type of black person promoted upper-class Jack and Jill clubs was that 'well-to-do blacks knew that they needed to bring together kids that might have felt like outsiders when they were with other black children who might have been less privileged'.[29]

Second, these divisions mean that upper-class blacks together with upper-class women have an interest in maintaining the present system. Their primary interest lies in keeping their own privileged position and, by extension, creating more space for blacks or women to join the elite. This defence of privilege, however, puts them in conflict with the majority of other women or blacks. Wendi Deng, for example, the Chinese-born executive of the News International media empire, has no interest in increasing the maternity leave of her female Chinese staff. Nor do the many rich women who employ nannies have an interest in increasing the minimum wage or allowing their domestic employment arrangements to be subject to public scrutiny.

The class divide between women was most evident in Marx's time during the Paris Commune. In the aftermath of the first workers' uprising, a great fear spread among the privileged about the women fighters who were supposed to have poured burning petrol on their victims. This hatred of female revolutionaries is often a feature of right-wing propaganda because they challenge stereotypes of traditional gender roles. In the aftermath of the Commune, Lissagray recounts how 'every woman who was badly dressed, or carrying a milk-can, a pail, an empty bottle, was pointed out as a *pétroleuse*, her clothes torn to tatters, she was pushed against the nearest wall, and killed with revolver-shots'.[30] Another historian claimed that 'According to reports, the elegantly dressed ladies were the most violent, especially against their own sex'.[31]

Class Struggle

Class struggle is an inevitable feature of our divided society no matter how much it is denied. It arises both because there is a conflict of interest between workers and capitalists and because capitalists intensify exploitation in order to respond to competition. As Marx put it, it:

> does not, indeed, depend on the good or ill will of the individual capitalist. Free competition brings out the inherent laws of capitalist production, in the shape of external coercive laws having power over every individual capitalist.[32]

The reality of class struggle is reflected at many levels in modern society. The mere existence of trade unions whose organisation depends on the exclusion of one class of people – the employers – is one indication. So too is the organisation of politics along the lines of a left–right axis. Even though left social democratic parties try to manage capitalism and typically disappoint their supporters when in government, their primary voting base comes from more class-conscious workers and their funding often comes from trade unions. Employers also organise on class lines, forming employer confederations to coordinate strategies against unions or using elite lobby groups such as the European Round Table of Industrialists to promote their interests.

Class struggle implies that there is some resistance to exploitation but the scale and quality of that resistance varies. At its lowest level, non-union workers may use absenteeism or informal sanctions to enforce their interests against their employers. Unionised workers employ a variety of tactics, ranging from work-to-rule or go-slows, to systematic non-cooperation, to strikes and occupations. Sometimes these generalise into highly political confrontations that convulse the wider society and at other times there are long periods of seeming social peace. The reality of class struggle is best captured by an image of trench warfare during the First World War. Occasionally, there are great battles when one side charges the other's defences and considerable casualties ensue, but for much of the time the opposing forces hunker down and individuals try to avoid being picked off. Yet the trenches remain and the war continues.

WHY THE WORKING CLASS?

The largest and most oppressed class in the world today is still the peasantry. In the past, figures like Mao Tse Tung and Che Guevara looked to this class as a base from which to build their revolution. In present-day India, the anti-capitalist writer Arundhati Roy has also praised the efforts of the Naxalite peasant movement in West Bengal to bring about change.[33] Given this revolutionary history, why did Marx focus on workers as the main agents of revolutionary change?

To answer this we need to debunk some myths. The first is that of the romantic peasant who has been uncorrupted by city life and who, therefore, might appear more revolutionary. This image motivated Che Guevara, who sought to build a base in a remote rural area of Bolivia rather than among the militant Bolivian working class in the cities.[34] Yet despite this mythology about incorruptibility, the peasant population can often provide the social base for urban dictators or right-wing populist politicians. In Marx's time, the dictatorship of Louis Bonaparte drew its main support from smallholding peasant proprietors. Despite the fact that they were crushed by mortgages and could have seen the urban working class as their natural ally, they turned to Bonaparte. The Bonaparte dictatorship represented, Marx wrote, 'the conservative, not the revolutionary peasant; the peasant who wants to consolidate the condition of his social existence, the smallholding, not the peasant who strikes out beyond it'.[35] More generally, Marx suggested that 'by its very nature, small peasant property is suitable to serve as the foundation of an all-powerful and innumerable bureaucracy'.[36] The independence of small cultivators, their highly parochial outlook, their isolation from each other can lead to an apolitical attitude where civil organisation is weak. Moreover, the lack of employment means that they look to state posts as a source of work.

This need not be the case because the peasants could also form the basis of revolutionary movements. Where the peasants challenged the old order, Marx championed an alliance between peasants and workers. His paper, the *Neue Rheinische Zeitung*, attacked the moderate liberal government of 1848 for not immediately abolishing all feudal burdens on the peasantry and betraying the peasant revolution. However, Marx also thought that their conditions of life made it harder for peasants to form and control national movements which exclusively represented their distinct interests. Their geographical dispersal and the criss-crossing of conflicting interests within the peasant 'community' often meant that the impetus for national organisation came from the outside. What are sometimes termed peasant revolts are, therefore, often ones where the peasantry provide the basis for a movement that is led by other forces. The Maoist movement in China, for example, mobilised the countryside to bring revolt to the cities, but it was led by a declassed, urban intelligentsia of the Communist Party.[37] Similarly, the revolt in India's 'tribal areas' today is led by an extremely hierarchical and authoritarian Maoist party.

Marx's focus on the working class as the revolutionary agent of change arose from a hard-nosed assessment about its capacity for change. It has nothing to do with a claim that workers are morally superior or noble or even less subject to reactionary ideas sometimes. Rather it rests on four interlinked features of working-class life under capitalism.

First, workers tend to organise collectively because of their conditions of life. They are brought together in large workplaces where they must cooperate to produce goods or services. They must work together and, as a class, are often concentrated in large cities. As Draper put it, 'workers are taught organisation not by their superior intelligence or by outside agitators, but by capitalists'.[38] Even if workers do not believe in class struggle, they are forced to organise in order to advance their interests. Typically, people who previously felt they were respectable workers join unions and take industrial action. At the start of the twentieth century, skilled engineering workers in Britain and Germany felt themselves to be a labour aristocracy who were above striking. Yet, when the First World War brought about a 'dilution' of their skills through their replacement by a semi-skilled workforce, they became one of the more militant sections of the working class. Since the 1960s a similar pattern has ensued with teachers, nurses and office workers so that today the strike figures in many countries are dominated by the activities of the so-called professional salariat.

Second, the spontaneous outlook of many workers contains ideas which implicitly challenge the framework of capitalism because they want security in their lives. In Marx's day, the focus of that struggle was a demand for a ten-hour working day to curb the capitalist 'appetite for surplus labour which appears in the drive for an unlimited extension of the working day'.[39] Today, most workers want some form of 'industrial legality' which undermines the absolute power of capital to treat them as flexible objects. They want grievance procedures to deal with individual cases and some legal protections to give them 'fairness' at work. Similarly, most opinion polls in Western Europe show strong support for a welfare state where workers are entitled to health care, pension provision and education. Yet the system undermines these modest requests because of what David Harvey has called its quest for 'perpetual accumulation at a compound rate'.[40]

Workers can, of course, achieve some victories in these struggles and capitalism may not only survive, but in some instances prosper. This is because the regulation of capital can help prevent its most destructive tendencies and is dictated, as Marx put it, 'by the same necessity as forced the manuring of English fields by guano'.[41] Guano was an expensive fertiliser that helped to prevent the exhaustion of the soil and in a similar way the legal limit on the working day helped stop the exhaustion of workers. Yet these temporary victories of workers are often undermined by the relentless drive for profit. A decade ago, most workers in industrialised societies thought they had a right to a defined benefit pension in their old age, yet today they must take the risk of investing their savings in the stock market. Equally, most thought they could retire at 65 but now workers have to work until they are at 67. In this sense, therefore, workers' demand for social responsibility comes up against a system that institutionalises economic irresponsibility.

Third, workers are the only class that have the power to bring change because their social situation puts them at the heart of an economy from where profit is pumped out. When workers stop work en masse, their power is easily demonstrated. In 1996, for example, 3,000 workers at the GM plant in Dayton, Ohio struck over outsourcing, causing company losses of $50 million a day. Despite the mythology about the 'death of the working class' every major strike calls forth a veritable onslaught from the authorities. The corporate media are mobilised to attack 'greedy workers'; the police are deployed to prevent militant pickets; the courts stand ready to introduce special injunctions.

There is a direct relationship between real economic power and the social psychology of workers. The famous aphorism of Lord Acton that 'power corrupts but absolute power corrupts absolutely' may have been applicable to debates within the Catholic Church about papal infallibility.[42] Applied to the struggle of the social classes, however, it is the opposite of the truth. Far from power corrupting, it is powerlessness that corrupts and absolute powerlessness that corrupts absolutely. Being ground down continually, with no hope of successful resistance, is more likely to turn people inward so that they seek scapegoats or imagined conspiracies to explain their plight. The ability to wield power in successful resistance, however, creates the possibility for a broader political vision that makes change seem achievable.

Fourth, other classes may engage in struggles, but the nature of their social position means that they are unable, as a class, to provide an alternative mode of organising the economy. The Italian writer Ignazio Silone, for example, argued that Italian fascism drew its principal base of support from the petty bourgeoisie who were attracted to a nationalist rhetoric that offered an escape from rapacious finance capital and 'Bolshevik' unions. But this 'third way' was only a rhetorical device because a petty bourgeois utopia is impossible under present conditions. Instead 'fascism, the strongest movement that has ever emerged from the petty bourgeoisie, resulted in the open dictatorship of high finance and in an unprecedented repression of the petty bourgeoisie as a class'.[43] By contrast, victory for workers could only be linked to a new collective way of organising the economy.

All of this meant that Marx was an enthusiastic supporter of the self-organisation of workers in trade unions and a virulent opponent of political sectarianism. Workers, the sectarians claimed, should wait to be educated 'in order to be the better able to enter into the new society that they have prepared for them with such foresight'.[44] Against this pessimism, Marx argued that the trade unions perform a number of vital functions. They bring together workers, so 'eliminating competition among themselves while enabling them to make a general competition against the capitalist'.[45] Instead of workers fighting each other, the unions promote an ideal of solidarity. They also teach workers the value of organisation so that the maintenance of a united organisation in the face of capital becomes more important than even the limited gains the unions might make. They provide schools of struggles where workers learn the value of tactics and strategy in their battles with employers. More importantly, they can help to politicise workers because, as Marx predicted, when union struggles moved from the local workplace to demands for legal rights, a qualitative change takes place:

> Out of the separate economic movements of the workers there grows up everywhere a *political* movement, that is to say a movement of the *class*, with the object of achieving its interests in a general form, in a form possessing a general social force of compulsion.[46]

Marx was writing, however, before a bureaucracy took control of the unions. This tier of full-time officials no longer experience the hardships of the workplace and define themselves as professionals who deserve to be paid more than those they represent. Increasingly, the union bureaucracy does away with regular elections and occupies permanent positions where they are no longer subjected to grassroots control. Their negotiating skills, their knowledge of the law and their relationship with employers becomes more important than the fighting spirit of those they represent. The penchant of the union officialdom for stability and for preserving the apparatus of the organisation at all costs leads them to acquiescence in and support the capitalist system itself. Today, Marx's arguments about the potential of unions to unite the working class and to prepare it for political advancement, therefore, can only be realised in the course of a long struggle against this deeply entrenched bureaucracy.[47]

Marx did not advocate a narrow, syndicalist approach that only championed workers' interests. He believed that the working class was unique because it was capable of giving voice to the grievances of all in society. As it became political, it could come forward as the representative of the whole of society, capable of organising a new economy that served people not profit. But a consciousness of this historic role did not develop automatically as workers sometimes accepted conservative ideas which aided the oppression of others. Such a consciousness could only emerge in struggle where workers learnt to remake themselves as a class capable of liberation. Marx contemptuously dismissed the idea that revolutionary change was simply a matter of willpower. He summarised this form of *desperado* politics under the slogan 'We must come to power immediately or else we might as well go to sleep'.[48] Against this Marx argued that workers would need to go through 15, 20 or even 50 years of struggle 'to change the conditions and make yourselves capable of government'.[49] Here, then, was a profoundly democratic and realistic view of the actual and potential conditions of workers.

BUT ARE WE NOT ALL MIDDLE-CLASS?

It is sometimes claimed that class conflict is at an end because the majority of people in industrialised countries are middle-class. The problem with this argument is that the term 'middle-class' is extremely confusing and has changed meaning many times. In the late eighteenth century, it was used to describe city dwellers who distinguished themselves from both the peasantry and the aristocracy. Later the term came to be used in a way that was similar to French term 'bourgeoisie'. In the early twentieth century, 'middle-class' was used to describe clerical employees who were thought to share a common cultural world that was different from that of manual workers. Later again, the term was used in a highly political way in the US to mask the reality of class conflict. In this usage, working-class referred only to the very poor while approximately 70–80 per cent of American society is supposed to be middle-class.

The cultural power of the US media has meant that the term 'middle-class' is now more commonly used to describe any employee who does not conform to the cultural stereotype of a manual worker. But this raises another problem: how can one lump together routine clerical workers who earn low wages with top managers who boss them? How could both groups have an interest in common as middle-class?

Contrary to Galbraith's argument about the contented two-thirds majority in industrialised societies,[50] many formerly 'middle-class' occupations are becoming part of the working class. A century ago, clerical employees had a similar social position to Uriah Heep, in Charles Dickens' *David Copperfield*. They were overwhelmingly male; they worked in close proximity to their employers; there were very few of them (they comprised only about 4 per cent of the working population of Britain);[51] and they often aspired to marry into their boss's family. A sociologist of the 1930s, Lewis Corey, described them accurately as 'honoured employees' who had close, confidential relations with their employer. Their relatively high income allowed them 'to reside in a fairly genteel neighbourhood, wear good clothes, mix in respectable society, go sometimes to the opera, and shrink from letting their wives do household work'.[52] The latter point indicates that many of these clerical employees had domestic servants.

The manner in which clerical workers have been proletarianised is illustrated in *The Blackcoated Worker*, a celebrated sociological text written by David Lockwood in 1958. This was an explicitly anti-Marxist book which argued that the 'clerk and manual worker do not, in most cases, share the same class situation at all'.[53] Lockwood argued that they differed on three dimensions: their status, their market situation and their work situation. Clerical workers were so positively advantaged on all three of these dimensions that they could not be seen as part of the working class. Yet the cruel irony of history is that Lockwood's anti-Marxist text provides a suitable baseline for illustrating how 'privileged' white-collar employees of the late 1950s have been proletarianised in the twenty-first century.

First, if status is defined as a measure of social esteem, there is little evidence to suggest that a routine white-collar employee is held in higher regard than a skilled or even semi-skilled manual worker. Status is not an issue that Marxists focus on, but it is doubtful if a clerical occupation generates a higher level of respect in modern society. Moreover, it is quite commonplace for a clerical employees to have been born into a manual working-class family and to reside in areas where many manual workers also live.

Second, Lockwood claimed that clerical workers had better incomes, career prospects and job security than manual workers and he called this their 'market situation'. However, this is not true today. By 1971, the median wage of a full-time clerical worker in the US was lower than many types of so-called blue-collar worker.[54] As clerical work came to be dominated by women, career prospects consisted mainly of moving between grades rather than being promoted out of clerical work into management. Differences in job security between white- and blue-collar workers were also lessened as both experienced the increased use of temporary contract employment and redundancies.

Third, Lockwood had claimed that in their 'work situation', white-collar employees had greater autonomy and experienced a more intimate, personal relationship with their managers compared to the 'harsh, impersonal and purely instrumental character of command', which manual workers experienced.[55] Again, this has changed. Information technology has allowed managers to take greater control over the design of office work and to press for greater productivity. Personal relations have increasingly given way to impersonal rules and procedures. Lockwood's celebrated refutation of Marx's theory has, therefore, ironically been overtaken by the very system he was defending.

A similar transformation has occurred in many lower 'professional' occupations such as teaching or nursing which are subject to new forms of managerialism. In the past, a 'trust culture' existed where it was assumed that these groups had internalised a professional ethos and could be trusted to get on with their jobs. In many instances, this has been replaced by an 'audit culture'[56] where, under the guise of rhetoric about 'transparency' and 'accountability', these employees are forced to produce quantitative measurements for their 'outputs'. An intense form of micro-management is often enforced through competitive benchmarks or key performance indicators, which subject their working life to greater scrutiny.

All of this would indicate that the category middle-class might more appropriately be dissolved into working-class. However, while the majority of white-collar employees have become 'proletarianised' there has been a growth of a distinct 'new middle class' that occupies a different position from most white-collar workers. In *Class, Crisis and the State*, the American Marxist E. O. Wright drew attention to occupations which occupy a 'contradictory class location'.[57] While Wright later retreated from his analysis, Alex Callinicos has taken up and developed the argument.[58] A contradictory class location refers to a social position that combines contradictory elements so that someone may formally sell their labour like other workers, but control the labour of others like a capitalist. In other words, there can be a separation between the two central dimensions that define class – sale or purchase of labour and control or subordination in the labour process.

An obvious example of such a contradictory class location between workers and capitalists are middle managers. Sometimes these simply receive a wage for carrying out the main function of capital: controlling workers. They are usually paid very high wages and have a delegated relationship of trust with owners of corporations. Another example of those who hold a contradictory class location are university professors and lecturers in some countries. These are paid a wage but, like the artisans of the past, have almost complete control over their own labour and sometimes the labour of a few others. By contrast, in other countries lecturers have been effectively proletarianised.

Overall, therefore, the term middle-class needs to be deconstructed into its constituent elements. The majority of routine clerical workers are in a similar class situation to manual workers, and other occupations formerly known as lower professionals are rapidly undergoing a processing of proletarianisation as greater control is exercised over their labour. Still other groupings retain a high level of autonomy and are often engaged in the control of other people's labour. Only the latter category could accurately be called a 'new middle class', even if their social and political trajectory is quite contradictory.

The global working class has expanded dramatically since Marx's day. In 1850, just after the *Communist Manifesto* appeared, the US labour force was 8 million but only 3.7 million were employed outside agriculture. By 1999, it had grown to 134 million, of whom 34 million were employed in manufacturing alone.[59] Even if around 10 per cent of this sector belonged to managerial grades, this leaves a lot of employed workers. For much of the nineteenth century, the largest occupation in Britain for women was domestic service yet today the vast majority of women work directly for corporations or the state. When Marx was writing, factory workers made up only 2.5 per cent of the economically active population of Germany[60] and countries like Japan or South Korea had hardly any waged workers, yet today however there are more workers in South Korea than in the whole world in Marx's day. His vision, therefore, about the capacity of workers to bring change is more relevant then ever.

5
Gender and Race

Many of the dramatic struggles that changed the face of the modern world were not class struggles. The black civil rights movement challenged racism in the US and eventually led to the previously unthinkable – the election of a black president, Barack Obama. The Stonewall Riot of 1969, which broke out after the police raided a Mafia-controlled bar in New York, gave rise to the gay movement which has made same-sex marriages a real possibility. Some of the greatest changes came from the women's liberation movement of the 1960s. These struggles arose in the context of a wider challenge to capitalism, but in the US – although not elsewhere – the links with workers' struggles were minimal. Subsequently, this led to academic claims that Marxism is too reductionist because it cannot account for oppression that is not based on class.

The central argument is that Marx's analysis of capitalism cannot explain why sexism or racism exists. More broadly, it is suggested that Marxism allows 'little or no theoretical room for conceptualising ... other types of social differentiation such as social divisions and contradictions arising around race, ethnicity, nationality and gender'.[1] Marx, it is asserted, ignored the oppression of women and blacks because it did not fit into his class schema. While this critique has often arisen from a post-1968 generation of ex-students who became academics, it does have important political implications for current strategies for change. If there is no clear link between capitalism and oppression, then a workers' struggle to overthrow the system will not remove racism and sexism. The future, it is suggested, lies in a rainbow coalition of the oppressed or 'the multitude', a vague term used to define groupings that develop an anti-capitalist consciousness.[2] If the diverse movements retain their 'autonomy', it is claimed, they can also operate a system of checks and balances on each other. This will help to both prevent USSR-style tyranny and ensure that the struggles against sexism, racism and other forms of oppression continue in a post-capitalist society.

This chapter challenges that approach by indicating that Marx laid the basis for a distinct and powerful analysis which located oppression in the specific nature of capitalism and its inability to match its human rights rhetoric with its actual practice.

GENDER

Marx and Engels' writings make frequent reference to the oppression of women, and their opposition to sexism was well in advance of most writers of their day. In *The Holy Family* they explicitly endorsed Charles Fourier's view that 'The degree of emancipation of woman is the natural measure of general emancipation'.[3] In his short, popular *Principles of Communism*, Engels outlined how a socialist society would transform the relations between the sexes into a purely private matter which concerns only the persons involved and into which society has no occasion to intervene. It can do this because it does away with private property and educates children on a communal basis, and in this way removes the two bases of traditional marriage, the dependence, rooted in private property, of the woman on the man and of the children on the parents.[4]

This means that present-day Marxists share with feminists a deep loathing of sexism and suggests that, despite the huge legal gains for women since the 1960s, no genuine liberation has been achieved. Although the position of the housewife has declined considerably, most societies have made little provision for childcare outside the family. Typically, it is assumed that children of the age of four have a right to schooling but before then their upbringing is the sole responsibility of their parents, and their mothers in particular. While Western women are no longer expected to be sexually inactive until they find 'the right man', even greater pressure is applied to younger women to conform to a body image that makes them attractive to men. More generally, the distorted nature of sexuality in modern capitalism is illustrated by the fact that spending on pornography in the US may be higher than the combined receipts of professional football, baseball and basketball.[5]

Feminists explain these phenomena through the concept of patriarchy, by which is meant a structure of male power that transcends class societies. This, however, begs the question: how did men get such power and why do women let them get away with it? A variety of answers are offered which range from men's psychological needs to biological explanations. Simone de Beauvoir, for example, claims that there is a psychic need to dominate the Other in the human consciousness and that this is at the root of men's oppression of women.[6] In other words, men affirm life by mastering women. Others, such as Susan Brownmiller, locate patriarchy in man's ability to rape, which she sees as 'a conscious process of intimidation by which all men keep all women in a state of fear'.[7] However, if patriarchy is located in male biology – whether that is testosterone or the ability to rape – then there can be no realistic hope of changing the relations between the sexes. Similarly, if male domination arises from psychic, existential doubt or jealousy about childbirth, then the cultural change needed to reorient men will take a very long time indeed.

Marx and Engels' analysis was very different and offered more hope. The primary text is Engels' *The Origins of the Family, Private Property and the State* published in 1884. Engels drew on notes that Marx had made on anthropological material from Lewis Henry Morgan's *Ancient Society* which had appeared seven years earlier. While some of Engels' detailed claims have been questioned by later writers, the fundamental argument still represents a valid critique of permanent male dominance.[8]

Engels argued that in pre-class society women were not subordinate to men because the division of labour in hunter-gatherer societies did not give males a dominant role. Women were not confined to nuclear families over which a man ruled but were part of wider lineage groupings. There was no separation between the private world of the home, where violence against women could occur, and the public world of work. Children were not just the responsibility of individual parents but of the nomadic group as a whole and so the concept of an 'orphan' did not have the same meaning as it does today. These societies were often matrilineal, in that descent was reckoned through the female line, and were sometimes also matrilocal because the man moved into the household of the woman. Engels did not claim, however, that these societies were matriarchies where women held the power, but merely that they were more equal. This rough equality persisted until the early stages of the development of agriculture.

Engels overemphasised wider lineage groups as against the more flexible networks of the smaller nomadic bands and he was probably wrong in his notion of a primitive promiscuity. But his more general argument was that 'The lady of civilisation, surrounded by false homage and estranged from all real work, has an infinitely lower social position than that of the hard-working woman of barbarism.'[9] Support for this argument about the higher social status of women in primitive societies has come from modern anthropologists such as Karen Sachs, Christine Gailey and Ernestine Friedl.[10] The existence of female goddesses and the widespread use of female statuettes also testify to this marked difference in position. However, in classical Greece, the situation was entirely different. Women were excluded from the *polis* – the political decision-making community – in Athens from the seventh century BC and were confined within the home. The exposure – *ektesis* – of newborn female infants to the natural elements was widespread and the playwright Posidippus, who lived between the third and second centuries BC, noted that 'a poor man brings up a son, but even a rich man exposes a daughter'.[11]

Engels argued that you cannot simply look to 'attitude' or biology as an explanation. If there was a biological basis for women's oppression, then it should have existed in pre-class societies, and if oppression arose from attitude, you have to explain why attitudes changed. He therefore focused on how the rise of class society was linked to the formation of monogamous families that loosened their ties to wider tribal networks. Class societies arose, as we saw, when humans became capable of producing a social surplus and this was appropriated by a small number of individuals. This normally developed in later agricultural societies when the plough was introduced to produce greater quantities of food from the land and when there was a shift to herding animals.

In the early Neolithic period women played a key role in production as they were mainly responsible for the discovery of edible plants and appropriate methods for their cultivation. They also had to devise special implements for tilling the soil, reaping and storing the crops and converting them into food. Owing to this contribution to the collective economy, descent is often reckoned through the mother's line.[12] However the changes in later agriculture involved the use of the plough and herding of animals and this gave men a greater role in production. These changes coincided with the growth of a surplus and the possession of wealth measured in cattle. A small minority of men had a direct interest in keeping this wealth for themselves and in ensuring that it was passed on to their offspring. This, however, was impossible while descent was reckoned according to mother right and they therefore gradually broke away from older kin ties. They created their own families established along rules of monogamy and this gave them a means of establishing inheritance for their offspring. While it was strictly enforced for women, the rules of monogamy were only hypocritically accepted for men. Engels argued that:

The overthrow of mother right was the *world historic defeat of the female sex*. The man took command in the home also; the woman was degraded and reduced to servitude; she became the slave of his lust and a mere instrument for the production of children.[13]

And so:

> the first antagonism which appears in history coincides with the development of the antagonism between men and women in monogamous marriage, and the first class oppression with that of the female sex by the male.[14]

Engels' book was deeply subversive because it fundamentally challenged the idea that the domination of men in traditional families was somehow natural and this helps to explain why it has often been dismissed by conventional male anthropologists. As Sachs has pointed out, the founding fathers of anthropology such as Bronislaw Malinowski and Alfred Radcliffe-Brown often portrayed 'primitive woman' as naturally accepting a subservient position in order to give credence to their own deeply held prejudices. Malinowski, for example, thought that women should not have the vote because it would impose a 'begrudged equality' on men.[15] By debunking the myth of natural male domination, Engels won the enduring hostility of those anthropologists who wanted to dismiss notions of equality between the sexes.

Engels opened the way to a more critical examination of the family and its role in determining the status of women. Here is his discussion on how the word first arose:

> The original meaning of the word 'family' (*familia*) is not that compound of sentimentality and domestic strife which forms the ideal of the present-day philistine; among the Romans it did not at first even refer to the married pair and their children but only to the slaves. *Famulus* means domestic slave, and *familia* is the total number of slaves belonging to one man ... . The term was invented by the Romans to denote a new social organism whose head ruled over the wife and children and a number of slaves, and was invested under Roman paternal power with rights of life and death over them all.[16]

Engels' starting point was that the shift from a kinship system to a more private-based family was both a 'great historical step forward'[17] which opened the promise of relationships based on individual sex love, and simultaneously contained, in microcosm, the contradictions of the wider society. The family promised love and respect, but it is based on the supremacy of the man: 'its express aim is the begetting of children of undisputed paternity, this paternity being required in order that these children may in due time inherit their father's wealth as his natural heirs.'[18]

This brought about hypocritical sexual relations as official monogamy was inevitably accompanied by the widespread use of prostitution. In Ancient Greece, for example, an upper-class man was entitled to have relationship with three women – the mother of his children, slave girls and *hetaerae* – effectively paid prostitutes.[19] In modern capitalism there is, according to Engels, both a 'conjugal partnership of leaden boredom, known as "domestic bliss" and widespread adultery'.[20] Family values are constantly promoted but there exists alongside them a huge sex industry that promises sexual fantasies and purchased domination. Engels suggested that if class society is abolished, the historically progressive shift to individual sex love could occur on a more equal and free basis. Whether that will be based on monogamy or alternative forms of relationships can only be answered by a new generation that grows up in a free society.

Engels' book triggered a rich vein of modern Marxist writing on women's liberation which links the status of women to the construction of gender roles in the family. The family is viewed as both the site of individual relationships and as an institution shaped by the wider society. These relationships, which are built on received ideas of masculinity or femininity, are also shaped by the 'economic' function that the family plays in a wider society. The embedding of the family in a wider class society had important consequences.

One is that the family is a changing institution that cannot simply be defined by permanent emotional needs to care for children. In pre-modern families, for example, children were not the focus of emotional life and were largely treated as immature adults. There were few toys; apprenticeships often began at age seven; and there appears to have been more of an emotional distance between parents and children than in present-day society. Although it may seem shocking to modern sensibilities, infants were often knocked to sleep through 'forceful shaking', boarded out to wet nurses and left alone for long periods.[21] Today families, however, often stay together for the sake of their children. So dramatic are its changing forms that it is barely possible to talk about 'the family' but it is necessary to examine the different families of different social classes in different societies.

Before the rise of capitalism, the family was a productive unit in which a male patriarch organised the work of women and children. Contrary to later images of femininity, women engaged in work as diverse as brewing, pig rearing or spinning. Marx and Engels thought that this patriarchal family had died out among workers after the industrial revolution, as men, women and children were employed in factories and the authority of the father was replaced by the authority of the boss. *The Communist Manifesto* noted 'the practical absence of the family among the proletarians'.[22] Later, Engels suggested that

> now that large-scale industry has taken the wife out of the home into the labour market and into the factory, and made her often the breadwinner of the family, no basis of any kind of male supremacy is left in the proletarian household except, perhaps, for something of the brutality toward women that has spread since the introduction of monogamy.[23]

He viewed the entry of women into the world of work as a necessary precondition for the decline of male dominance because it gave women economic independence. However, the above passage also indicates that paid work was not a sufficient condition for ending male dominance because the centuries-old traditions of 'brutality toward women' in marriage persisted.

Marx and Engels' prediction of the demise of the working-class family proved to be wrong and the older patriarchal family was replaced by a breadwinner family from the mid-nineteenth-century onwards. The male worker was provided with a family wage and women were excluded from certain occupations defined as men's work. The family's primary function was to reproduce the next generation of workers, at no cost to capitalists. The woman was to clothe, feed and socialise the children from the proceeds of her husband's wage. Of course, the family's function was not simply economic in the narrow sense. Beyond attending to the material needs of the family, women were assigned responsibility for imparting values that would enable future workers to take up their allotted role in the wider society. Among those primary values were obedience, respect for authority and a discipline that made one content with one's lot. In the breadwinner family, Engels argued:

The wife became the head servant, excluded from all participation in social production. The modern individual family is founded on the open or concealed domestic slavery of the wife, and modern society is a mass composed of these individual families. In the great majority of cases today [1874], at least in the possessing classes, the man is obliged to earn a living and support his family, and that in itself gives him a position of supremacy without any need for special legal titles and privileges. Within the family, he is the bourgeois; the wife represents the proletariat.[24]

However, while this male breadwinner family was once held up as a natural unit, the needs of capitalism changed again and so too did the family. The long economic boom which lasted from just after the Second World War to 1971 in most Western countries created a huge demand for labour and so married women were encouraged to join the workforce. By the 1990s most young women could expect to work ten years longer than their counterparts in the early part of the century due to spending less time at home looking after children.[25] Simultaneously, the growth of consumer durables such as washing machines, televisions and microwaves reduced the cost of reproduction of the next generation of workers. The coincidental availability of the contraceptive pill also allowed women to control their own fertility and undertake paid employment. In almost every industrialised country, the breadwinner family was, therefore, replaced with the dual-earner family. Marxist writers such as Lindsey German and Johanna Brenner have analysed how this shift took place in ways that suited capitalism in two fundamental ways.

First, despite the entry of most married women into the workforce, capitalism still insists on the privatised reproduction of the next generation. Corporations do not want to fund the cost of caring for the young or the elderly through taxation. So few resources are made available for provision of subsidised crèches or care homes for the elderly. The relentless drive for profit means that corporations provide the most minimal maternity leave or flexitime and the result is, therefore, an extremely contradictory mix. On one hand, the modern female is supposed to become a super-woman who can go to work and juggle childcare responsibilities. Yet, on the other hand, the traditional family is still held up as the ideal. Women continue to be defined as the primary carers and right-wing politicians often try to guilt trip them with talk of family values. Women, it is strongly suggested, have a particular responsibility to domesticate young men through family life and, as parents, may even be held legally responsible for failure to control their children.[26] These traditional ideas are bolstered by the real material fact that women earn less than men and this encourages families to do everything to 'hold down' the better paid jobs.

Second, the breakdown of the breadwinner family has produced a new alienated sexuality to replace traditional repression. The crisis of masculinity, for example, is now supposed to find its relief in the commodified culture of laddism as capitalism sells back fantasised images of female sexuality that still assures male dominance. Lads' magazines, lap dancing clubs and popular porn are all retailed under the supposed cover of irony to promote a new sexism and women are encouraged to prove their liberated attitudes by engaging in this culture by 'choice'. In reality, late capitalism has commodified sexuality to a degree unknown in all previous history. As German puts it, 'a human relationship, which should bring pleasure to the vast majority of men and women, has a price like a piece of meat or a second hand car and has been turned into another commodity'.[27]

Marxists, therefore, argue that an alternative to capitalism is necessary to challenge this new sexism. 'With the transfer of the means of production into common ownership', Engels argued:

> the single family ceases to be an economic unit of society. Private housekeeping is transformed into a social industry. The care and education of children becomes a public affair; society looks after all children alike, whether they are legitimate or not. This removes all anxiety about the 'consequences' which today is the most essential social – moral as well as economic – factor that prevents a girl giving herself completely to the man she loves.[28]

In today's terms, such a society would take responsibility for social reproduction through an extended system of public childcare and by reducing the drudgery of housework. Resources would be available for cheap, high quality restaurants and free 24-hour crèches to facilitate both working and leisure-time activities. (A 24-hour crèche does not imply that children are left in crèches for 24 hours, only that such childcare is available.) Similarly, if housing was not a private but a public responsibility, women would find it easier to leave abusive relationships, confident that they could find somewhere to live. If these measures lessened anxiety about the consequences of bringing children into the world, 'would that not suffice', Engels asked, 'to bring about the gradual growth of unconstrained sexual intercourse' alongside removing the 'inseparable contradiction' of prostitution and monogamy?[29] If sexual relationships were separated from property and economic insecurity, might they not blossom in ways different to the present?

RACE

Despite the election of a black president, clear patterns of racism in modern US society persist. The prison statistics alone demonstrate this as Afro-Americans are incarcerated at a rate seven times higher than whites and 23 per cent of all black males in their twenties have been in prison or are on parole, on probation or awaiting trial. Police killings of black people were also four times higher than whites in 1998 – which is an improvement on 1976 when it was eight times.[30] Deep-seated racist structures clearly remain in the most economically advanced capitalist country, but how is this to be explained?

Some have again argued that Marxism cannot adequately analyse the persistence of racism because it is over-focused on workers and capitalism. David Roediger, for example, claims that Marxism is inadequate because it does not acknowledge that white supremacism has been created by the working class and cannot accept 'why so many workers define themselves as white'.[31] Similarly, Cedric Robinson has suggested that Marxism itself is 'Eurocentric' and is unable to deal with the fact that racism pre-dates capitalism.[32] These views, however, ignore the way that the Marxist tradition has developed from its early foundations.

Marx actually wrote very little on racism and the main reason was that the black population of Britain at the time was tiny and mainly confined to the dockland areas of Liverpool, Cardiff and London. One of the main issues of his day was the fight against slavery during the American civil war and Marx was fully on the side of the abolitionists. Whereas *The Times* newspaper campaigned for British intervention on the side of the Southern pro-slavery states, Marx and the First International were resolutely pro-Abraham Lincoln. Marx argued that if the slaveholders' rebellion was victorious, it would 'sound the tocsin for a general crusade of property against labour'[33] and so the workers' movement had to support the Northern states, even if that meant economic hardship because of a cotton shortage for British factories. Later in *Capital* he spelled out his position when he stated simply that 'Labour cannot emancipate itself in white skin where in black it is branded'.[34]

The other main issue that Marx confronted was anti-Irish prejudice in England which arose from a huge influx of Irish immigrants after the famine of 1847–48 and the subsequent emergence of the Fenian movement which engaged in a bombing campaign. Like the current Muslim population in many European countries, the Irish were identifiable by their supposedly more traditional religion (Catholicism) and framed as violent fanatics who could not accept British values. Marx, however, did not make the slightest concession to chauvinist attitudes and argued that the main problem was not Irish 'fanaticism' but British landlordism which had destroyed the country. He argued that 'Any nation that oppresses another forges its own chains' and that therefore it was the special task of the First International[35]

> To awaken a consciousness in English workers that *for them* the *national emancipation of Ireland* is no question of abstract justice or humanitarian sentiment but *the first condition for their own social emancipation.*[36]

These strong sentiments gave rise to a vibrant tradition of Marxist writings on racism and anti-imperialism. Like the pattern of writings on gender, it forged a strong link between racism and class society and suggested that racist attitudes were damaging to the workers' movement.

One key text of this tradition is Alex Callinicos' *Race and Class* which significantly updates Marx's account.[37] The foundation stone of this account was that racism was not simply a matter of individual attitudes. It did not result from a lack of education or ignorance or prejudice, but arose from the specific history of Western capitalism. Nor did racism arise from the fear of the Other or a 'productive ambivalence' that mixed 'desire and derision'.[38] These social-psychological explanations claim that racism arises from a need to define one's own identity in opposition to 'the Other' and assumes there is a constant need to assert that difference. However, each summer, most Western cities are crowded with tourists from many distant countries but the local populations do not engage in great displays of hostility to reaffirm their own identity. Nor does the fear of 'the Other' explain how a language about 'race' or 'national culture' emerged or why 'the Other', who had a different skin colour or ate different kinds of food, should be considered more significant than 'the Other' who had a different hairstyle or wore glasses. In other words, supposed psychological laws are so general that they explain very little.

Racism is a modern phenomenon that may be defined as discrimination against a group of people on the basis of characteristics which are held to be inherent in them and so racists claim to be able to 'sum up' the character of a social group in terms of negative stereotypes. So some groups are typically defined as being lazy, cunning, mean or over-sexual. None of these supposedly inherent characteristics have any biological basis and the use of terms like the Irish 'race' or the White 'race' has no basis in fact. Any two unrelated human beings differ by about three million distinct DNA variants but, as Lewontin points out, about 85 per cent of this variation is among individuals within the same local, national or linguistic populations. Most remaining variation has to do with skin colour, hair form or a few proteins like the Rhesus blood type and none of it can be related to any social characteristics of particular groups.[39] Racial differences were, therefore, invented by specific societies and particular groups were 'racialised'.[40]

These differences have not always existed and 'whiteness' was by no means always assumed to be a mark of superiority over blacks. The Roman emperor Septimus Severus (193–211 AD) may have been black and the Romans did not discriminate between Britain and North Africa in taking slaves. Africans were sometimes used as mercenaries in the Greco-Roman world but others resided there for educational or commercial purposes.[41] The principal distinction was drawn between 'barbarians' and those who engaged in Greco-Roman culture, rather than any particular skin colour.

The sociologist Zygmunt Bauman has made a useful distinction between 'heterophobia' and modern racism in order to discuss hatreds in pre-modern societies. By heterophobia he means a generalised fear or suspicion of outsiders and he uses this concept to discuss how people in small, localised areas reacted to contact with strangers. These fears or suspicions, however, were not based on a belief about the inherent inferiority of a particular type of people. The one exception was the religious persecution of the Jews, but even these could escape anti-Semitism through conversion to Christianity. Only in sixteenth-century Spain were the *conversos* (Jews who converted to Catholicism) made subject to the doctrine of *limpieza de sangre* (purity of blood).[42] What is unique about modern racism is that people are defined as having inherently inferior qualities which exclude them from the national community. As Bauman put it:

in a world that boasts an unprecedented ability to improve human conditions by reorganising human affairs on a rational basis, racism manifests the convictions that a certain category of human beings cannot be incorporated into the rational order, whatever the effort.[43]

The basis for this modern form of racism was the specific manner in which Western capitalism was forged through slavery and imperialism.

Twelve million people were taken from Africa to the Caribbean and North America to build an economy that laid the basis for early capitalism. In what Eric Williams has called the triangular trade, Britain and France supplied the ships; Africa the human merchandise; and the Caribbean and America the raw materials from the plantations.[44] The profits from this trade accounted for between 21 per cent and 55 per cent of Britain's fixed capital formation in the 1770s.[45] Some of the greatest names in modern capitalism acquired their original money from the slave trade, including Lloyds Bank which insured the slave expeditions; Lehman Brothers who were the middlemen for slave-grown cotton; and Barclays Bank, one of whose original constituents enslaved more than 30,000 Africans. Without the triangular trade, the primitive accumulation of capital would have taken much longer.

Yet while slavery helped to provide the economic basis for capitalism, the early ideologues of the system claimed it would usher in a new era based on the rights of man. In order to dismantle the old aristocratic society, the advocates of a new society claimed that all men were born equal and that wealth should only accrue to those who could compete in the market rather than to those who were born with 'blue blood'. The contradiction between the new discourse about equal rights and the material reality is best exemplified by two US presidents, George Washington and Thomas Jefferson. These were slave plantation owners but they pursued a war with a Declaration of Independence that proclaimed 'that all men are created equal, that they are endowed by their Creator with certain inalienable rights'.[46] The great philosopher of constitutional liberty, John Locke, was also a shareholder in a slave ship.

These intense contradictions could only be resolved by excluding black people from the category of full human beings. They had to be denied equal status because, it was asserted, they possessed some extraordinary deficiency that made them less than human. They were supposed to have descended from the children of Ham rather than Adam and so destined to be 'hewers of wood and carriers of water'.[47] Later pseudo-scientific racists dropped the Biblical justifications and claimed that Black people were further down the evolutionary chain than White people.

Notions about the inherent inferiority of certain races grew even more dramatically with imperialism. Between 1876 and 1914, for example, Britain gained an extra 4 million square miles of the earth's surface; France got 3.5 million, Germany 1 million and Italy 1 million. These conquests were justified by the claims that the imperial powers were civilising the natives and had to take on the 'white man's burden' in order to bring semi-savage peoples into the modern world. The imperialist mind-set had a deep impact on Western culture because it fostered a notion that the 'free world' had a responsibility to lead backward peoples. The original culture of empire was expressed through writers such as Rudyard Kipling, who described the population of the Philippines as 'half devil and half child', or Charles Kingsley, who claimed that the Irish were like 'white chimpanzees'.[48] While this crudeness has largely disappeared, imperialism continues to feed into racism with repeated images of Western civilisation protecting itself against Muslim 'fanaticism'. Once again the West is presented as reasonable and moderate while the Muslim world is emotional and extreme.

Balibar put it well when he argued:

> The colonial castes of the various nationalities (British, French, Dutch, Portuguese and so on) *worked together* to forge the idea of 'White' superiority of civilisation as an interest that had to be defended against savages. This representation – the White Man's burden – has contributed in a decisive way to moulding the modern notion of European or Western identity.[49]

Modern Marxist writers have, however, not simply defined racism as a cultural hangover but have sought to locate it in real structures of experience in capitalist society.

Two structural elements within this society foster racist views. The first has been the role of the modern nation state. Over time it has grown from an external relation with its population where it functioned mainly as a tax collector to a more intrusive role where it registers, categorises and forges the identities of its population. This process is summarised well in Eugen Weber's *Peasants into Frenchmen* where he shows how school education is used to forge new loyalties to the nation rather than simply to the local community.[50]

In 1863, for example, at least one fifth of the population did not speak French and so the state had to adopt a deliberate policy to mould them into the ways of French civilisation. Contrary to its own myths, national identities do not emerge naturally among populations but are often created by the state. The state tries to establish a unified national history; to produce a selected version of a national culture; to inculcate a sense of patriotism. It is successful because it can wield real material power to back up the categories that it imposes on people.

One of the key powers of the state is the right to issue a passport and so concretely define who is and who is not a citizen. This power is deployed in ways that are highly functional for capital, even though individual capitalists sometimes rail against restrictions on importing labour. By defining some workers as 'non-nationals' and subjecting them to immigration controls, corporations are enabled to hire workers with restricted legal rights and to subject them to greater forms of exploitation. Workers can be forced to remain with a particular employer for a set period of a year or two to enjoy a work permit. Others may be forced to take on illegal work and so accept atrocious conditions. Capital as a whole benefits from this politico-legal oppression of migrant workers because it reduces the cost of their wages. Corporations in metropolitan countries can also benefit because they get a ready supply of surplus labour in periods of boom but are not required to contribute to the cost of its social reproduction as families in the migrant home countries have already borne the cost. These double standards on globalisation and migration help to explain why more than eleven million people are deemed to be illegal in the US. Modern capitalism demands more migrant labour but wants it on conditions that give less legal independence to workers.

State policy in promoting citizenship and then controlling the movement of labour in this hypocritical way has a huge impact on 'native' populations – particularly in an era of economic insecurity. The contradictory claim that the state looks after 'its own' citizens, while managing immigration in ways beneficial to capital, has produced a white defensive nationalism that targets migrants and asylum-seekers. This new racism claims to have moved beyond empire and can even evoke folktales of how their hard-working ancestors faced discrimination themselves, but it still wants migrants excluded. Instead of a focus on skin colour, exclusion is framed in terms of a defence of national culture and the 'refusal' of migrants to integrate into that culture. Typically, this new racism develops a victim psychology to claim that native culture is being 'swamped' or that a country is being 'colonised' by Muslim invasions. In response to this populist backlash, the political establishment has retreated from the liberal ideas of a multicultural society and demands greater effort by migrants to 'integrate'. This new racism rests on a claim that minority groups are guilty of 'self-segregation' and so it demands language and culture tests to curtail the legal status of migrants.

The second structural element that gives rises to racism is the way the market simultaneously unites and divides workers. Under capitalism, individual workers are forced to compete for jobs, social housing or promotions. They live in fear that the social security provided by the state will be cut or that they will be asked to pay more taxes to fund it. When these fears coincide with both a Western culture that was forged by empire and state structures that reduce the legal rights of migrant workers, it is no wonder that racism flourishes.

In the nineteenth century Marx had to confront conflicts between English workers and Irish migrants. In the 1860s a number of anti-Irish riots took place in Britain and Marx wrote of its effects on working-class politics:

Every industrial and commercial centre in England now possesses a working class divided into two *hostile* camps, English proletarians and Irish proletarians. The ordinary English worker hates the Irish worker as a competitor who lowers his standard of life.

In relation to the Irish worker he regards himself as a member of the *ruling* nation and consequently he becomes a tool of the English aristocrats and capitalists against Ireland, thus strengthening their domination *over himself*.

He cherishes religious, social, and national prejudices against the Irish worker. His attitude towards him is much the same as that of the "poor whites" to the Negroes in the former slave states of the U.S.A. The Irishman pays him back with interest in his own money. He sees in the English worker both the accomplice and the stupid tool of the *English rulers in Ireland*.

This antagonism is artificially kept alive and intensified by the press, the pulpit, the comic papers, in short, by all the means at the disposal of the ruling classes. *This antagonism* is the secret of the *impotence of the English working class*, despite its organisation. It is the secret by which the capitalist class maintains its power. And the latter is quite aware of this.[51]

This lengthy passage summarises some of the main elements of the modern Marxist approach to racism and immigration. It recognises that capitalism has historically drawn in a migrant reserve army of labour, which it tries to use to gain advantage. It notes that workers can have racist attitudes both because of economic competition and because workers sometimes embrace imperialist ideas. It also points to what du Bois called the 'psychological wage'[52] – the desire to be seen as part of the 'national community' as against a 'non-citizen'. And crucially, this perspective focuses on how such racist attitudes are consciously stoked to keep workers divided.

But while all of these factors underline the structural causes of racism in a capitalist society, there are equally good reasons why racism is against the interests of workers and why many workers come to recognise this. Marx's reference to the 'poor whites' in the Southern states of America was actually quite prophetic. Despite their own notions of privilege, the racism of Southern white workers rebounded on them because it weakened union organisation and allowed employers to impose low wages. One study conducted in the early 1970s noted:

> In each of these blue-collar groups, the Southern white workers earned less than Northern black workers. Despite the continued gross discrimination against black skilled craftsmen in the North, the 'privileged' Southern whites earned 4 per cent less than they did. Southern male white operatives averaged ... 18 per cent less than Northern black male operatives. And Southern white service workers earned ... 14 per cent less than Northern black male service workers.[53]

It is in the interest of workers to oppose racism and indeed workers' organisation can only be sustained if they mount a fight against racist ideas. This conflict between the interests of workers and the acceptance by some of racist ideas explains why clashes occur within the workers' movement. Even in the Southern states of the US, the history of labour is not one untrammelled assertion of white supremacy, but rather of a clash between the pull of race and class.[54] Attempts to forge a class identity have to be made in a society where elites try to incite division and whether or not they are successful depends on the way workers develop political understandings of the world.

6
How We Are Kept in Line

If Marx's description of capitalism is accurate, why do people put up with it? The capitalists are a tiny minority and if workers banded together, they could easily be ousted. Why has it not happened already? Marx provides two answers to this question: capitalists can dominate through ideas and use the threat of force. The former takes us to Marx's theory of ideology and the latter to his theory of the state.

IDEOLOGY

The term ideology was coined by Destutt de Tracy during the course of the French Revolution to mean the science of ideas, but later changed to a more pejorative use – how ideas might be used to hold on to power. Machiavelli had written on how ideas were linked to techniques of political power in the fifteenth century. He argued that power is rarely exercised simply through force and that much more can be achieved by fraud. He advised rulers to conceal their actions and appear – but not actually be – merciful, faithful, humane, honest and religious. These techniques, known today as 'spin', were possible because rulers lived in isolation, in castles or great houses, surrounded by security guards. The privilege of power was, as Machiavelli put it, that 'everyone sees what you appear to be, few really know what you are'.[1]

Fraud or deception is, therefore, one way ideology might work and writers of the Enlightenment thought that religion was the prime example. The priests deliberately concocted the doctrine of the divine right of kings so people would accept monarchy. This allowed Louis XIV, for example, to claim a direct connection to God and proclaim that 'He who gave men kings desired that they be respected as his lieutenants'.[2] The priests also inculcated ignorance and superstition in the population. As Holbach wrote:

In fixing men's eyes continually upon heaven; in persuading them, that all their misfortunes are effects of divine anger; in providing none but ineffectual and futile means to put an end to their sufferings, we might justly conclude, that the only object of priests was to divert nations from thinking about the true sources of their misery, and thus to render it eternal.[3]

This view of ideology sees it as brainwashing and the solution was to provide an education to overcome religious doctrine.

Marx thought, however, that a 'conspiracy to brainwash' model could not adequately explain how ideology worked because the ideas which held people in thrall could not just be produced by a tiny minority. Pro-capitalist ideas were secreted from the pores of the system itself and there was not just one locus where they were generated. They were produced not only by professional ideologists in a variety of institutions but also from people's experience of living under capitalism. The latter element was important because the 'conspiracy to brainwash' model could not explain why people accepted ideas that were clearly against their interests. It had to assume an induced stupidity or ignorance but, if this was the case, there was little hope of change coming from the mass of people. They had to be led by an enlightened minority who could educate the rest of the population.

Marx's own theory of ideology sought to escape these cruder implications. Although there is no one systematic presentation of his theory, the elements can be constructed from the *German Ideology* and his theory of commodity fetishism in *Capital*.

WHERE DO IDEAS COME FROM?

Marx did not think that ideas that were held by large numbers of people, and became the common sense of society, arose accidentally. Nor did he think, as intellectuals sometimes imagine, that there is a distinct 'history of ideas' which operates within its own sphere, with one idea reacting and responding to another that preceded it. For Marx, however, 'the phantoms formed in the human brain are … sublimates of their material life process'.[4] The more complicated the division of labour in society, the more removed people are from immediate, sensuous nature, the more abstract their system of concepts became. Consciousness and thought, however, cannot be fully separated from the world in which they occur. They arise from problems, issues and experiences that we encounter in the world. In other words, ideas must have a material base even if they are at a high level of abstraction and not directly based on the use of the senses.

In a class society, not all interpretations of the social world are equal and the upper class is in a much better position to shape the dominant ones. There is a connection, therefore, between ideas which become the common sense of society and economic power. Here is how Marx put it:

> The ideas of the ruling class are in every epoch the ruling ideas, i.e. the class which is the ruling *material* force of society, is at the same time its ruling *intellectual* force. The class, which has the means of material production at its disposal, has control at the same time over the means of mental production, so that thereby, generally speaking, the ideas of those who lack the means of mental production are subject to it.[5]

A complex argument is presented here and we need to distinguish between two themes. One is a claim that ideas can in some sense belong to a class, that they are the ideas *of* a particular group. Here Marx is not simply referring to their origin or who first thought of or articulated them. He is rather arguing that there are interpretations of the world which suit a ruling class and which articulate their particular class interest. Such interpretations provide a legitimate justification for their privilege and will help intellectually to disarm their potential opponents. The statements that 'we need more competitiveness' and that the 'private sector is more efficient' belong to this category. 'Competitiveness' is a jargon word repeated constantly in the media to imply that rivalry leads to the best economic results for everyone. 'Private sector' is another term for capitalist ownership of industry. When you join the two statements into an argument, you conclude that capitalism is best for an economy because it is linked to efficiency. Clearly, this set of ideas will help to win acceptance for the current form of class rule and so we can legitimately argue that it is an idea *of* the ruling class – meaning that it serves their interests in so far as it perpetuates their system. Conversely, if the opposite idea were to prevail – namely that cooperation increased efficiency and so public ownership is better – the position of capitalists would be undermined.

This is an example of how a simple set of ideas serves ruling-class interests, but ideology can also work at subtler levels. Marx claimed that it often functions as 'an ideal expression of material relationships'.[6] By this he means that the real experience of market competition is given an 'ideal expression' through a much broader philosophical outlook which defines humans as 'selfish'. We are, it is often claimed, greedy and competitive and our present arrangements for running society are only an expression of deeper characteristics of the human personality itself. The concept of 'natural greed' appears now as an 'ideal expression' to our material reality, and individual advancement seen as what naturally motivates everyone. Similarly, an image of God in heaven surrounded by saints and angels who are ranked by how close they are to Him is an ideal reflection of feudal power relations. Broader, more abstract concepts help to lay an intellectual foundation for a wider paradigm which guides our day-to-day interpretations of the world. By selecting facts and interpreting them in a certain way, this thought paradigm shapes how we see the world and colours the judgements we make. It is like contact lenses – after wearing them for a while you barely notice them.

The second theme in Marx's quotation above is that economic power makes it easier for the ruling class to promote their ideas – that there is a link between material production and 'mental production'. Although there are many arenas where ideas are produced, these are influenced, directly or indirectly, by economic power.

Ideas are clearly not things which are 'produced', but they go through an analogous process as they are often written down, debated and crucially disseminated. Intellectual reflection and working out ideas in detail also require time and mental space that not everyone in society has. Dissemination of and debate on ideas take place in certain material institutions which are shaped by class relations, and these in turn impact on them. In modern society, there is a host of diverse ideas on what is best for humanity, but only a small number are taken seriously and debated in the mass media. In this way, the mass media have replaced the church or the village schoolmaster as the main source of ideas about society.

Yet the mass media are organised through corporations which are controlled by boards of directors and are answerable to shareholders. They are run as a business with a declared aim of profit and, naturally, this leads to an intrinsic bias to support the capitalist system. In the US, just five conglomerates – Time Warner, Disney, News Corporation, Bertelsmann and Viacom – own most of the newspapers, magazines, books, television and radio stations.[7] They have had a big influence in supporting right-wing politics and a value system that underpins rampant consumerism. To cater for a mass audience, the media present an image of balance but the limits are set by the acceptable level of dissent within the dominant paradigm. During a crisis, pretence at objectivity is often dropped so when George Bush launched a war on Iraq every one of the 175 newspapers owned by Rupert Murdoch came out in support.[8] The raw material which forms our daily news passes through what Herman and Chomsky called five interrelated filters. These are 1) the size, concentrated ownership, owner wealth and profit orientation of the dominant mass media firms; 2) advertising as the primary income source of the mass media; 3) reliance of the media on information provided by government and business 'experts' funded and approved by these primary sources and agents of power; 4) 'flak' as a means of disciplining the population; and 5) 'anti-communism' as a national religion and control mechanism.[9]

'Flak' refers to a systematic attack on alternative views or the individuals who hold them and 'anti-communism' is increasingly being replaced with a new enemy – 'Islamic fundamentalism'. With these filters in place, the population are subjected to a view of the world that approximates to the broad interpretation of their rulers.

But while the mass media are a key arena for idea production, they are not the only one. At a more sophisticated level, universities also promote the ruling-class view of the world. Professors of economics and the social sciences are usually drawn from respectable academics who function as the intellectual 'watchdogs' for the status quo.[10] The peculiar division of knowledge that separates history from economics and sociology mirrors a fragmented understanding of the world which denies there is even 'a system' that can be defined as capitalist. Today universities look more like corporations than places of learning: McDonalds sponsors research, IBM decides the content of computer degrees and Pfizer run drug trials in university labs. It is hardly surprising that across university campuses in every department the ideology of business predominates with a uniformity that even ten years ago people would have found shocking. More basically, schools also support dominant ideology, often through a 'hidden curriculum' that exists alongside training children in literacy and numeracy to promote the type of socialisation that capitalism needs. Most schools set store on obedience, timekeeping and respect for experts who know better – ideal qualities to fit adults for their future role as wage workers. In elite schools, however, the emphasis is on confidence and leadership skills.[11]

As well as shaping the production of ideas, economic power has a bearing on how they sound. If I argue that a small-time drug dealer who sells marijuana should be jailed, this may sound a little tough on law and order but it is debatable. If, however, I suggest that directors of tobacco companies should be incarcerated for causing cancer, this sounds 'extreme'. The latter suggestion appears to go against the grain of 'reality' because directors of tobacco companies are respectable people 'who provide jobs' and 'shore up the economy'. The ideology of capitalists has, therefore, a 'positional advantage' because their ideas appear practical.[12] As Meszaros put it,

> since they identify themselves 'from the inside' so to speak with the ongoing processes of socio-economic … reproduction, they can stipulate practicality as the absolute prerequisite for choosing between alternatives.[13]

Alternative ideas are more easily defined as 'negative' and 'impractical' because they challenge the economic powers that really dominate people's lives.

One way of appreciating Marx's theory of ideology is to locate it within the three-dimensional model of power developed by the sociologist Steve Lukes.[14] The first dimension concerns overt conflicts and can be measured by calculating who wins most of the visible outcomes. However, this is a crude measure because it does not take account of how some people are able to block items from even being discussed. The second more covert dimension of power is about controlling agendas to ensure that some items just fall off. The third dimension, however, is the most invisible but most effective because it works by influencing how people articulate their desires and interests. If one can stop people articulating a certain demand or get them to define a barely articulated demand as 'impractical', then you have real power. Marx's theory of ideology belongs to this third dimension.

How might such ideological control work? Here we can detect a number of patterns in the promotion of ideas that help uphold capitalism. These patterns may be summarised under five headings.

Capitalist Ideology Presents Current Social Arrangements as Part of the Natural Order

They either have no history or are just an expression of tendencies that have always been there. While commodity exchange is a feature of capitalist society, 'common sense' ideology will read this concept back in time to claim that the primitive hunter is also 'exchanging' his produce with female gatherers.[15] In this way, hunters, merchant traders in goods, capitalists who hire workers are all doing what comes naturally – exchanging goods and services.

This method works by providing abstract descriptions. Real 'exchange' activity is taken out of its historical context, denuded of the class relations that surround it and defined in purely formal terms. Modern conventional economics works primarily with this sort of abstract conceptual definition. Concepts such as capital, for example, are defined as 'savings' and, as every society must use 'capital' in this sense, it is not necessary to examine what specifically happens when wage labour is hired. The aim, as Marx put it, is to present production as 'encased in eternal natural laws, independent of history, at which opportunity *bourgeois* relations are then quietly smuggled in as inviolable natural laws on which society in the abstract is founded'.[16]

Another way that this technique of naturalising works is by presenting an image of human motivation which dovetails neatly with desired social behaviour within capitalism. In the nineteenth century, Herbert Spencer coined the phrase 'the survival of the fittest' as the natural law to underpin capitalism.[17] By this he meant that all species, including humans, had to compete against each other in a brutal endeavour to survive and prosper. Today evolutionary biologists such as Richard Dawkins have developed concepts such as 'the selfish gene' to imply that some behaviours that are common in a capitalist society are rooted in our genes.[18] This has clearly an ideological function because if certain behaviours are rooted in human nature, there is no scope for real change. Dawkins' view of the world merits prime-time viewing on TV while opposing views from biologists such as Steven Rose, Richard Lewontin and Leon Kamin are confined to specialist audiences.[19]

Ideology Deals with Appearances, with How Things Seem – Not How They Are

Conflict in human relations is not always immediately visible and this is particularly relevant to understanding capitalism. In a feudal society, every peasant knew when their exploitation started – they had to work for a certain number of days for the lord or hand over some of their produce. Under capitalism, the working day is divided, as we saw, between necessary labour and surplus labour, but there is no visible demarcation. Exploitation is hidden and a broader understanding of how the system works is required to unearth it.

The current ideology seeks to deny further that fundamental conflicts of interest exist. At a popular level, workers are continually told to 'give a fair day's work for a fair day's pay'. They are encouraged to think of themselves as 'social partners' with their employer or 'stakeholders' in a company. They are supposed to pull together with their management to fight the threat of competition from other companies. A dense institutional structure of 'industrial relations machinery' exists to reconcile workers and employers so that they reach shared understandings on common interests. The last question anyone is encouraged to ask is 'who benefits?' because this often leads to an inquiry into how a supposed common endeavour is appropriated by the few. Increasing productivity, for example, is almost universally agreed as a 'good thing'. But if one asks who benefits, more embarrassing issues may arise.

One way that the fundamental conflict of interest between workers and employers is concealed is by drawing a veil over what happens in production. Despite a vast explosion of information and images, the world of production remains largely invisible in the mass media. While consumption patterns and the latest fashion crazes are regularly reported, journalists are effectively barred, often under the guise of 'commercially sensitive information', from entering factories and offices to report on how employees feel about their boss. Where detailed material on workers' productivity, for example, is published it often becomes a dense, technical discussion that abstracts the issue from real conflicts.

Through some of these mechanisms, it is made difficult for workers to generate a broader view of how the system works so as to organise against it.

Capitalist Ideology Assumes that People Should Identify Naturally with Their Nationality or Their Government

Every ruling group tries to represent its sectional interest as the general interest of society. Instead of claiming that profits are good for Bill Gates and Microsoft, profit-making is deemed to be good for Western civilisation. As they rise to power, an aspiring ruling class debunks the claims of the old and offers a new vision to the rest of society. When the capitalist class was challenging the aristocracy, they presented them as slothful, luxury-seeking parasites who could not advance the economy. But when they in turn are challenged, they try to claim that there is no other possible way of organising society. In other words, they try not to focus on their privileges or on the fact that they won them from a former ruling class, but on their role as eternal representatives of the general society. Marx summed up the ideological manoeuvre as follows:

For each new class, which puts itself in place of one ruling before it, is compelled merely in order to carry through its aim, to represent its interest as the common interest of all members of society. It has to give its ideas the form of universality, and represent them as the only rational, universally valid ones.[20]

When this claim to represent the good of society starts to break down, ideologists often adopt a more defensive strategy and claim to be standing up for their 'national community'. Attacks on BP following a catastrophic oil spill are presented, for example, as attacks on British society; high food prices are not just good for farmers but for the Irish or the French as a whole; and what is good for General Motors is really what is good for America. More broadly, an imagined threat is often projected to 'our culture and way of life' so that the political elite step forward to defend society against hordes of 'outsiders' who want to 'milk' our welfare state.

In an unequal society, our rulers will always represent themselves as standing for the interest of the mass of people.

Ideology Seems to Become Fixed in Language

Marx did not discuss how language is used to give an emotional charge to particular ideas. This gap – understandable in an era where there was no surfeit of images – has been used in academic circles to promote an analysis of 'discourse'. This often suggests that there is no reality outside texts because knowledge of the material world is only possible through language.[21] Such views tend to place language and ideology in a realm of their own. Nevertheless, it is clear that language often sums up ideological slants and certainly the media today exploit this to the full.

Labels are a convenient way of summing up a complex association of ideas and so words are sometimes chosen for their effect. If someone is labelled a 'terrorist' – as Nelson Mandela once was – this conveys a different connotation from 'freedom fighter.' If a candidate is called a 'moderate' politician, it can be assumed that she is practical, gets things done and is (wisely) middle of the road; if an 'extremist' wins support, there is a need for a re-education programme. A 'moderate' trade unionist is a polite word for someone who accepts capitalism, but 'militants' are usually presented as mindlessly dogmatic. The governments of Iran or Pakistan impose 'censorship' but ours 'withholds information'. A crowd 'streams out' from a football stadium but immigrants 'flood in'. Such selective use of emotive words shows how language is often highly charged ideologically. Language gives a recognisable stamp to the dominant ideology and instant access to the prescribed modes of thought. As the Russian Marxist Volosinov argued, the social nature of language means that words vary their ideological meaning according to the context and can thus become an ideological battleground.[22]

Capitalist Ideology Promotes Negative Freedom and Choice

Capitalism and freedom are often inextricably linked by ideologists such as Milton Friedman, who claimed that the market is the only way to guarantee liberty.[23] During the Cold War this theme was used to suggest that despite its inequalities, at least capitalism gave 'freedom'. After the demise of the USSR, however, it was necessary to state what exactly this freedom meant because it could no longer be defined in terms of its opposite and so Friedman's writings came into their own.

The neoliberal definition is of an abstract freedom which refers primarily to freedom from government control. It is an idealised version of freedom of exchange because individuals are said to be free when they can pursue their self-interest and enter into relations with others only when it suits their purpose. However, this is a negative definition because it sees it as freedom *from* external authority. This is by no means the same as a positive freedom *to* carry out desires. You could be free from government control but be forced to work for low wages because you need to eat. Rich and poor people may both be free from state control but only the rich can choose to live in large houses while the poor must 'choose' tiny bedsits. Real choice for a poor person requires social measures which enable them to overcome their poverty. The same abstract definition of freedom is mirrored in laws which treat people equally. Everyone is supposed to be a citizen with equal rights and duties, but the limitation of this formal equality was explained by Anatole France, who quipped that 'the majestic quality of the law prohibits the wealthy as well as the poor from sleeping under bridges, from begging in the streets, from stealing bread'.[24]

The equation of freedom with a purely individual choice is a particular feature of capitalist ideology. As Marx put it:

> The liberty we are here dealing with is that of man as an isolated monad ... [it] is based not on the association of man with man, but on the separation of man from man. It is the *right* of this separation, the right of the *restricted* individual, withdrawn into himself.[25]

However, if each individual pursues exclusively self-interested goals, none may achieve what they desire. When everyone relies on a car to get to work as quickly as possible, they fail because their individual choice has caused traffic jams.

REIFICATION

How do we explain how these patterns of thinking come to be accepted? Even if economic power allows our rulers to freely disseminate their ideas, how can this determine how they are received and endorsed? Marx's discussion of commodity fetishism and its development by Lukács as reification helps in this.

Although capitalism breaks down individual self-reliance and creates a great dependency on each other, it does so through an anarchic exchange of things. As Marx put it:

> It is, however, this finished form of the world of commodities – the money form – which conceals the social character of private labour and the social relations between individual workers, by making these relations appear as relations between material objects, instead of revealing them plainly.[26]

Once the social character is concealed through commodity exchange, we enter a world where we are controlled by anonymous forces. There is ever greater pressure to produce more commodities and so 'the process of production has mastery over men instead of the opposite'.[27] The markets for commodities take on a life of their own and they appear to be governed by laws over which we have no control. Particular commodities assume supra-human qualities as they 'rise' or 'fall' or even 'attract investors'. Finance, which 'no longer bears the birth marks of its origin' in human labour, becomes imbued with a magical property of yielding dividends or interest, much like 'it is the property of pear tree to bear pears'.[28]

Since Marx's day the control that finance exercises has grown to nightmarish proportions. Our lives are dictated by interest rates, share price movement on stock exchanges and flows of global finance. Even the former German President, Horst Kohler, a former head of the IMF, has stated that the 'international financial markets have developed into a monster that must be put back in its place'.[29] In almost every part of the globe, people wake up to morning news reports about how 'the markets' are feeling about national debt or their economic policy.

Under the shadow of three revolutions – in Germany, Russia and Hungary – Georg Lukács wrote *History and Class Consciousness* in 1922 to develop Marx's theory. Lukács had frequented the circles of the German sociologist Max Weber, and was familiar with discussions on how a new, cold, calculating culture of 'instrumental rationality' was enchaining human beings in a maze of bureaucracy.[30] Lukács, however, concluded that these sociological descriptions, while perceptive, did not get to the root of the problem.

By reification, Lukács meant the social relations between people appear as relations between things. It is as if we were part of a complex machine which is subject to its own laws and which escape our control. He argued that as capitalism expanded, 'the structure of reification sunk more deeply, more fatefully and more definitely into the consciousness of man'.[31] People became 'contemplative' and watched passively as their economy took on a life of its own. But while the details of their lives were subject to external laws which compelled obedience, the total system appeared to be ruled by chance.[32] So, because of 'globalisation' workers are told that they have to accept lower wages and that this is just how things are. Yet even if they comply, there may still find themselves out of work due to chance developments in stock markets thousands of kilometres away. Economic crises appear from nowhere, like volcanic eruptions. This sense of a lack of control and helplessness was compounded by the growing fragmentation of work. As work is 'rationalised' into smaller and smaller parts, more and more disconnected from other parts of the productive process, people literally feel like cogs in an immense machine. All of this produces a culture of passive contemplation of an objective external world. Lukács summarised it thus:

> Man in capitalist society confronts a reality 'made' by himself (as a class) which appears to him to be a natural phenomenon alien to himself; he is wholly at the mercy of its 'laws', his activity is confined to the exploitation of the inexorable fulfilment of certain individual laws for his own (egoistic) interests.[33]

In other words, people's experience of capitalism induces a feeling of fatalism. The dominant impression is that 'There is nothing that can be done because we are in the hands of the market'. If the word 'monster' were substituted for 'markets' and people spoke in hushed tones about pleasing the Great Beast, it still would not capture the sense of powerlessness before this anonymous force.

In this situation, all that is left for people to do is to look after their own individual needs. This experience of the overall social world helps to explain why Marx rejected the idea that ideology was just a form of deception or that people were mere dupes of ideological conditioning. The 'phantoms' which dominate the human mind come from a real experience under capitalism. They may be produced by priests, professors or media hosts, but they gain a hearing because they fit with how people actually experience the world.

Marx was under no illusion that his description of commodity fetishism would in itself tear away the veil of illusion. Even if there was more education in socialist arguments, it would still persist because reification is deeply rooted in the reality of life. It cannot be abolished simply by realising how bad it is. It requires a real struggle where people break free of fatalism to assert that they are taking control of the world. It must be abolished in a 'practical objective way for man to become man not only in *thinking*, in *consciousness* but in mass *being*, in life'.[34]

But how could this occur if people were brainwashed? Here Marx made a further break with the tradition of the Enlightenment. People may be dominated by the ideology of their society but this did not amount to total control because ideologies cannot suffocate all ability to think critically. For one thing, the dominant ideology is a contradictory phenomenon because of the society it emanates from.

In order to be effective, some elements of the outlook of subordinate classes often have to be incorporated into the dominant ideology. Governments that came to power by overthrowing colonial rulers through mass movements often claimed that they were building 'a republic for all the people'. Liberal Western governments that want the support of the post-1968 generation will try to 'recuperate' and co-opt oppositional ideas that grew out of social movements that promoted sexual liberation or anti-racism. Even though these elements play a subordinate role, they can give rise to tensions within the ideology. Questions will arise over what exactly is meant by 'rule of the people' or 'sexual equality' or why official anti-racism is not more evident in police behaviour or in social institutions. This contestation can lead to wider challenges as contradictions within the dominant ideology are unearthed.

The dynamic and crisis-prone nature of capitalism means that it is often forced to undermine earlier certainties and make sudden ideological shifts. Up to 2008, for example, most governments had a policy of 'non-interference' in the market. After the crash, however, many raced to bail out the banks, even though they had told their population that they could not 'interfere' to save jobs or develop a better welfare state. These sudden shifts help to undermine the 'hegemony' or leadership of the political elite.[35]

A real weak spot for any dominant ideology, however, arises from the effects of struggles mounted by workers. The system functions by turning labour into a commodity but, unlike other commodities, it cannot detach its use from the human being who sells it. As Lukács put it:

> While the process by which the worker is reified and becomes a commodity dehumanises him and cripples and atrophies his 'soul' – as long as he does not rebel against it – it remains true that precisely his humanity and his soul are not changed into commodities.[36]

This elementary fact means that struggles break out against the rule of capital even when those waging them are not clear about an alternative to it. Many workers who strike or join unions continue to endorse the dominant ideas of society. Yet the very experience of banding together in a society that promotes individual competition leads to a deeper questioning. Workers find, for example, that the police, whom they previously thought were neutral, are used to break their strike. Or the media, which they thought reported objectively, branded them as greedy. They come to understand that it is only through solidarity that they can win.

For these reasons, it is more accurate to say that workers, rather than accepting the whole of what dominant ideology dictates, accept some parts of it and reject others. For example, their experience in capitalist society leads to seeing themselves *both* as individuals in competition with other workers *and* as members of a collective class with the same conditions. This was what Gramsci meant by workers having a 'contradictory consciousness'.

> One might almost say that he has two theoretical consciousnesses, or one contradictory consciousness: one which is implicit in his activity and which in reality unites him with all his fellow workers in the practical transformation of the real world; and one, superficially explicit or verbal, which he has inherited from the past and uncritically absorbed.[37]

As Gramsci well understood from his time as a socialist organiser among Turin workers in the early 1920s, from this contradictory consciousness could spring the possibility of revolt.

THE STATE

When such revolts occur, the state plays a key role in safeguarding capitalism. It is the last line of the defence. But even before that point is reached, the power of the state operates as an iron fist inside a velvet glove. No supermarket would survive if there were not the threat of force that states can deploy to defend capitalist property relations.

The state may be defined as a complex of institutions that claims a monopoly on the use of force through one of its specialised agencies. It is much larger than a government which, as Ray Miliband points out, speaks 'in the name of the state and is formally invested with state power [but this] does not mean it effectively controls that power'.[38] Within the apparatus of the state, the government is surrounded by the administration, military, police and judiciary.

Coordination and a degree of force are features of most societies, but in some distant pre-class societies this was undertaken by the community as a whole. Sometimes the tribe gathered in an assembly to make decisions or to ostracise someone as punishment, but no special institution had an exclusive use of force. As the productivity of these societies expanded and a more elaborate division of labour developed, this changed. New bodies emerged to coordinate society, but these developments either coincided with or were followed by the division of society into classes. Once this split occurred, a whole community could no longer spontaneously organise itself to collectively administer punishment. When there are slaves and masters, who is to decide what is theft and what isn't? The masters believe that a slave who stole bread was guilty of theft, but the slaves believe that their masters who captured them committed a worse theft! No wonder Greek society had to invent a special body of bowmen to guard against its slaves.[39] The state, therefore, according to Engels:

is a product of society at a certain stage of development; it is the admission that this society ... has cleft into irreconcilable antagonisms which it is powerless to exorcise.

But in order that these antagonisms, classes with conflicting economic interests, might not consume themselves ... in fruitless struggle, a power, apparently standing above society, has become necessary to moderate the conflict and keep it within the bounds of "order" and this power ... is the state.[40]

The very existence of a state expresses the 'irreconcilability of class antagonisms'.[41] As long as these divisions persist, there will be a state.

This view stands in marked contrast to two other commonly held views. The first sees the state as standing above sectional interests to represent the 'common good'. Hegel, for example, thought that the state separated itself off from the particular interests of civil society to promote universal goals. Marx derided this view because it took at face value the image the state bureaucracy had of itself. These 'Jesuits of the state' hid behind a dense official language to promote their own careers and interests.[42] They presented a false and abstract solidarity of citizenship that could not overcome the real conflicts in civil society. Far from the state imposing reason on civil society, its whole legal structure had its roots in political economy.

The more modern 'pluralist' theory of the state is a variant of the first. It suggests that no one social group can achieve governmental office in a liberal democracy and so coalitions have to be constructed. The state, therefore, has to respond to competing interests and everyone, including those at the back of the queue, eventually gets served.[43] In this roundabout and somewhat accidental manner – a little like Adam Smith's 'invisible hand' of the market – the state works for the good of all. This ignores, however, how the wider state apparatus that surrounds elected governments imparts a bias to decision-making. The individuals who dominate this apparatus are often drawn from unelected elite networks and their decisions are coloured by this. Moreover, states rest on, and have to manage, a capitalist economy from which they derive their tax revenue. Despite conflicting views among political parties, this reliance induces an eventual consensus on promoting profit-making for the good of society.

The class nature of the modern state is demonstrated in four main ways.

First, the state fuses the individual interests of competing capitalists into a common perspective. In a phrase, it becomes the management committee for their common affairs.[44]

The capitalist class is the most divided ruling class in all of history. Internally, they are like a snake pit with conflicting interests – finance versus manufacturing; small enterprise versus large monopolies – continually fighting each other. They need a state to develop a national economic strategy and to defend themselves against common enemies. In the 1980s and 1990s, for example, US capitalists were under growing pressure from their Japanese rivals and could only develop a counter-strategy through the medium of the state. That state used its military power to pressure Japan to revalue its currency and to open its markets to US imports.[45] On the home front, it helped to reorganise capitalists around a new industrial policy to promote manufacturing and open up financial markets. Without the cohesive intervention of the state, many capitalists would have been eliminated. Even though the state attempts to develop a common ruling-class strategy, it can at times be riven by conflicts within that class. In periods of crisis, differences about how to save capitalism from the capitalists themselves can open up deep cracks within state structures.

Second, the state guarantees the conditions for the reproduction of the capitalist economy. Without these the market would degenerate into a dog eat dog world where capitalists would not be assured of any stability or even a supply of workers to make their profits.

The state guarantees and underpins the financial arrangements that facilitate the circulation of capital. It provides a coherent system of law to resolve disputes between capitalists and protects their property. Engels remarked that the individual capitalist knows that 'even if the particular law may injure him as an individual, still the complex of legislation as whole protects his interests'.[46] The law expresses the 'mean average interest' of the ruling class and that is why they preach its sanctity.[47] The state also undertakes costly infrastructure projects that no individual capitalist would do. While these can benefit society at large, they often suit the specific needs of capitalist reproduction. The Indian government, for example, has borrowed huge sums from institutions like the World Bank to build dams that will supply industry with water and electricity. Yet despite the fact that 50 million people have been displaced, droughts and flooding are more prevalent today than when the state was founded in 1947.[48]

States also undertake some of the social reproduction and care of workers to ensure a smooth and timely supply to the labour market. Children are educated to make them fit for work, workers are kept fit through a healthcare system and a minimum degree of contentment is secured through a social security system. Despite the fact that the bulk of the money to pay for these services comes from working-class taxes and social insurance schemes, capitalists deeply resent any imposition on their profits. The neo-liberal demand to shrink the state expresses their resentment but, despite these cries, they still need state support. Despite more than two decades of Thatcherite attacks on state spending, the overall ratio of public spending to GDP stands at 41 per cent in OECD countries.[49]

Third, states supervise the subordination and suppression of the lower classes. For most of the time people accept the system due to 'the dull compulsion' of economic necessity and so 'direct extra-economic force' is the exception rather than the rule.[50] But the wealthy cannot always rely on workers fearing the loss of their jobs to achieve compliance and need to have the power of the state in reserve:

> The possessing classes ... keep the working people in servitude not only by the might of their wealth, by the simple exploitation of labour by capital, but also by the power of the state – by the army, the bureaucracy and the courts.[51]

Every major working-class uprising comes up against the power of the state. In these confrontations, all pretence at neutrality is swept aside and brute physical force is used to protect the privileged. The riot police and even the army are deployed to break strikes, protect strike-breakers and intimidate large gatherings.

The use of force is, however, costly and unpredictable. The state, therefore, tries to keep it in reserve and to use the threat of force to add to the effectiveness of other tactics for disorganising workers as a class. It uses secrecy and surveillance to monitor potential opponents and forewarn employers in major battles.[52] Crucially, it employs the tactic of co-option to disrupt movements that resist the rule of capital. Labour leaders are regularly flattered and bought off with seats in the House of Lords or positions on state boards. Protest movements are invited to become compliant NGOs with official funding to keep them in check.[53]

Fourth, the state performs a vital ideological function for capitalism. During a crisis, it mobilises the central themes and arguments for the ruling class. Pretence at independence in the media is dropped and the main television networks adopt the same attitude as that promoted by the BBC director general, John Reith, during the 1926 General Strike: 'Since the BBC was a national institution and since the government in this crisis were acting for the people ... the BBC was for the government in this crisis too.'[54]

In more normal times, the state funds research outlets that promote conventional ideas and even subsidises the employment of chaplains in universities to ensure support for religion. More crucially, it gives legal sanction to expropriations undertaken by capitalists. Marx noted how 'conquerors attempt to give a sort of social sanction to their original title derived from brute force, through the instrumentality of laws imposed by themselves'.[55] He was referring to how landed aristocrats enclosed the common land and established their legal title deeds. Today corporations want similar legal sanction to take control of water, natural resources and intellectual property.

The state is both an institution of class rule and a centre for the coordination of society at large. In the latter capacity, it performs non-class functions to maintain cohesion in society. It promotes public health, delivers a sanitation system and organises rescues when major accidents occur. The mere fact that it performs such functions enables it to mystify its role as a protector of capitalist rule. The police, for example, are presented as a 'service' to help old ladies cross the road or to deal with traffic management rather than as protectors of capitalist property. However, while the state clearly performs non-class functions, it undertakes them in ways that are filtered by the needs of capitalism. Thus the police concentrate on crimes against property and often ignore domestic violence or corporate crime. The public health system is not primarily focused on preventative care to prolong life but on drug treatment and hospital care. The US rescue effort after 'Hurricane Katrina' revealed a deep racism and contempt for the poor. Increasingly, non-class functions such as the maintenance of the roads or the water system are franchised out to private companies, with effective guarantees of minimum rates of profit.

Sometimes the links between governments and business are too visibly close and intimate. Goldman Sachs, for example, has been nicknamed 'Government Sachs' because of the number of its executives who have found their way into the US Treasury Department and the Federal Reserve. Former Goldman chief executive Henry Paulson was Treasury Secretary from 1999 to 2006; Robert Rubin, Goldman's chairman, had the job before that.[56] In other countries, there is a pattern of revolving doors as top politicians who leave office go on to serve as non-executive directors on the boards of large corporations. Broadly, however, the current captains of industry do not play an active role in politics. Most are simply too busy to have even the mental head-space to exercise such control. But just as they hire individuals to take on particular roles such as public relations, the wider capitalist class relies on policy strategists and professional politicians to serve its interest. The fact that profits are, in the main, made in the market rather than by holding political office allows for a certain distancing between economic and political power.

These factors, plus the need for an 'outside' force to impose a common strategy on the ruling class, help to explain 'the relative autonomy of the state'.[57] In Marx's historical writings a number of examples of this phenomenon appear. Sometimes, control of the state can fall to a *fraction* of the ruling class. After the 1830 revolt in France, for example, Marx suggested that under the regime of Louis Philippe, 'it was not the bourgeoisie as a whole which ruled but only one fraction of it'.[58] This was mainly a financial aristocracy drawn from bankers, railways barons and stock market barons. On other occasions, the governing elite can be drawn from an aristocratic element. In Britain, Marx noted that the Whig Party were 'the aristocratic representatives of the bourgeoisie'.[59] The unification of Germany and the conditions necessary for capitalist development were carried through by the aristocratic *Junkers* led by Otto von Bismarck. According to Engels, the bourgeoisie bought 'its gradual social emancipation for the price of immediate renunciation of its own political power'.[60]

Marx thought that the strongest example of this pattern lay in a phenomenon he called Bonapartism. This was a reference to the period in French history between the *coup d'état* of Louis Napoleon Bonaparte in 1851 and his fall in 1871. Bonaparte was a classic political adventurer who spoke an ambiguous political rhetoric and consolidated his rule as a dictator through periodic plebiscites. Marx believed that the secret of his success lay in 'the mutual prostration of the antagonistic parties'[61] – the bourgeoisie and the workers had fought each other to the death and none could achieve a decisive victory over the other. Neither of the two classes could take French society forward, so Bonaparte rose above the contending classes to carry through the modernisation of France along capitalist lines. The cost to society was a state machine that grew like a gigantic boa constrictor to strangle society.

These examples indicate that distinctions can arise in certain circumstances between the governing elite and the ruling class. More generally, state autonomy provides a certain flexibility to maintain the domination of capitalists over society. It provides a space for 'statesmen' to emerge who can stand above the immediate interests of capital to impose a wider strategic vision. It allows them to deal more flexibly with discontent from below. Draper puts it well: 'If the bourgeoisie were capable of keeping the state on a short leash, and always did so, that state would have been strangled long ago.'[62]

The fact that they can extend the leash explains why they prefer parliamentary democracy as the normal form of rule. This allows party competition around economic choices determined by the economic rule of capital. The governing A team is set up against its B team, but the leadership of the opposing parties share a consensus on fundamentals. By its very nature this gives a political flexibility – but only insofar as it conforms to the needs of capital.

7
Historical Materialism

The rulers of our society promote the belief that real change will never happen. According to the new mantra, no matter how outraged you are at injustice, you have to accept that 'we are where we are'. Marx developed his theory of history or historical materialism to challenge such fatalism.

In some ways it is a misnomer because his concern was not to help academics do better research on history and it had nothing to do with the type of history which Marx dismissed as 'high sounding dramas about princes and states'.[1] His theory was not even primarily about the past because his aim was to discover a pattern in the human story that showed how real change became possible – in the future. Instead of being mystified by forces beyond our control, understanding how they were created could help change them. The purpose of historical materialism was, as Perry Anderson put it, 'to give men and women the means with which to exercise a real popular self-determination for the first time in history'.[2]

WRONG THEORIES OF HISTORY

Some deny there is any pattern in history and assert that change results from a series of accidents. The First World War was supposed to have been triggered by the assassination of Archduke Ferdinand and if the assassin's bullet had missed, presumably that great tragedy could have been avoided. Similarly, some of the great wars of the Roman Empire were apparently fought over a beautiful Egyptian pharaoh and so, as Pascal remarked, 'if Cleopatra's nose had been shorter, the whole face of the earth would have changed'.[3] A more sophisticated version of the accident theory focuses on diplomacy or the political skills of rulers as the main explanation of events. Change seemingly occurs due to cock-ups caused by the lack of these skills and this allows mobs, who are swayed by their passions, to rule. The historian Richard Cobb, for example, suggested that the movement of the *sans-culottes* during the French Revolution was 'a freak of nature, more a state of mind than a social, political or economic entity'.[4]

This approach fails to make an elementary distinction between an event that acts as a trigger and an underlying cause. The First World War would have broken out even if Archduke Ferdinand had escaped because the real crux of the matter was not his assassination, but the growing rivalries between the imperial powers.[5] Similarly, the lack of political skill of political leaders might only be a symptom of a wider loss of control over their societies so that far from the 'mobs' being swayed by emotion, their intervention on the political stage often reflects deeper underlying problems.

Another popular approach is the Great Man or great leader theory of history. According to this view, the Russian Revolution was created by Lenin; the French Empire was established by Napoleon; and the evil genius Hitler caused the Holocaust. The cult of hero worship was most clearly articulated by the conservative writer Thomas Carlyle when he suggested that 'the history of what man has accomplished in this world, is at bottom the History of the Great Men who have worked here'.[6] It was in many ways a secular version of how God came down from heaven to help men perform His tasks. A variant of this theme can be found in the writings of the German sociologist Max Weber, who believed that modern society was imprisoned in an iron cage of bureaucracy and that change would only come from 'charismatic' individuals who could break the bars.[7] The word charisma, which was taken from Christian theology, means 'a gift of grace' and implies that great leaders have exceptional individual qualities.[8] Accordingly, they were able to create a collective excitement, so that 'masses of people respond to some extraordinary experience by virtue of which they surrender themselves to a heroic leader'.[9]

The Great Man theory is a deeply elitist reading of the past because it ignores how leaders would achieve nothing without the many whose names never appear in history books. The German left-wing poet Bertolt Brecht gave the classic putdown of Great Men in his poem A *Worker Who Reads History*:

Who built the seven gates of Thebes?
The books are filled with names of kings.
Was it the kings who hauled the craggy blocks of stone?
And Babylon, so many times destroyed.
Who built the city up each time? In which of Lima's houses,
That city glittering with gold, lived those who built it?

In the evening when the Chinese wall was finished
Where did the masons go? Imperial Rome
Is full of arcs of triumph. Who reared them up? Over whom
Did the Caesars triumph? Byzantium lives in song.
Were all her dwellings palaces? And even in Atlantis of the legend
The night the seas rushed in
The drowning men still bellowed for their slaves

The Great Man theory cannot explain why the mass of people sometimes respond and sometimes do not respond to 'great leaders'. Contrary to an image of the dumb masses, most people do not respond like the spellbound followers of the Pied Piper of Hamelin and instead weigh up what they hear. They often look to particular individuals to express powerful moods that have developed in their ranks. Hitler, for example, was originally regarded as an eccentric living in a hostel in Vienna and even by 1923, when he launched his failed *putsch*, he acknowledged that 'They always said I was crazy'.[10] But after the economic crash of 1929, the terrible anger of a large part of German society found its expression in this odd character. In the 1920s and 1930s, the Irish republican leader Eamon de Valera was so honoured that he was the subject of children's songs which were recited for decades. Today, however, a different generation regards him as a symbol of boredom and conservatism. The social context is all when it comes to the effects of 'charisma'.

Another conservative view of history is that nothing ever really changes but simply repeats set patterns. This was most clearly expressed by the Enlightenment philosopher David Hume:

Mankind are so much the same, in all times and places that history informs us of nothing new or strange in this particular. Its chief use is only to discover the constant and universal principles of human nature.[11]

History is read as shadowy replica of current motives and these in turn arise from a fixed human nature. Hunter-gatherers may have lived in nomadic groups, but they really wanted to get away with their own families at the first opportunity. The commercial activity of Ancient Greece was just as 'capitalist' as modern society. Always there is the same drive for acquisitiveness, it is only the specific directions and forms that change according to the unique culture in which they occur. More broadly, this view suggests that hierarchy and domination are eternal in human society because, according to the philosopher Mary Midgley, domination springs from the child–parent relationship: 'Our natural interest in dominance is not just a lust for oppression. It is a taste for order ... Based on the relationship of child to parent, it is essentially protective.'[12]

One problem with this view is that it cannot account for the variety of human behaviour. If human nature were fixed, it should be constant in all societies. Yet the social activity of humanity is extremely varied and what is today considered to be an essential feature of human nature is not in other societies. John Molyneaux provided a simple refutation:

> To the American Indian private ownership of the land was 'unnatural'. To the eighteenth century landowner it was the most basic human right. To the Ancient Greek, homosexuality was the highest form of love. To the Victorian English it was the lowest. To the traditional Hindu, arranged marriages have been the norm for centuries. To most people in the West it now seems 'unnatural'. Change the social conditions and change the human nature.[13]

However, while social behaviour varies from society to society, this does not imply that people are infinitely malleable or that there are no connecting threads. Marx argued that interaction between people and nature in the labour process is an 'everlasting nature-imposed condition of human existence' and is 'common to all forms of society in which people live'.[14] It is the material basis on which all human society is founded and is at the core of our nature.

The labour process makes us social animals and so production by an isolated individual outside society 'is as much an absurdity as is the development of language without individuals living together and talking to each other'.[15] Our capacity to produce means that we engage in 're-directive activity' and constantly examine how we are using tools and how these might create new items from nature.[16]

But this very process gives rise to new needs and ensures that our social behaviour changes. If nature was an Arcadia where our food dropped into our laps and there was no need to produce, there would be no history. History, as Cohen graphically put it, is the human substitute for nature.[17] Conservative writers miss this key feature of human nature because they want to freeze its development within the limits of the existing society. They ignore its dynamic quality which accounts for both variety and development of human behaviour.

The simple fact that we have to produce in order to live tells us very little about particular societies. Or as Marx put it, the taste of porridge does not tell us who grew the oats, whether it took place under a slave owner's brutal lash or the anxious eye of the capitalist.[18] We still have to examine the different and specific social forms in which we undertake material production. Human history is about the way we produce in different ways and how we form different social relations to do so. Once we describe this 'active life process', history 'ceases to be a collection of dead facts' or Big Ideas which sweep up humanity in its wake.[19] It becomes a story about how we could become really free by consciously recognising and collectively organising our interaction with nature.

METHOD

Marx's method of understanding history involved an attempt to get at underlying structures. 'All science', he claimed, 'would be superfluous if the outward appearance and the essence of things coincided.'[20] It was a warning against a common sense or empiricist understanding of the world that simply accumulates facts.

The fundamental problem with these approaches is that elements of reality are not always directly recognised by our senses. Take, for example, the notion of continental drift originally formulated by Alfred Wegener in 1912. This asserted that the present shape of the world had arisen because continents, which once formed a single landmass, had drifted apart and were continuing to do so. The theory was rejected for nearly 50 years until new discoveries about plate tectonics established that the continents were indeed subject to movement. Common sense thought the continents could not move, but a science based on getting at underlying realities showed that they did.

When trying to grasp the realities that were beneath the surface, Marx used dialectics. This was a way of seeing the world that stretched back to Ancient Greek philosophers such as Heraclitus and was developed by Hegel. The dialectical method means, first, understanding that *things or events do not occur in isolation but are part of a web of interconnected relationships*. Together, these relationships constitute a 'totality'. From this perspective, the very idea that an historical event, a person or a social relation exists in isolation is itself an abstraction. The dialectical approach tries to place individual historical phenomena in the totality of their relationships.

The second element of dialectics recognises *that everything is transitory – in other words, it has come into existence and will eventually go out of existence.* It is in process, having had a past and about to have a possible future. This is best expressed by the simple aphorism of Heraclitus – you cannot step into the same river twice. By the time you have raised your toe a second time, the water has moved on – and, a little more depressing, you too have moved a little closer to your inevitable demise.

Third, the reason why there is constant change is because *a totality is riven with contradictions.* By contradiction we do not simply mean that there are two ideas which stand in formal, logical contradiction, but that contradictions exist in reality itself. In fact, all that exists is held together by a contradictory unity of opposing elements. As Hegel put it, 'Contradiction is at the heart of all movement and life, and it is only insofar as it contains a contradiction that anything moves and has an impulse and activity.'[21] Change is the unleashing of forces which were originally held in mutual dependence but which then evolve.

Fourth, a dialectical thinker is sensitive to that fact that *quantitative change can at some point change into qualitative change.* Processes often contain moments that 'build up' and a certain 'tipping point' that brings decisive change. Let us say I produce food from my garden for my own family and sell any surplus on the market. If that surplus increases, there is only quantitative change – I remain a subsistence farmer but I am becoming increasingly open to the market. However, if the quantitative change continues to develop, there comes a 'tipping point' where my relationship to why I produce changes. I now produce for the market and this in turn changes the social relationships with those around me.

Fifth, certain features which occur at a lower stage in history may reappear in a more developed form at a higher stage. Marx called this pattern the 'negation of negation', but did not claim that it was historically necessary.[22] It was a pattern of possibility. Originally, communal life was the main way humans organised production this but was 'negated' through the creation of private property. Later, petty property in tools and workshops was in turn 'negated' as large capitalist enterprises wiped them out by competition. Today, however, there is a new possibility of 'negating' capitalist property relations and restoring common ownership but at a more developed level. There can be an interesting pattern whereby previous features of human life can be both overcome and preserved.

But Marx never saw this as 'The March of History' and despised writers who invoked history as proof of their theories. He claimed that for these writers 'history exists to serve as an act of consumption for theoretical eating'.[23] They lived in a world of intellectual elitism where they claimed to have discovered the 'truth' of history and then explained the real lives and struggles of people as an involuntary movement towards that truth. They saw real 'human individuals as merely bearers' of history, which was conceived as a real subject, a person.[24] Against this intellectualising gibberish, Marx argued that

> *History* does *nothing,* it 'possesses *no* immense wealth', it 'wages *no* battles'. It is *man,* real, living man who does all that, who possesses and fights: 'history' is not, as it were, a person apart, using man as a means to achieve *its own* aims, history is *nothing but* the activity of man pursuing his aims.[25]

Marx's approach to history was therefore to examine how people entered into struggles on the basis of wider contradictions thrown up by that society.

PRODUCTION AND SOCIETY

In 1859, Marx wrote a *Preface to a Contribution to the Critique of Political Economy* where he traced the guiding principle of his intellectual development. His inquiries led him to conclude that 'neither legal relations nor political forms could be comprehended by themselves or on the basis of a so called general development of the human mind'.[26] This amounted to a fundamental attack on an idealist interpretation which sees social institutions as emanations of big, influential ideas or values. The reason why there is a parliamentary democracy in the US, for example, is not because Thomas Paine wrote *The Rights of Man* and introduced the idea of democracy. Still less has it to do with Alex de Tocqueville's suggestion that Protestant sects promoted a version of Christianity which facilitated democracy.[27]

Most academics instinctively reject Marx's argument as 'reductionist' and insist on the autonomy of values and ideas. But academics are subject to a structural bias because they work in institutions that separate legal studies from politics and economics and so will naturally conclude that their particular subject matter has its own unique importance. Moreover as their job is to produce ideas, they are somewhat insulted by the suggestion that these do not simply pop out of the human mind and win popular acceptance through the power of intellectual persuasion.

Nevertheless, an idealist interpretation faces some difficulties. If American democracy had its roots in a Christian heritage, why did it take so long to discover the idea? If it is assumed that the Puritan tradition was responsible, why did their idea of a community of believers which dispensed with priests only arise in the seventeenth century? Had no one thought of attacking the power of the priesthood before that? And why did this particular religious idea have such a profound political impact when many others, such as the injunction to love thy neighbour, were ignored? If Paine was the originator of democracy, why was his other book, *Age of Reason*, which attacked religion, ignored? In other words, even if Big Ideas are important, you still have to explain where they come from and why they lead to the creation of certain institutions and not others at a particular moment in time.

Against this idealist view of history, Marx summarised his own materialist approach as follows:

> The specific economic form, in which unpaid surplus-labour is pumped out of direct producers, determines the relationship of rulers and ruled, as it grows directly out of production and reacts on it in turn as a determining element.
>
> Upon this, however, is founded the entire formation of the economic community which grows up out of the production relations themselves, thereby simultaneously its specific political form.
>
> It is always the direct relationship of the owners of the conditions of production to the direct producers – a relation always naturally corresponding to a definite stage in the development of the methods of labour and thereby its social productivity – which reveals the innermost secret, the hidden basis of the entire social structure and with it the political form of the relation of sovereignty and dependence, in short, the corresponding specific form of the state.[28]

There is a lot in this very compressed formulation, so let us try to disentangle some of its elements.

Marx is suggesting that there is 'an entire social structure' which includes 'a specific form of state'. A social structure means a pattern of arrangements that link together different institutions and dominant ideas. In modern society, there is an intricate link between capitalist ownership, the abstract ideas of free citizens and parliamentary democracy. Conversely, you could not expect to have an official Declaration of Human Rights in a society founded on slavery any more than you could have parliamentary democracy in a society based on feudalism. Society is, therefore, a totality with implicit 'rules' that govern its parts. The rules constrain the possible options and enable certain developments to occur.

The 'innermost secret' of social structure is the relationship between the producers and those who own the land, machinery or workplaces. This relationship determines 'the way the unpaid surplus is pumped out' and this in turn underpins the society. In all class societies, producers do both necessary labour and surplus labour. Necessary labour refers to the amount of labour time required to feed and clothe each other, whereas surplus labour provides for their exploiters. The way the surplus is extracted – whether through slavery, serfdom or wage labour – shapes the wider political and legal forms. Under slavery, surplus is extracted from unfree individuals who are owned by their masters. Under feudalism, the surplus is extracted through the political threat of violence from semi-free individuals. Under capitalism it occurs through 'free' labour that is sold to employers. Each of these different ways of exploitation requires a different legal system and different type of state.

This, however, does not imply that political or legal arrangements cannot react and affect the tempo of economic development or block some of its directions. Nor is it suggested that legal arrangements or political ideologies do not play a vital role in real struggles. When Marx wrote *The Eighteenth Brumaire of Louis Napoleon*, for example, he concentrated on the special role of political battles and ideas. In a letter to clarify what they meant by historical materialism, Engels later wrote:

Political, juridical, philosophical, religious, literary, artistic etc development is based on economic development. But all these react upon one another and also upon the economic basis. It is not that the economic position is the *cause, solely active* while everything else is only passive effect. There is, rather, interaction on the basis of economic necessity which *ultimately* always asserts itself.[29]

This qualification aside, Marx and Engels still asserted that the way people organise production is the foundation on which society is organised. Why should this be the case?

One reason is that the system of production places limits on the realisation of ideals. The aspiration for a better world, where property is shared in common, is by no means a modern phenomenon. During the Peasant War in Germany in 1524–25, radical ideas began to take hold among some of the estimated 300,000 rebels, with Thomas Munzer and his followers demanding the immediate establishment of God's kingdom on earth. By that they meant 'a society with no class differences, no private property, and no state authority independent of, and foreign to, the members of society'.[30] Just over a century later a similar radical fringe developed during the English civil war as groups like the Diggers took seriously Gerard Winstanley's words that 'the earth should be made a common treasury of livelihood to the whole mankind, without respect of person'.[31]

While Engels had tremendous sympathy and admiration for Munzer, he noted that 'this sally beyond the present ... could be nothing but violent and fantastic and was bound to slide back at its first practical application'.[32] If Munzer had won collective ownership of the land at that historic juncture and abolished classes, economic development would have halted. The communal land would have been cultivated with a low level of technology and people would have spent at least twelve hours a day on backbreaking labour to meet their needs. They would have had few resources left over to develop new technologies and even less time to study the science which made them possible. Social development at this stage could only have taken place through a minority freeing themselves from labour and extracting a surplus from the rest of the population which was then used to expand the productive forces. Most likely, the sheer hardship of eking a living from the land would have given rise to new authorities to take on the task of guaranteeing a supply of food. Some of Munzer's movement would have been compelled to transform themselves into that class of rulers. The aspirations of Munzer and the English radicals were inspirational and brilliant, but the 'tragedy of history' meant they could not be realised.[33] Put simply, the economic structure set limits on their aspirations.

Production systems develop and this exerts pressure on static legal and political structures. Sometimes through great convulsions and at other times though smoother transitions, the latter are brought into conformity with the former. In the Middle Ages in England a landed gentry enclosed common lands and displaced people to make way for sheep in order to engage in an expanding wool market. At first, only a small number of merchants could obtain a royal charter and urban guilds laid down strict rules on how production would be carried out. However, as commerce and industry grew, these practices, which once offered a form of protection, became a burdensome restriction. As Marx put it:

> The fruits [of economic growth] would themselves have been forfeited if men had tried to retain the forms under whose shelter these fruits had ripened. Hence came two thunderclaps – the revolutions of 1640 and 1688. All the old economic conditions which were the official expression of the old civil society were destroyed in England.[34]

The revolutions were fought with great religious and political passion. Oliver Cromwell and the parliamentary forces were by no means guaranteed victory and had the royalists won, they could have done 'great damage' to England's economic development.[35] Nevertheless the economic structure developed and this then created the framework in which key issues had to be fought out between different social classes.

The pressures exerted by the production system can also work in less dramatic ways, when older political and legal forms are retained but their content changes. Some of the concepts of the modern law on property, for example, date back to ancient Rome. The Roman legal system contained some elements concerning the regulation of contracts that were sufficiently general to allow adaptation and development. More than any other society, capitalism needed coherent laws to create stable conditions for the exchange of commodities between strangers and sometimes the legal system took the form of Roman law as long as

> the legal subject [who] is the abstract commodity owner [is] elevated to the heavens. His will – will understood in a legal sense – has its real basis in the wish to alienate in acquisition and to acquire in alienation. For this desire to be realized it is necessary that the desires of commodity owners be directed to one another. Legally, this relationship is expressed as a contract or an agreement of independent wills. Therefore, contract is one of the central concepts of law.[36]

As long as it enables individuals to buy, sell and establish contracts regardless of status or rank, the law can seemingly work according to its own internal logic. Yet the content of contracts is still set by the needs of the capitalist economy rather than simply by formal legal logic.

Consider the case of property rights in plants. Until the early twentieth century, plant seeds were considered part of the common heritage of humankind. Even after independence, former colonies allowed seed collections to be sent freely to research centres in metropolitan countries. But as the market in hybrid plants increased, the US introduced a Plant Patent Act in 1930 and in other countries Trade Secrets Acts were used to establish property rights. Many exceptions were allowed and farmers and researchers could continue to develop new hybrids without authorisation. However, as advances in biotechnology made it possible to produce plants with specific traits, giant corporations pressed for more property rights. The Diamond and Chakrabarty judgment of the US Supreme Court granted them their wish in 1980, and the Trade Related Intellectual Property Agreement of 1995 extended this to all member countries of the World Trade Organisation. Henceforth, as an EU directive put it, 'biological material which is isolated from its natural environment' could be subject to the rules of invention and patented.[37] These legal judgments adversely affected farmers but they sanctioned the commodification of plant life for the benefit of large corporations. The law, in this instance, directly reflected the needs of a late capitalist economy and reacted back on it by leading to the further commercialisation of knowledge. It could hardly be argued, however, that these developments sprang from the formal legal logic.

The interaction between property relations in society and the level of the productive forces helps shape ideas and cultural forms. This can occur even in those spheres of life that seem furthest from production. Instead of explaining human social practice by ideas, it is necessary to explain ideas by people's material practices. Even when whole epochs are characterised by religious struggles, there is no need to take its illusions at face value but one could inquire into their real roots.

The Protestant Reformation is a case in point. Weber was one of the first to see a link between the rise of Protestantism and capitalism and he used the example to attack the 'more naïve historical materialism' that assumed that ideas 'originate as a reflection or superstructure of economic situations'.[38] His argument focused on how Martin Luther's doctrine of 'the calling' and John Calvin's doctrine of predestination had the unintended effect of creating a capitalist 'spirit'. Luther had rejected the idea that holiness meant retreating from the world and had asserted that one should honour God by good works. Calvin claimed that people were predestined for heaven or hell and this created a terrible anxiety that could only be relieved by a sign that one was successful in the world. Together, these doctrines led, according to Weber, to a belief that a methodical approach to money-making was compatible with Christianity and so laid the foundations for capitalism.

Weber was correct to emphasise the fact that the Protestant religion was more conducive than Catholicism to the rise of capitalism. But he failed to examine why these doctrines won such wide support or how they fitted into people's experience of the world. Previous heretical movements such as the Hussites in Bohemia had offered ideas that were similar to Luther's but were crushed. Missing from Weber's account is any concrete explanation of what was happening to people's lives in Germany at the time. Yet sixteenth-century Germany was a society in transition as market relations started to encroach into many aspects of life. Land was increasingly being used to produce goods for exchange; merchants were using a putting-out system to undercut customary prices; new trading cities were developing; money was pervading the economy. The Catholic Church responded to the growing dominance of money by selling indulgences and increasing pressure for tithes.

This peculiar combination of a growing market and feudalism affected many social classes badly and they sought solutions. In these circumstances, the Protestant Reformation won a huge following because it attacked the power of the Catholic Church and called on people to fulfil their inner calling. However, Weber neglected all these material factors and instead argued that capitalism grew out of the spiritual logic of Protestantism. While this was certainly one element of the story, its effect was to give capitalism an ideological cover because it is supposed to arise from a search for a new relationship with God. This explanation goes no further than the illusions held by the leaders of the Reformation, with Luther himself claiming that 'The Word did it all. While I sat drinking beer with Philip and Amsdorf, God dealt a Papacy a mighty blow.'[39] Marx's method by contrast did not imply that religious ideas were simply a 'reflex' of material conditions. Real battles were fought over religious symbols, but these battles grew out of real contradictions in the system of production in the old society.

A less portentous example of how changes in property relations and systems of production can affect culture may be taken from art history. In the seventeenth century there was an extraordinary flourishing of Dutch realist art which represented a break with a tradition of painting religious images, often for didactic purposes. House interiors, portraits, group pictures of everyday scenes of food and still life became commonplace subject matters. The paintings often became smaller so that they could fit in domestic houses rather than cathedrals or public buildings and one of the key techniques used was oil painting. This technique was distinguished from other forms of painting by its ability to render the tangibility, texture, lustre and solidity of the objects it depicted. This shift in the Dutch art world could only be explained by a profound change in class relations. As the Dutch won independence from Habsburg monarchy, the patrons of the art market became the city burghers and traders rather than the aristocracy and the Church. Their primary interest was in displaying and almost possessing the subjects of their paintings. As the Marxist art critic John Berger put it, 'Oil painting did to appearance what capital did to social relations … All reality was mechanically measured by its materiality.'[40]

BASE AND SUPERSTRUCTURE

In his 1859 Preface, Marx gave a more precise outline of his theory of historical materialism in order to show how it was linked to social change. This is known as the base and superstructure model. According to this, the economic structure of society can be analysed in terms of two elements: the forces of production and the relations of production.

The *forces of production* include both human labour power and the objects on which it is expended. Human labour power can be enhanced by science, skill and cooperative organisation. Nevertheless, labour has to be applied with, and to, the means of production. These include machinery, tools, buildings, raw materials and energy supplies. Together, labour power and the means of production constitute the material conditions for production no matter what society we live in.

The *relations of production* refer to the bonds we form with each other to carry out production. They are the social forms through which human labour and the means of production are united. 'The particular form and mode in which this connection is effected' Marx argued, 'is what distinguishes the various economic epochs of the social structure.'[41] Once a class society arises, the relations of production refer to the specific ways in which a surplus is exacted from the producers for the benefit of the upper classes. In legal terms they are the property relations, but it is important also to look at effective control. They are, therefore, relations of control and ownership.

These relations of production pre-exist the individual and they are entirely independent of his or her will. In a capitalist society, for example, workers cannot choose to make their own produce or give over part of it to a lord in return for land. They may choose not to work for this or that employer, but they must sell their labour to *some* employer. In other words, the elements may change but the dominant capitalist–wage labour relationship persists.

Marx's argument is that there is a certain correspondence between the relations of production and the level of development of forces of production. This correspondence is not automatic and it is possible to find many anomalies or combinations in history. The US cotton plantations of the nineteenth century were linked to the most advanced form of capitalism of the day, but they used slave labour. But broadly speaking, certain types of class relations are more appropriate to different levels of the forces of production, and at some point non-class relations become more appropriate.

Up to the tenth century in Western Europe, for example, forms of slavery lingered on in great estates but after that it generally declined. One of the key reasons was that productive techniques had developed which made slavery inappropriate. The heavy wheeled plough and the extensive use of cow dung led to improvement in soil fertility. People learnt to harness horses and use them instead of oxen. They also discovered how to plant beans and legumes to replenish their soil. Monasteries brought water mills into greater use to grind corn for flour and all of this led to a significant rise in productivity. Slaves, however, had no incentive to embrace any of these new agricultural techniques, but serfs, who could control their own land and keep a part of the produce for themselves, did. Even the stupidest landlords found that if their peasants were free to produce more, they in turn could grab more of the surplus. Serfdom, therefore, became a more common practice in this era.

The fit between certain relations of production and the forces of production is not simply about technology. One of the key elements in raising productivity is how labour is organised to co-operate. Marx argued that:

> the sum total of the mechanical forces exerted by isolated workers differs from the social force that is developed when many hands co-operate in the same undivided operation ... Not only do we

have here an increase in the productive power of the individual, but the creation of a new productive power, which is intrinsically a collective one.[42]

Developments in cooperative labour required a shift away from domestic production to capitalist production. As capitalism was able to expand its markets through the sale of commodities, it provided, for a period, the most appropriate form of property relations for these large-scale cooperative units.

The particular combination of the relations and forces of production constitutes a distinct mode of production that is the foundation for each particular society. Broadly speaking Marx distinguished four major modes of production.

Asiatic Mode

This was the least satisfactory of Marx's typologies because his information was very inadequate. This was a tributary mode where the surplus flowed to a state bureaucracy rather than to individual landlords. Marx thought that the hallmarks of this society were the absence of private ownership. Based on contemporary accounts he assumed people lived in small villages which were relatively isolated from each other and were dominated by a state bureaucracy.[43]

Ancient Mode of Production

This was primarily based on slavery, which meant that the producer owned neither their own labour nor the means of production. In Greece there were not the large plantations that were typical in Rome but most classicists now recognise that Greece and Rome were slave societies. Orlando Patterson notes that 'Ancient Greece and Rome were not simply slaveholding societies; they were what Sir Moses Finley calls "genuine" slave societies, in that slavery was very solidly the base of their socio-economic structures.'[44] Estimates from modern scholars for the number of slaves in classical Athens vary from 20,000 to 120,000. The one ancient source who gives us some figures is usually dismissed as unreliable, but Athenaeus wrote in his 'The Banqueting Sophists' that in the fourth century BC there were 21,000 Athenian citizens, 10,000 metics (resident foreigners) and 400,000 slaves. The silver mines at Laureon, which helped to finance the construction of the Athenian fleet, were worked by gangs of thousands of slaves who had a life expectancy of only a few years. Xenophon, in his work *The Poroi*, describes Athens' need for a constant supply of slaves to work the silver mines.[45]

Feudal Mode

In this system, tenants pay rent, either in kind or in labour, to a lord who is their political master. A variety of social formations can develop within this mode of production and often they can be influenced by the outcome of class struggle. In some cases, serfdom is enforced, with the producer being tied to the land and forced to provide a range of services to the lord. But when the population was depleted during the Black Death, there was a loosening of these ties and feudal rent became the main connection between the classes. Later again, labour services were commuted for money rent.

Capitalist Mode

Here workers are free to sell their labour power but do not receive the full value in wages. The surplus is expropriated by capitalists who are driven to accumulate for accumulation sake.

Each of these modes of production provides the base on which a superstructure is formed. This refers in the first instance to non-economic practices such as the political system or the law, but beyond these core institutions, there are wider ideological beliefs that also uphold the system. The base–superstructure model was a metaphor used by Marx to describe a complex social process and it was not envisaged as a neat line across a thing called society. It was devised to help clarify concepts for analysis and for this reason it has been the subject of much discussion.

Cohen, for example, extends Marx's architectural analogy to portray the base as four struts that are driven into the ground. They are unstable and sway in the wind but when a roof is attached they stay more firmly erect. The roof, or superstructure, is supported by the base but also renders it more stable. The point of his metaphor is that the political and legal systems are founded on the economic structure but then add support to it. They help to conserve property relations and in some cases to ossify them so that change is minimised.[46]

Harman argues that exploiting classes form a network of non-economic relations to safeguard their position. They use laws, customs and ideology to turn might into right in order to ensure their wealth is safeguarded. The superstructure is, therefore, not a distinct set of institutions but relations formed outside of production to conserve privilege. Some institutions will belong in both domains. If the medieval Church is viewed as a producer of ideas, it clearly belongs to the superstructure, but when we look at its monasteries, which were one of the main sources of wealth creation, it belongs to the base.[47]

THE FETTERS THAT CAN BREAK

The purpose of the base–superstructure metaphor was to examine how social change occurred. Marx argued that the forces of production tended to develop and, at a certain point, this posed problems for the wider class relations that surrounded them. The property relations acted as a brake on the material process of production and this eventually threw society into turmoil. When these contradictions ripened, class struggles and social upheaval reached a new pitch. Here is how Marx put it:

> At a certain stage of development, the material productive forces of society come into conflict with the existing relations of production or – this merely expresses the same thing in legal terms – with property relations within the framework on which they have operated hitherto. From forms of development of the productive forces these relation turn into fetters. Then begins an era of social revolution. The changes in the economic foundation lead sooner or later to the transformation of the whole immense superstructure.[48]

The first argument here is that there is a tendency for the forces of production to develop over time. One simple reason is that people generally want to spend less labour time on producing goods and will seek to produce more goods for the same amount of labour time or the same number of goods for less labour time. Once they achieve either of these goals, they will rarely forget how particular technologies work. While individuals may forget, the wider collectivity is unlikely to do so. Discussions on productive techniques will, therefore, normally be about improving rather than reversing efficiency. Moreover, once new technologies and new forms of labour organisation are employed, it becomes difficult to reverse out of them. The use of fertilisers and tractors has revolutionised agriculture and by doing so helped to increase life expectancy, but this made it harder to return to more primitive forms of subsistence farming. In addition, as Marx repeatedly pointed out, man's engagement with nature engenders new needs and these in turn further stimulate the search for new discoveries.

Economic regression, however, is possible on rarer occasions. Many different social strata develop an interest in conserving society as it is and will sometimes seek to hinder economic development if it threatens their privileges. Courtiers, police officers, state officials who engage in tax farming all inhabit the superstructure but they can develop an interest in stopping change. One of the classic cases of stagnation and regression occurred in China in the seventeenth century. Impressive centres of industrial activity had appeared at Soochow for silk textiles, Sung kiang for cotton goods and Chingtechen for porcelain but the Ming dynasty put a sudden stop to naval voyages to India and Africa and restricted overseas trade. The reason, it appears, was that they were frightened of the rising merchant class which might destabilise their rule. In this instance, the superstructure reacted dramatically on the base and impeded development. The Chinese example, however, also illustrates the problems when this occurs because, as a result of its stagnation, the country was eventually overrun by a drug-dealing British empire which had initially been more backward.

Marx's overall point then is that the productive forces generally develop – often slowly and imperceptibly in pre-capitalist societies and at a much quicker rate in capitalist societies where they are constantly revolutionised. For long periods, the wider class or property relations facilitate their growth but, at a certain point, these developments stretch the existing relations of production too far and society at large is thrown into chaos. More intense class struggles break out and sometimes the ruling elite are no longer able to cope with the surrounding environment. The key question becomes who can resolve these contradictions and offer society a new way of organising its relations of production.

At this point there is a problem in Marx's formulation in the 1859 Preface because he suggests that 'sooner or later' the changes in the economic foundation will lead to a change in the political structure. This is a very formulaic expression and was occasioned by Marx's desire to escape the Prussian censor. Missing from the whole Preface, for example, is any reference to class struggles.[49] On one reading, therefore, Marx's argument might be taken to imply an inevitable victorious revolution. And, unfortunately, many of his followers in the period known as Second International Marxism – roughly, from his death to the First World War – understood it that way. They also 'forgot' about revolution and concentrated on waiting for the inevitable alignment of the relations of production with the forces of production.

However, there is no need to stick to this particular formulation because Marx's wider argument may equally be presented through two simple propositions: first, that the productive capacity of human beings comes up against limits imposed by a particular class society at a certain point; and second, whether or not society regresses or moves forward to provide a better world depends on the outcome of the class struggles that arise in these conditions.

Today, for example, it is becoming evident that modern production, which relies on immense cooperation, is coming up against the barrier imposed by private corporate ownership. It is possible to start reducing the working week and the number of years that individuals must work. But neither of these objectives is possible due to the present social relations. Work intensity and the time spent at work have even grown despite the enormous expansion in productive capacity. If account is taken of festivities and holy days, the average US worker probably spends as much time at work each year as the peasant in the Middle Ages. This occurs because, as Cohen points out, capitalism must prioritise the production of ever more goods over reduction in labour time.[50] Increased profit only comes if ever more commodities are produced and sold regardless of their actual use value. But if the immense productive capacity of humanity is driven in this direction, it will have dramatic effects on the environment. The contradictions, therefore, between the real productive possibilities and the fetters of private ownership pose huge problems for society.

There are no guarantees that these contradictions will be resolved. It depends on whether a new social class has the energy, political insight and combatitive spirit to make itself the focal point for society's grievances. Marx had every confidence that the working class could do this and had contempt for all theories that paralysed revolutionary action or encouraged a passive contemplation of the inevitable. People, he argued, make history not economic forces, but they do so in conditions not of their choosing.

> Men make their own history, but they do not make it as they please; they do not make it under self-selected circumstances, but under circumstances existing already, given and transmitted from the past.[51]

The central issue for modern society, therefore, is whether the working class can organise itself politically to bring about change. If it does, it can unlock the productive capacity of society, but if it does not, there can be terrible social regression.

8
Crash: How the System Implodes

In 2009, the leaders of the world met in L'Aquila, Italy in a G-8 conclave. Before them was a report from the UN Food and Agriculture Organisation which indicated that over 70 million additional people were experiencing chronic hunger because of rising food prices. They decided to allocate $20 billion over three years for their relief. But a year later it was revealed that less than one third of the L'Aquila pledge constituted new money. Germany included funds that had already been allocated for biofuel projects in South Africa, while Spain added figures for naval patrol boats donated to Nicaragua. One NGO, Actionaid, discovered that no additional funds had been made for agriculture.[1] Banks, however, are treated differently. The bail-out of one small bank, Anglo-Irish, cost at least €29 billion – more than the pledge to feed the entire world's hungry – and was delivered immediately by just one government.[2]

A major economic crash, such as occurred in 2008, can reveal the underlying dynamics of any society. It can also expose the expertise of experts.

Take Ben Bernanke, chairman of the US Federal Reserve, who is entrusted with oversight of the world's largest economy. In 2005, he claimed that 'we've never had a decline in house prices on a nationwide basis' and that any change would not drive the economy 'too far from its full employment path'.[3] In February 2008, he claimed that 'among the largest banks, the capital ratio remains good, and I don't expect any serious problems'.[4] Bernanke was not alone in his miscalculation. Britain's then Chancellor of the Exchequer, Gordon Brown, introduced his 2007 budget with the statement: 'We will never return to the old boom and bust'.[5] In the same year, the IMF claimed that 'output volatility has been significantly lower than the 1960s'.[6] After the crash of 2008 shattered these illusions, Professor James Galbraith wrote to a US Senate Committee to explain why only a handful of economists saw it coming:

> I write to you from a disgraced profession. Economic theory as widely taught since the 1980s failed miserably to understand

the force behind the financial crisis. Concepts including 'rational expectations', 'market discipline' and the 'efficient market hypothesis' led economists to argue that speculation would stabilize prices ... Not all economists believed this – but most did.[7]

The economic experts got it wrong because they thought that capitalism is a self-regulating system. They start from the assumption that there are insatiable human wants but only limited availability of resources. Only the 'laws of supply and demand' can regulate this greed efficiently. When there is too great a demand for a particular item, prices rise and send a signal to capitalists to invest in producing more of this good or service. Conversely, when demand is low, prices fall and capital migrates to a different sector of the economy. In this way the 'invisible hand' of the market is said to allocate scarce resources efficiently.[8]

This means that economic crises cannot be an intrinsic part of the system. They only occur because of an external cause which is blamed on either Nature (e.g. crop failures) or Human Nature (e.g. bouts of over-optimism, herd instinct or political blunder).[9] The source of this optimism can be traced back to Say's Law, named after a nineteenth-century French economist, Jean-Baptiste Say, who suggested that, since exchange is a two-way process, there could never be a general excess of products. For every item sold, there was a buyer who would buy products of a similar value. In that way, the supply of goods was said to create its own demand. As James Mill stated:

> A nation's power of purchasing is exactly measured by its annual produce. The more you increase the annual produce, the more, by that very act, you extend the national market ... The demand of a nation is always equal to the produce of a nation'.[10]

Say's law was taken up by David Ricardo, the leading classical economist, who claimed that as a man 'never sells but with the intention to purchase some other commodity' general over-production was impossible.[11]

BREAKING THE CIRCUIT

Marx challenged the very core of this dogma by asserting that capitalism is not a system that is geared to consumption. This is not its central purpose or what drives it forward:

It should never be forgotten that the production of surplus value – and the transformation of a portion of it back into capital, or accumulation ... – is the immediate purpose and the determining motive of capitalist production. Capitalist production, therefore, should never be depicted as something that it is not, i.e. production whose immediate purpose is consumption or the production of the means of enjoyment for the capitalist. This would be to ignore completely its specific character, as this is expressed in its basic inner pattern.[12]

As the system is not driven by consumer need – whether of the mass of the population or even the luxury consumption of the rich – its primary purpose is not to allocate scarce resources rationally as a simple example illustrates. Each day, 5,000 children die because of lack of clean water and that could be remedied, in the short term at least, if they received water purification tablets which cost less than €2 for a packet of 50. Yet capitalism cannot provide for this modest need even though there is an abundance of water purification tablets. It is clear, therefore, that the law of supply and demand does not work for the poor.

It makes more sense to view the central dynamic of the system as the self-expansion of capital. Capital, however, is not a thing but 'a process by which money is sent in search of more money',[13] and it achieves this by being joined, directly or indirectly, by human labour to produce commodities. The immediate purpose is profit, but this is then reinvested to accumulate more capital in order to make more profit, in order to accumulate more capital, and so on. It is a system built on competitive accumulation and will only serve some human need when its fits in with that goal.

Typically, there is a circuit where the different forms of capital undergo a metamorphosis. Money is first assembled, normally through the credit system, and the means of production – machinery, premises, resources – or the physical capital is gathered. Workers are hired, wages are paid and supplies or parts are purchased from other capitalists. When the finished goods are produced, they are passed on to commercial capitalists, such as Wal-Mart, who organise the sale in the shortest possible time because the faster the turnover the more profit that can be achieved. After the goods or services are sold, a high proportion is reinvested to accumulate more capital and more profit.

If we take any specific good or service that is produced and sold, we can view it as a circuit. Within this circuit individual capitalists have to cooperate to buy raw materials or machinery from each other, to hire transport companies that move their products, or to avail of the services of outsourcing agencies that take care of pay roll organisation or marketing. The circuit, therefore, involves separate decisions being taken by autonomous enterprises even though these directly affect each other. The sole purpose of each of these enterprises is profit through the sale of their commodities. Should the market price of these commodities fall below their cost price or endanger profit rates, these autonomous entities will curtail production and this creates the possibility of breakdowns at many points. Alternative suppliers can often be found, but it is not just a matter or production but sales as well. A firm producing brake systems or mother boards for computers is affected not only by the decisions of their immediate purchasers but also by all other capitalists whose actions impact the market for the finished product. If bankers in America, for example, cause a crash in the property market, this will affect the sales of computers or cars from Chinese companies. While economists are correct to emphasise how competitive accumulation imposes laws that enforce a certain order, they are wrong to see this as balanced growth and equilibrium. Disorder and disruption are built into its very nature.

Say and Ricardo had assumed a harmonious unity between sale and purchase existed. Marx's dialectical approach, however, assumed the opposite: that such a unity only occurred through contradictions that were resolved through crisis. 'We see then that commodities are in love with money but that the course of true love never did run smooth,' he quipped.[14] Far from a smooth equilibrium arising from a stable 'balance' between supply and demand, there is often chaos and breakdowns. There are a number of specific reasons for this.

First, as the interval between sale and purchase lengthens, lack of coordination increases the possibility of breakdown. Construction involves a vast social division of labour where builders must purchase cement, timber, electrical equipment and copper. Additionally, they have to find land in areas where planning permission is required. They have to hire subcontractors to organise gangs of carpenters, bricklayers and plumbers. Each capitalist who controls these distinct operations wants to achieve the maximum rate of profit, yet no one has organised the circuit to achieve this harmoniously. No one planned to make extra land, labour or raw materials available to facilitate a quickening tempo of construction. So when a boom develops there are shortages of land, labour and materials and each capitalist will try to drive up prices to maximise their profits. The result is an inflationary spiral that sends some builders out of business. They will try to save as much of their investments as possible by selling their houses at below the market rate. But this in turn triggers a chain reaction causing house prices to fall further because of over-supply.

Marx summarised the general pattern as follows:

> No one is forthwith bound to purchase because he has just sold. Circulation bursts through all the restrictions as to time, place and individuals, imposed by direct barter, and this it affects by splitting up, into the antithesis of a sale and a purchase, the direct identity that in barter does exist between the alienation of one's own and the acquisition of some other man's product ...
>
>   If the interval of time between two complementary phases of the complete metamorphosis of a commodity become too great, if the split between the sale and purchase become too pronounced, the intimate connection between them, their oneness, asserts itself by producing – crisis.[15]

Second, concrete labour, which is embodied in particular skills and operations, can only be aligned to the wider system of production as abstract labour. Through the exchange of commodities, it becomes established *which* unit was produced at a socially necessary average labour time and which was not. As none of this is known in advance, the possibility of devaluation and disruption exists.

Firms start production by purchasing machinery of the appropriate level of technology as elsewhere. As long as they match this with the labour power of average skill, they assume that they can make a profit. But the circuit of capital, which begins with this initial purchase of machinery and ends with the eventual sale of goods and return of profit, can be lengthy. Within that time, other firms can develop newer, cheaper and more efficient technology. In the 1990s, for example, there was a spectacular surge in capital investment because computerisation led to a rapid turnover of equipment. Yet these technological advances, which should be a boon to society, devalue older capital equipment.

Finding that their abstract labour is now priced above the social average, some firms become increasingly concerned about risky investments and may cut back on new investments for a period. This in turn reduces demand from their intermediate suppliers and some of these too will cut prices to maintain sales. This leads to the sacking of workers and attempts to squeeze more productivity out of those who are retained. Once again, therefore, technological advances come up against the social relations they are imprisoned within in a capitalist society. Instead of less pressure on workers, there is more pressure and disruption.[16]

Third, the movement of capital occurs through the circulation of money. Money, however, functions both as a medium of circulation and as a source of social power. This means that it can be withdrawn from circulation at any point, either to be held as savings or turned into speculative items such as the purchase of an Old Master or precious metals. Moreover, as soon as the system receives the slightest shock, there is a rush to money – and to secure money at that. At this point, Marx argued:

> Commodities are thus sold not to in order to buy commodities, but in order to replace their commodity form by their money form. Instead of being merely a way of mediating the metabolic process, this change of process becomes an end in itself ... The money is petrified into a hoard and the seller of commodities becomes a hoarder of money.[17]

The withdrawal of money from circulation undermines the idea that every sale creates its own purchase. It reduces demand in an economy and, by cutting back on investment, leads to job losses and further reductions in demand.

Fourth, capitalists strive continually to raise productivity and cut unit costs. The more successful each one is, the more surplus value they can achieve. However, when this is generalised, it leads to a lack of demand for the goods and services. The less each worker has to spend, the fewer products he or she can buy. So a contradiction emerges between the expansion in productivity and the realisation of profit through sales. As Marx put it:

> There must be a constant tension between the restricted dimensions of consumption on the capitalist basis and a production that is increasingly striving to overcome these immanent barriers.[18]

In a later chapter of *Capital*, Volume 3, he put the matter even more starkly:

> The ultimate reason for all real crisis always remain the poverty and restricted consumption of the masses in the face of the drive

of capitalist production to develop the productive forces as if only the absolute consumption capacity of society set a limit to them.[19]

Some Marxists such as Rosa Luxemburg took this argument about the restricted consumption of the mass of people to imply that the system needed to expand into 'outside', non-capitalist zones to dump its surplus produce.[20] Others, however, have labelled this an 'under-consumption' explanation and rejected it.[21] One reason for this hostility is that under-consumptionist arguments originated with writers such as Thomas Malthus and Simonde de Sismondi.[22] While the latter wanted some reform of the system, the former used it as a justification for the luxury consumption of the aristocracy. The landed gentry, Malthus argued, performed the vital social function of spending widely thereby plugging the gap in demand.

A variation of the under-consumptionist argument was taken up by Keynesian economists. They disputed Say's Law and suggested that if 'aggregate demand' was reduced through savings or lack of confidence, this could lead to economic crisis. Their conclusion, however, was not to overthrow capitalism but to manage it through state intervention. When there was a risk of a downturn, the state had to step in to stimulate demand by cutting interest rates or by initiating new infrastructure projects to create demand.

The problem with the Malthus/Sismondi argument was that they treated working-class consumption as an independent variable rather than being itself shaped by the rate of accumulation of capital. A high level of investment in producing machinery for capitalists, for example, is not directly affected by working-class consumption but it can provide jobs and so increase demand throughout the wider economy. So even if wages were held down, the economy could still progress because investment in the capital goods sector helped indirectly to create alternative demand. The key issue, therefore, is the rate of profit which may either encourage or discourage investment. This was also the weak point of the Keynesian argument because it failed to acknowledge that even if the state stimulates demand, the capitalist might not invest because profit rates were not high enough. A capitalist cannot be forced to invest.

However, if the issue of under-consumption is seen as just one aspect of the wider problem, then it can fit into Marx's rather than Keynes' schema. Long before Keynes, Marx was arguing that the ultimate basis for crises is the contradiction between the huge productive capacity created by capitalism and its inability to match this to real needs. In late capitalism, the gap between the rising productivity of workers and wage compensation has sharpened dramatically. Since 1973, for example, total productivity growth in the US has risen by 83 per cent while the overall compensation package for workers grew by only 9 per cent.[23] Clearly, the restricted compensation of workers will play a role in causing economic downturns. Marx's solution, however, was not simply to manage demand at the onset of a downturn but for society to take control of the economy and organise it rationally.

Far from the system being stable, then, it moves from crisis to crisis. There is considerable evidence to suggest that economic crises are intrinsic to capitalism. According to the World Bank, there were 117 banking crises in 93 countries between 1970 and 2003, the crash of 2008 being unusual only in its scale.[24] Nor is economic disruption confined to banks. In the United States, there have been 35 economic cycles in the 150 years since 1834. Two of these – the Great Depression of 1873–93 and the Wall Street Crash of 1929 whose effects lasted until 1941 – qualify as general crises.[25] This record has forced even conventional economists to make some reference to 'business cycle' theory, but they see this mainly as adjustments, where there is some periodic expansion and contraction leading again to equilibrium. Most fail to understand Marx's next argument about how the system has a central flaw that helps both to trigger and deepen many of the mechanisms described above.

RISING MASS AND FALLING RATES

Marx regarded the law of the tendency for the rate of profit to fall as 'in every respect the most important law of modern political economy' yet 'despite its simplicity, [it] has never before been grasped'.[26]

The classical school of economics, which developed with the birth of capitalism, agreed that rates of profit tended to fall, but there was confusion about why. Despite being claimed by right-wing politicians such as Margaret Thatcher, Adam Smith thought that a high level of profit was a sign of economic backwardness. It would decline as more capital was invested and workers hired, thus causing wages to rise and profits to fall.[27] Ricardo worried that this explanation posed difficulties for the defence of capitalism because it indicated a fault-line in the system. He was involved in a long drawn-out battle against the landed gentry in Britain and sought the reason for declining rates of profit outside the industrial economy. Like Smith, he suggested that rising wages were the cause, but claimed that this resulted from a decline in agricultural fertility. As more workers were employed, they needed more food from the countryside but, due to diminishing returns from the soil, this pushed up prices. This in turn led to higher wages that reduced profit rates.[28]

Marx did not start from wages but from his theory of surplus value. As was explained in Chapter 2, he argued that profit arose from the surplus value provided by workers. Capitalists sold goods on the market at values determined by the amount of socially necessary labour time they contained. If they contained more labour, the value would be higher and prices would fluctuate around this higher point. Less labour brought a lower value and often a lower price. However, even though workers bestowed value on these goods, they were not paid the full value of their labour power. Instead they provided free surplus labour time to capitalists.

In their drive for profits, capitalists do battle on two fronts: in the labour process, they seek to create extra surplus time; and on the market, they try to gain an increased share.[29]

The key to victory in the labour process lies in greater productivity. They will try to increase work effort but there are limits set by the physical exhaustion of workers. There are no limits, however, to the technology that can be used to get workers to produce more goods in less time. If a firm invests in computer numerical control machinery, its workers will carry out vastly more cutting and welding of metal than those using traditional lathes no matter how much harder the latter work. The drive to raise productivity, therefore, leads to the mechanisation of production. Machines replace workers, materialised labour replaces living labour and more fixed capital is employed per worker.[30] The first firm to embrace the latest technology will gain a particular cost advantage. They can produce goods at a cost that is below the value which is still set by older forms of technology. This will give them extra profit because they can both slightly reduce their prices and gain extra market share but still make higher profits because they benefit from the technology.

However, this development eventually has an impact on their rivals. The key to gaining market share is to reduce unit costs. Marketing and advertising can certainly help, but ultimately cost emerges as the crucial variable. If a competitor has introduced new technology that reduces their costs, a rival must do the same. As a result, the level of machinery that is employed in any one sector rises compared to the number of workers. This leads to a change in the technical composition of capital because there is now a greater mass of machines or, as Marx calls it, 'dead labour' compared to living labour. Marx refers to this change in the value of capital as the *organic composition of capital* because there has been a change in the ratio of its two components. *Constant* capital, which is locked up in machinery and the physical means of production, rises compared to *variable* capital, which is the amount spent on the wages.

This, however, creates a problem because the source of profit is living labour. The fall in the number of workers compared to fixed capital means that there will be a fall in the rate of profit. Technology will help the firm produce more goods for less but, as these methods become generalised throughout the sector, their price will fall. Computers that are made today are much cheaper than those made ten years ago. Radios, televisions, video recorders have also fallen in value. Yet in each of these sectors capitalists have to spend more on plant and machinery while the number of workers has decreased. Each capitalist must, therefore, seek to gain a profit from products that cost less with a smaller workforce and much higher initial investment.

They may still manage to increase the *mass* of profit – in other words, the figure on the bottom line. As additional capital is employed, more workers may even be hired, even if their number compared to the fixed investment has fallen. And generally, a capitalist controlling a large capital will make more profit in absolute terms than a smaller one because they command a greater market share.[31] Nevertheless *the rate of profit,* by which we mean the return on investment employed, will drop. In technical terms, the ratio of the net operating surplus to the capital stock, as measured by the replacement value of the gross fixed capital stock, will decline.[32] Marx expressed it like this:

> the same reasons that produce a tendential fall in the general rate of profit also bring about an accelerated accumulation of capital and hence a growth in the absolute magnitude or total mass of the surplus labour (surplus value, profit) appropriated by it.
>
> Just as everything is expressed upside down in competition, and hence in the consciousness of its agents, so too is this law – I mean this inner and necessary connection between two apparently contradictory phenomena.[33]

Why, however, do capitalists choose to produce at a lower level of profit? The point, of course, is that they don't – they are compelled to by competitive dynamics. If they want to maintain or expand market share, they have to keep pace with technological advances introduced by their rivals.

However, they will still try to do something about their falling rates of profit. If they can intensify the rate of exploitation, this will help compensate for the decline of living labour compared to dead labour. By squeezing more from fewer workers, they get more surplus value and so offset a decline in the rate of profit. This gives rise to what Marx called a number of 'countervailing tendencies' that seek to reduce or even reverse the tendency for the rate of profit to fall. If we think of these as *strategies* employed by different capitalists, we can start to see the power of Marx's theory. Three methods may be typically employed here.

One is to increase the *absolute level of surplus value* by ensuring that a smaller number of workers work longer hours. They can force workers – within legal limits – to work an extra hour or so a week. They can introduce a system of annualised hours that ensures there is no downtime throughout the working year. They can eliminate overtime rates and shift premiums to achieve round-the-clock production, thus serving their heavy investment in machinery. They can move production to countries where longer working hours are legal.

A second method is to increase the *relative level of surplus value* through an intensification of work effort. Here the working day stays the same but instead of producing goods to the value of their own wages, in say four hours, workers do so in three or even two. In this way, more of the working day is devoted to working for nothing for their employer. If we imagine the working day as a piece of Swiss cheese, in which there are several holes called 'downtime', the employer will try to fill as many as possible. Under the cry of 'flexibility' all sorts of methods are used to achieve this. Workers will be told to 'multi-task' to increase their skill levels. Team working may be used to enforce a collective effort to meet group bonuses. The overall result, whichever method is employed, is that downtime is reduced and work effort is increased.

A third method is *wage cuts*. Economic crises provide employers with an opportunity for 'downward adjustments', but even in normal times more subtle methods may be used. Younger workers may be hired at lower rates than older workers; wage increases may be granted below the rate of inflation; pension contributions may be reduced; special holiday bonuses may be eliminated; workers can be sacked and rehired on lower pay rates; production can be moved to countries with cheaper labour. As the increased use of machinery leads to job losses, workers can be compelled to accept these changes.

All of these strategies have become familiar features of modern society but few conventional economists can explain why work has become harder, more stressful and worse paid even though technology exists to make it easier. In the 1960s, for example, there were academic debates about how people would fill increased leisure time caused by automation. Today, however, many people live with the paradox that they are more stressed than before automation was introduced. Only Marx's theory of how capitalists respond to the falling rate of profit can help to explain it.

In addition to these strategies, Marx suggested that foreign trade could be used to reduce a decline in the rate of profits. Goods sold to other countries might achieve a higher mark-up or labour could be purchased at much cheaper rates. He also suggested that there was some 'capital-saving' technology that could reduce the cost of constant capital. Sometimes, for example, the capital investment required to introduce new technology might have reduced due to cheaper ways of making this machinery. However, there are relatively few cases where capitalists cut physical investment per worker.[34]

The tendency towards a decline in the rate of profit and its countervailing tendencies were not, however, of equal strength. The latter, Marx noted, 'do not annul the law but weaken its effect'.[35] The former is 'decisive only under certain particular circumstances and over long periods'.[36]

CONCENTRATION AND FINANCE

The expansion of the system, even as the rate of profit tends to fall, produces a number of important effects that have become evident in the twenty-first century.

There is, first, a shift towards the concentration and centralisation of capital. As greater levels of fixed capital are employed per worker, it becomes harder for smaller capitalists to thrive. Small shops, internet cafés and restaurants may certainly multiply, but the main sectors of the economy become dominated by a decreasing number of giant firms. By *concentration* Marx meant bigger firms that use massive amounts of capital to put production in motion. By *centralisation* Marx meant the swallowing up of small capitalists by the big.

Both trends are evident in late capitalism as only a handful of corporations dominate the different sectors of the global economy. Of the top 100 entities in the world today, 52 are now corporations and 48 are countries.[37] A company such as General Motors or Shell controls more economic resources than entire countries such as Denmark, Indonesia, Greece or Poland. In one celebrated case, the top people at Goldman Sachs shared out money that was equivalent to the national income of Tanzania.[38] The centralisation of capital was accelerated in the 1990s because there was a huge spate of mergers and acquisitions as the assets acquired grew five-fold to reach $2.7 trillion.[39] The result is that a small number of powerful corporations control vast areas of our lives.

Second, with the expansion of capitalism has come a huge surge in credit and speculation. Marx's writing on money and credit is quite abstract and rambling but writers such as David Harvey have extended some of the concepts he used to throw light on how modern finance works.[40]

When units of production were small, individual capitalists could fund expansion from their own resources. Now, however, they can no longer pay for machines, materials and energy supplies in advance and this is where the financial system develops to perform a number of vital functions for capitalism. It mobilises initial capital by combining savings from diverse sectors to start production. It reallocates capital that had been 'immobilised' due to lack of investment opportunities from one sector to another. In this way it helps to create great pools of finance which become 'the common capital of a class'.[41] This helps make the rate of profit transparent across the economy and to equalise those rates as investments flow from sector to sector. Credit also reduces turnover time by allowing capitalists to buy new materials on instalment rather than waiting for their circuit to be completed. This enables them to turn over the same capital several times during a single production period. Credit also facilitates the consumption of goods such as cars or houses, stimulating further production.

As the financial system grows, it too moves beyond barriers of money. In the past, paper money had to be directly convertible into gold but later this link was broken. Banks established the right to issue 'bills of exchange', credit cards, cheque-books and all manner of credit paper. Eventually, even more elaborate *fictitious capital* emerges. These are promissory notes that are put into circulation without any real basis in commodities or productive activity. The holder will simply have a piece of paper which promises an income stream in the future. One example is a piece of paper purchased on a futures market and promising payment for bushels of soybeans due for delivery in a year. Another is a collateralised debt obligation where a lender advances a large amount money in order for bankers or brokers to gain a stream of income from many people who will be paying their mortgages. These pieces of paper, however, may in turn be sold to someone who assumes that next year the prices of soybeans or interest rates on mortgages will be higher. They are, therefore, willing to pay more and so the gap between the paper and the original commodity grows wider. Or purchasers may simply buy the paper because they think they can sell it on to someone else at an even higher price. In either case, we have entered the murky world of fictitious capital.

Now comes the twist. As all this is becoming terribly risky, a few enterprising capitalists emerge to 'quantify' risk – they will put a figure on it and allow you to take out insurance to cover that risk. The insurance on the piece of paper – which, remember, was originally linked to soybeans or mortgage debt – is known as a credit default swap. But once again its price will vary according to different assessments of risk or because it can be sold on for a higher price. So even more enterprising capitalists purchase credit default swaps because they think they can make a profit from them.

This may all sound like a bizarre maze in a fantasy island, but this is how modern capitalism works. The largest insurance company in the world, AIG, for example, bought enough credit default swaps to ensure $441 billion of securities because they thought they could make huge profits on them. But after the crash of 2008, all the entrepreneurs who lost out on speculation on soybeans or mortgages or whatever came calling on AIG to cover their losses. AIG was badly stung and was only saved from going the way of Lehman Brothers by a bail-out from the US government. This, then, is the strange world of fictitious capital, which Marx suggested was the most 'fetishistic' of all forms of capital because 'All connection with the actual process of capital's self expansion is lost, right down to the last trace, confirming the notion that capital automatically expands itself by its own powers'.[42]

At the start of the twentieth century, Eduard Bernstein argued that a well-developed credit system would prevent a general crisis of overproduction.[43] It was the cornerstone of his argument for reform rather than revolution. Today many people take the opposite view and see the bankers and financiers as the cause of economic chaos. Marx, however, was deeply irreverent about all mystifications surrounding finance. He regarded it as neither the cause of capitalism's ills nor the solution to its woes. Finance, he argued, helped capitalism overcome its limits by stretching demand – only to lead to even more severe crises. He wrote that 'it suspends the barriers to the realization of capital only by raising them to their most general form'.[44]

Financiers demand profit to carry out functions for productive capital. But this profit is not the surplus value that is derived from production but is an interest charge that transfers wealth from one capitalist to another. Contrary to the mystified talk about 'financial engineering' it cannot generate wealth by itself, but represents a claim on wealth. As the financial sector seeks ever more profit, it will stretch itself beyond its own official reserves and will borrow to lend. Banks now go to the 'money markets' to borrow vast sums in order to lend out at interest. They will take ever greater risks because they assume that debts can be paid back later from rising asset prices. At first, all this helps capital to grow as it speeds up the circuit of capital and reallocates resources. The provision of extra funds for housing, for example, becomes a self-fulfilling prophecy which helps to stoke the boom.

But once the economic system is at full throttle, ever more credit is required to mobilise funds for apparently more profitable activity. Ever more fictitious capital is created and a widening gap opens between paper claims and real measures of value. Eventually, a point is reached where lending outstrips what can be paid back and the bubble in asset prices bursts. At first sight the crash appears to be merely a credit and money crisis because there is a rush for real money. But while the crash may have a financial form, its roots lie in a system that strives to overcome every barrier while restricting consumption.

CRASH

An economic crash represents a point when all these contradictions come to the fore. Typically, an over-accumulation of capital is matched by unemployment and underuse of labour power. The expansion of capital during a prior boom creates a surplus of capital that can no longer find profitable outlets. Although capital strives to overcome all barriers, it finds that

> The *real barrier* of capitalist production is *capital itself*. It is that capital and its self-expansion appear as the starting and the

closing point, the motive and the purpose of production; that production is only production for *capital* and not the reverse, i.e. the means of production are not simply means for a steadily expanding pattern of life for the *society* of producers.[45]

A crash is, however, not a departure from equilibrium; it is the equilibrium mechanism itself.[46] As Dobb suggested, it 'is seen as catharsis as well as retribution: as the sole mechanism by which ... equilibrium can be enforced, once it is broken'.[47] This occurs through the destruction of capital as production is blocked, machinery stops, raw materials are unused and labour remains unexploited. A depreciation of values also sets in as commodity prices collapse and the promissory notes of fictitious capital, which are claims on future profits, are written down. When the crash hits, the capitalist class start to behave like 'enemy brothers' because 'as soon as it is no longer a question of the division of profit but of loss, each seeks as far as he can to restrict his own share of the loss and pass it on to someone else'.[48] But difficult as it may be for capitalists, it is far worse for the rest of society who find themselves out of work and their living standards reduced.

Eventually, however, the crash prepares the ground for the economic cannibals to emerge. Equipment, plant and human labour may all have been devalued but as physical entities they still exist. The bigger capitalists – or those with friends in government – who survive can buy them cheaply and so resume production with higher levels of profit. And so the system returns to its path of capital accumulation.

Or so it should. However, a 'too big to fail' syndrome has developed in late capitalism. The system is now so concentrated and centralised that the bankruptcy of major firms threatens to create black holes that suck in other sizeable chunks of capital. In the early hours of Monday, 15 September 2008, Lehman Brothers collapsed and the leaders of the 'free world' saw the ripple effects from that black hole. AIG was next to tumble in and the system appeared to be in meltdown. Suddenly, US politicians, led by George Bush, who had previously railed against all government intervention in markets, rushed in with bail-outs. The system was saved – but at a cost.

Catharsis was halted, state debts ballooned – and the surplus capital stood there, petrified that profitable reinvestment might not be secure. Capitalism has entered a protracted period of uncertainty, crisis and suffering for the majority. The issue of how to lift the real barrier of capital itself has become more pressing.

9
Utopia or Revolution

The crash of 2008 destroyed an estimated €50 trillion of the world's assets, equal to one year of the combined labour of humanity.[1] As a direct consequence, millions of children face the prospect of 'long-term irreversible cognitive damage',[2] according to Patrick Montjourides, of UNESCO's Global Monitoring Report team. Rising food prices and growing unemployment have already led to the death of between 200,000 and 500,000 children and many more will suffer brain damage due to malnutrition.

Yet many still claim that there are no alternatives to capitalism. 'We cannot picture to ourselves a world that is essentially different from the present one, and at the same time better,'[3] claims Francis Fukuyama. This sentiment is echoed by left-wing critics who denounce the current system but suggest that 'it is easier to imagine the end of the world than it is to imagine the end of capitalism'.[4] The roots of much of this pessimism stem from a belief that the USSR was a form of 'actually existing socialism'. The fall of the Berlin Wall and the subsequent collapse of the USSR are taken as proof that public ownership of enterprises and socialist planning cannot work.

However, the USSR and the communist regimes of Eastern Europe were not an alternative to capitalism but a mirror image of it. They were controlled by bureaucratic elites who ran the economy as a military-industrial complex to compete with their Cold War rivals. There was no democracy, no independent unions and no element of worker control. The consumption fund to provide goods and services for the population was systematically squeezed to pay for a vast military machine. Equating those societies with socialism misses an elementary point made by the Irish socialist James Connolly:

Socialism properly implies above all things the co-operative control by the workers of the machinery of production; without this co-operative control the public ownership by the State is not Socialism – it is only State capitalism.[5]

What failed in the USSR was a state-run society shaped by military competition. More generally, neither Marx nor Engels ever thought that socialism could be equated simply with state control. Engels, for example, envisaged a situation where large corporations became monopolies and might be taken over by the state, much like the railway system had been. However, he thought that this would not lead to the abolition of capitalism but to the creation of a 'national capitalist',

> The modern state, no matter what its form, is essentially a capitalist machine – the state of the capitalists, the ideal personification of the total national capital. The more it proceeds to the taking over of productive forces, the more does it actually become the national capitalist, the more citizens does it exploit. The workers remain wage-workers – proletarians. The capitalist relation is not done away with. It is, rather, brought to a head. But, brought to a head, it topples over. State-ownership of the productive forces is not the solution of the conflict, but concealed within it are the technical conditions that form the elements of that solution.[6]

If the misconception about socialism and state ownership is removed, the claim that socialism has failed – and hence the 'There is No Alternative' motto – becomes palpably absurd. It assumes that a particular form of society – industrial capitalism – which has been in existence for just over 250 years will continue forever, despite the pattern of all previous history. The issue, therefore, is not whether an alternative is possible but what alternative is practical and how it might be achieved.

MARX AND UTOPIANISM

'Utopian' has become a term of abuse commonly used to imply that critics of the current order are wild-eyed idealists who have little 'practical' to offer. Their moral denunciations may be understandable but, it is suggested, their solutions are 'utopian'. By this is meant a desire to achieve a perfect but impossible society. This argument, however, misunderstands Marx's relation to utopia.

The word 'utopia' traces its origins to the title of a book written by Thomas More in 1515. At the time, a new elite was amassing wealth by enclosing common lands and *Utopia* was written as a damning critique. It attacked the practice of hanging thieves and denounced the king for ruling over a nation of beggars. 'For one man to abound in wealth and pleasure, when all about him are mourning and groaning, is to be a jailer and not a king'.[7] The second part described a land known as 'Utopia' that looked exactly the same as England but where property was held in common. In this land of Nowhere (the translation of the Greek word utopia) people led a serene and cheerful life because 'though no man has anything, yet all are rich'.[8] *Utopia* was not a programme for change but a brilliant literary device to hold up a mirror to existing society. The same technique was followed in other books such as Tomasso Campenella's *City of the Sun* (1602), Francis Bacon's *New Atlantis* (1627) and James Harington's *Oceana* (1657). At a time when class division was seen as an eternal, God-designed feature of human life, the more fantastic were the dreams of a better world.

This began to change with the early utopian socialists who were the first to highlight the flaws of the new society born with the French Revolution and the Industrial Revolution. Behind the proclaimed goals of 'liberty, equality and fraternity' Henri de Saint Simon, Charles Fourier and Robert Owen detected another form of class rule – with one difference. Instead of poverty arising from famine and scarcity, Fourier proclaimed that 'poverty is born of abundance itself'.[9] These writers suggested that class division could be replaced but, unlike their predecessors, they wanted to create practical experiments to show how their utopia might work.

The philanthropist Owen used his wealth to found the New Lanark commune where 1,800 people worked and children were given free education for the first time. Followers of Fourier founded colonies in the US known as 'phalanxes' which were designed for communal living. The experiments were often short-lived but the utopian socialists foretold new ways of thinking that were incredibly progressive. Fourier attacked the position of woman in marriage where 'people try to persuade her that her chains are woven with flowers'.[10] As a general thesis, he argued, social progress occurs 'by virtue of the progress of women toward liberty, and decadence of the social order occurs as the result of a decrease in the liberty of women'.[11]

Marx and Engels praised these early utopian critics of capitalism and were often inspired by the 'gems of thought'[12] contained in their sometimes fantastic forms. Engels watched with interest the founding of communist colonies that were supposed to be models of a new society. However, they saw these experiments merely as precursors of a real movement for change and when attempts were made to draw up detailed blueprints for a future society they became particularly critical. In a celebrated section of the *Communist Manifesto* they announced their break with all forms of utopian socialism. Their reasons are still relevant for thinking about how a transition out of capitalism might occur.

Marx and Engels argued that a utopian sees a new society arising from the 'personal inventive actions'[13] of individuals who use reason to redress the wrongs of society. How or why masses of people might embrace their particular model becomes a matter of chance or fantastic hope. The only strategy that utopians could adopt was propaganda and teaching by example. Despite a lack of resources available for their experiments, they aimed to overcome all obstacles to create a shining example for others to follow. At the heart of this model was, therefore, an inherent elitism. The model builders undoubtedly cared for workers, but they saw them only as the most suffering class, incapable of independent initiative. The path to a new world had to be hewn by brighter and morally better people who would set an example for others to follow.

The utopians were also mistaken in trying to follow the model of the transition from feudalism to capitalism. It was possible to construct islands of capitalism in a sea of feudalism when merchant cities, which grew in the crevices of society, successfully expanded and eventually overcame the old economic order. This occurred because merchant capital could be accumulated in more successful and dynamic ways than landed property. This method of transition out of capitalism is, however, not open to workers because they cannot accumulate wealth in a way that is superior to the economic power of capital. The main resource workers have is their ability to combine in solidarity, but this can hardly be accumulated. Creating islands of socialism in a sea of capitalism is, therefore, impossible.

Ironically, however, the utopian socialists underestimated the real elements of continuity with the older society. They assumed that a new society could start from scratch as if there was a Day One of an entirely New Way of Living. Against these fantastic imaginings, Marx thought that socialism would come into existence through human beings who are marked by their experience of capitalism. 'In every respect', Marx argued, 'economically, morally, intellectually, it is thus still stamped with the birth marks of the old society, from whose womb it has emerged'.[14]

This radically different vision located change in the struggles of workers because Marx thought they were not simply brainwashed by the system but were capable of transforming themselves in struggles. A new society would arise as *both* a continuity *and* a break from the experiences of workers. In the *German Ideology*, Marx and Engels neatly summarised their method:

> Communism is for us not a *state of affairs* which is to be established, an *ideal* to which reality [will] have to adjust itself. We call communism the *real* movement which abolishes the present state of things. The conditions of this movement result from the premises now in existence.[15]

In one of Marx's last letters he was even more emphatic in opposing schemes for the future and in focusing on the real struggles today:

> The doctrinaire and necessarily fantastic anticipations of the programme of action for a revolution of the future only divert us from the struggle of the present. The dream that the end of the world was at hand inspired the early Christians in their struggle with the Roman Empire and gave them confidence in victory. Scientific insight into the inevitable disintegration of the dominant order of society ... is a sufficient guarantee that the moment a real proletarian revolution breaks out the conditions (though these are certain not to be idyllic) of its immediately next *modus operandi* will be in existence.[16]

A related polemic that Marx conducted with Pierre-Joseph Proudhon and John Gray also sheds insight into how a change out of capitalism might occur. These used Ricardo's early formulation of the labour theory of value to claim that each individual worker should directly enjoy the full fruits of his or her labour. They envisaged a more just market where everyone worked and received labour notes that entitled them to the precise amount of commodities that were the equivalent to the labour they had expended. A National Exchange Bank would oversee the process to ensure justice in these exchanges. As money was abolished and replaced by labour time chits, society could be gradually transformed.

This assumed that markets could be regulated to bring about a just distribution and failed to see how real markets operate through a destructive process of adjustment to arrive at *average* values that are assigned to each commodity. Calculations based on individual labour time were, therefore, artificial and would require an immense bureaucratic machine. Proudhon and Gray also thought that one could maintain the independence of the individual commodity sellers while society as a whole pursued collective social goals. Against this market utopianism, Marx argued for the total overthrow of capitalism so that social labour, which is currently organised through the medium of commodity exchange, could be controlled democratically by the collective effort of the 'associated producers'.[17] That could only happen through the eventual suppression of the markets rather than a utopian vision of market justice.

Marx's discussions with the utopian socialists and the semi-anarchist Proudhon have taken on a new relevance today as an urgent desire for change produces great frustration about why it has not already happened. One symptom has been the revival of utopian thinking that stresses the importance of 'doing' something rather than 'waiting' for revolution. John Holloway, for example, who has inspired much of the autonomist movement, argues that there needs to be 'an endless multiplicity of screams' to solve 'the dilemma of the urgent impossibility of revolution'.[18] By this he means the creation of 'autonomous zones' such as community gardens or experiments in radical education or the Zapatistas' area in Chiapas, Mexico. Similarly, E. O. Wright has pointed to 'real utopias' such as the Mondragon cooperatives in the Basque region of Spain as prefiguring a new society.[19] Still others, such as Richard Wilkinson and Kate Pickett, who produced substantial statistical evidence on the inequalities in capitalism, advocate worker-owned firms because 'employee-owned companies might maintain higher standards of morality even with the profit motive'.[20]

Marx differed from all these approaches in advocating social revolution. This did not mean 'waiting' for the one Big Day but engaging with contemporary workers' struggles. In this scenario, 'doing something' meant contributing to the class struggle in the hope that it would usher in a new society if victorious. Instead of many different 'screams' it was necessary to link up with a social class that had the power to bring about change. The formation of any 'autonomous zone' was to be welcomed, but no matter how enthusiastic people are about these 'real utopias', they could not relieve the huge pressure imposed by the surrounding market economy.

The Mondragon Corporation of cooperatives is a case in point. Formed originally by a Catholic priest, it has grown to become the seventh largest firm in Spain. In the process, however, it has been forced to respond to the competitive pressures so that 20 per cent of the workforce is on part-time or temporary contracts.[21] One researcher, Sharryn Kasmir, who conducted a poll among workers, found that 'the co-operative does not seem to transmit a strong sense of ownership, except to those in high positions'.[22] Similarly, United Airlines, which was the largest employee-owned firm in the US, enforced pay and pension cuts on its own staff in a bid to survive. Tragically, the value of the employees' shares eventually tumbled and workers lost out badly. In both cases, the 'real utopias' could not break with the logic of capitalism.

Marx's approach, therefore, was not to build alternatives within the existing mode of production but to overthrow it.

REVOLUTION

In one of his early writings, Marx declared that 'without revolution, socialism cannot be made possible'.[23] In the *Communist Manifesto*, he and Engels were even more forthright, declaring that 'their ends can be attained only by the forcible overthrow of all existing conditions'.[24] A number of reasons were advanced for why revolution was necessary.

The machinery of the state could not be used for this purpose because it had been shaped by the dominant class and their economic goals. Marx, therefore, argued that his purpose was not to 'transfer the bureaucratic-military machine from one hand to another, but to *smash* it'.[25] While this point was made in relation to Continental powers and Marx held open the possibility of a parliamentary transition in the US and Britain, the 'bureaucratic-military machine' has now grown in all countries.

Unlike the capitalist class, workers need direct political power to begin the process of liberating themselves. In 1789, the bourgeoisie of France carried out a radical overthrow of the old feudal regime, but after the upheavals of 1848 in Europe they became ever more fearful of the growing class of workers below them.

> They are aware that in revolutions the rabble gets insolent and lays hands on things. The bourgeois gentlemen therefore seek as far as possible to make the change from absolute to bourgeois monarchy without a revolution, in an amicable fashion.[26]

They learnt that sometimes aristocrats could be left in political control as long as they, the capitalists, had the freedom to make money. However, a similar separation of political and economic power was not possible for workers because, unlike both the bourgeois and the aristocracy, they are an exploited class. Uprooting a system of exploitation that is embedded in the very nature of commodity exchange, therefore, required direct political force.

It was also only in the process of revolution that the mass of people learnt to clarify their own interests and develop a different understanding of their society. In normal times, the majority accept the legitimacy of their rulers and at least some of their ideas. This cannot be changed simply through preaching, teaching or good example. A new consciousness cannot emerge on a mass scale by workers 'waking up' and then passively following the teachings of their intellectual masters or clever television presenters. Experience of class struggle is the only way in which people can learn and, as Draper put it, 'revolution speeded up the curriculum and enriched the course'.[27] In the *German Ideology*, Marx and Engels summed up their views on how traditional ideas were changed:

> Alteration ... can only take place in a practical movement, a revolution; this revolution is necessary, therefore, not only because the ruling class cannot be overthrown in any other way, but also because the class overthrowing it can only in a revolution succeed in ridding itself of all the muck of ages and become fitted to found society anew.[28]

Revolutions are neither accidental nor planned. They may start in the most unpredictable way, often with spontaneous mobilisations, but they arise from deeper contradictions in society. As Engels put it, 'revolutions are not made deliberately and arbitrarily, but ... have been the necessary outcome of circumstances entirely independent of the will and leadership of particular parties and entire classes'.[29] They develop from a general tumult in society that affects all social classes. Typically, the lower class does not suddenly embrace a vision of a bright new world, but rather fights for aspirations it considers just in the old world. It is only when society has reached a massive impasse that it adopts revolutionary methods to achieve these 'moderate' demands. The Russian Revolution of 1917 was fought, after all, over 'land, bread and peace'.

It is not only the lower classes who are drawn into the maelstrom of revolution. The Russian revolutionary Lenin suggested that three conditions were necessary for revolution, but only one concerned the working class. The first was that the ruling class are 'sufficiently entangled and at loggerheads with one another'.[30] Splits at the top both create new spaces for people to question their rulers and ensure that the rulers are not able to act decisively to defend their privileges.

The Hungarian Revolution of 1956, for example, began because diehard Stalinists attempted to oust reformers in the Communist Party elite, and this split encouraged students and youth to mobilise in support of the latter.

The second condition was that the 'intermediate elements' not only break with loyalty to the elite but then subsequently show the 'practical bankruptcy' of their own policies.[31] Every major crisis in society is characterised by adventurers who emerge from sub-elites to propose apparently radical solutions. In the French Revolution of 1848, for example, radical republicans such as Alexandre Ledru-Rollin or Alphonse Lamartine made passionate speeches which won them working-class support but when the crackdown on the working class occurred, they sided with the party of order. A revolution is a major test for all political positions – and its dynamic exposes a moderation that hides behind radical rhetoric.

These two conditions, combined with the growth of a 'mass sentiment' among workers for 'the most determined, bold and dedicated revolutionary action', was, according to Lenin, what makes a revolution possible.[32] However this sentiment implies that a revolution is a process rather than simply a one-off event because normally only a tiny minority of workers favour 'bold, dedicated and revolutionary action'. Even after the outbreak of tumultuous struggles many continue to wish for compromise rather than 'going too far'. In one of his later letters, Engels argued that 'the big mistake is to think that the revolution can be made overnight. As a matter of fact it is a process of development of the masses that takes several years even under conditions that favour its acceleration'.[33]

The reference to several years may at first appear puzzling and so it may be useful to distinguish between a pre-revolutionary and a revolutionary situation. When a society enters a crisis, the prior traditions of struggle or passivity can have an immense impact. Where workers have gone through a long period of social peace and their unions have atrophied, an economic crisis can dramatically accelerate retreat and demoralisation before anger gives way to new forms of organisation. Conversely, where workers enter these new circumstances after a period of struggle, the economic crisis can increase militancy and generate a new political consciousness. Engels' reference to several years, therefore, applies to the conditions of struggle before revolutionary events occur.

But even when decisive confrontations are entered into, these are often only a prelude to a revolutionary situation that can last months or years. This is because the revolution is itself a learning process in which workers can come to the conclusion that only their rule can solve the problems of society. As this involves the immense majority who have different experiences of struggle, this realisation can take some time to spread. The standard image of a revolution involves street fighting, the erection of barricades and the final storming of a centre of power. While these elements may certainly be contained in a twenty-first-century workers' revolution, the process is also more complicated.

As capitalism is not based on a single command and control centre but is rooted in a myriad of social relations in the workplace and beyond, a workers' revolution must move from the streets to workplace occupations to strikes and insurrection. A workers' revolution will, therefore, naturally ebb and flow and will be constantly fuelled by battles over economic confrontations as well as 'big' political issues. In perhaps his most succinct and prophetic broad-brush summary, Marx tried to outline the differences between a bourgeois revolution to win democracy and a workers' revolution to achieve socialism:

> Bourgeois revolutions, such as those of the eighteenth century, storm quickly from success to success. They outdo each other in dramatic effects; men and things seem set in sparkling diamonds and each day's spirit is ecstatic. But they are short-lived; they soon reach their apogee and society has to undergo a long period of regret until it has learned properly to assimilate soberly the achievements of its period of storm and stress.
>
> Proletarian revolutions, however, such as those of the nineteenth century, constantly engage in self-criticism, and in repeated interruptions of their own course. They return to what has apparently been accomplished, in order to begin the task again; with merciless thoroughness they mock the inadequate, weak and wretched aspects of their first attempts; they seem to throw their opponent to the ground only so to see him draw new strength from the earth and rise again before them, more colossal than ever; they shrink back again and again before the indeterminate intensity of their own goals – until the situation is created in which any retreat is impossible, and the conditions themselves call out: Hic Rhodus, hic salta! Here is the rose, dance here![34]

While Marx's emphasis is on how workers learn and relearn, other groupings will engage in a similar process. Many people who are not workers are oppressed because of their nationality, sexual orientation or because they are migrants in a world hemmed in by nation states. Many shopkeepers or professionals, such as lawyers, auctioneers or doctors whose incomes are supplemented by 'savings', may be crushed in an economic crisis. Most crucially, in underdeveloped countries millions of peasants are squeezed between the demand for cash crops for the world economy and a type of globalisation that pits the poor against the poorest in a desperate bid to sustain an independent livelihood. A workers' uprising can only be successful when these layers of society are drawn to their movement. In *Class Struggles in France*, Marx argued that workers could:

> not move a step forward' or cause the 'slightest disruption in the bourgeois order' until they had 'aroused the mass of the nation, the peasants and petty bourgeois...against the rule of capital' and forced them to join forces with them.[35]

Echoing these comments, Lenin argued that the ideal socialist could not act as a 'trade union branch secretary' but as a 'tribune of the people' capable of giving a left voice to the accumulated grievances in society.[36]

Marx's view of revolution led him to reject all attempted *putsches*. He denounced those who imagined that a revolution was a technical feat prepared for by bombs and conspiracies and referred to them as 'alchemists' who lived in a fantasy world. A true revolution, he argued, 'is the exact opposite of the ideas of a *mouchard* [police spy] who, like the "men of action", sees in every revolution the work of a small coterie'.[37] Engels took this argument one step further, challenging the assumptions of Louis Auguste Blanqui's supporters. Engels argued that if

> any revolution may be made by the outbreak of a small revolutionary minority, [it] follows of itself the necessity of a dictatorship after the success of the venture. This is, of course, a dictatorship, not of the entire revolutionary class, the proletariat, but of the small minority that has made the revolution, and who are themselves previously organized under the dictatorship of one or several individuals.[38]

Real revolutions involve the mass of people who create their own organisations of 'dual power' which coordinate their actions and encroach on the power of the state. They move through great ebbs and flows until decisive confrontations are finally reached. At that point, either the lower class breaks through and reorganises society on a new basis or the old power consolidates itself on a more violent basis. While revolutionaries never create a revolution, their interventions in this process through an organised, mass party can have a major impact on the outcome.

10
After the Revolution

Ever since the birth of capitalism, there had been calls to end the class antagonism but until 1871, Engels acknowledged, 'no one knew how this was to be brought about'.[1] Marx and Engels had come to one general conclusion: a change from capitalism required a revolution. They also thought that this abrupt, dramatic upheaval would be followed by a slower set of economic stages required to transform society. In the *Communist Manifesto* they suggested that workers would use their 'political supremacy to wrest, *by degrees*, all capital from the bourgeoisie' (emphasis added).[2] They acknowledged that workers would take measures 'which appear economically insufficient and untenable but which, in the course of movement, outstrip themselves [and] necessitate further inroads upon the old social order'.[3] This gap between the pace of political change and economic change stemmed from their rejection of utopian thinking. The material conditions had not only to be ripe for socialism but its construction had to be undertaken in a practical way. There would be no Day One of the perfect world.

Moreover, Marx and Engels did not think that the old elite would simply accept the stripping of their privileges even after a victorious revolution. There would almost certainly be some form of 'slaveholder rebellion' or at least attempts to engage in economic sabotage. A degree of coercion – this time by the majority over the minority – would be necessary to break that resistance. They therefore saw 'a *class dictatorship* of the proletariat as a necessary intermediate point on the path towards *the abolition of class differences in general*'.[4]

Here confusion arises between how words are used in the nineteenth- and twenty-first-century contexts. Today most people understand the word 'dictatorship' as implying the personal rule of an autocrat. So when Marx uses the phrase 'dictatorship of the proletariat', this is taken to imply one-party rule presided over by a tyrant like Josef Stalin or a more benevolent dictator such as Fidel Castro. However, nowhere in any of Marx and Engels' voluminous writing is there a shred of evidence to support this interpretation.

The original meaning of the term dictatorship stemmed from the Latin word *dictatura,* which meant a temporary, constitutional form of legal power that acted in energetic ways. Marx consistently used the term in this way, so he argues, for example, that the elected National Assembly in Germany in 1848 should 'act dictatorially' to guarantee the victory of democracy over the monarchy – in other words it had to act energetically to consolidate its rule.[5] The term 'dictatorship of the proletariat' simply meant that the workers should take full political power to consolidate their revolution. Hal Draper, who wrote a book on Marx's use of the term, concluded:

> is not problematical if we adopt the only meaning of the term that corresponds to the way Marx actually used it: a 'dictatorship of the proletariat' is a state in which the proletariat exercises dominant political power – a 'workers state' the 'rule of the proletariat'. No more, no less.[6]

Before 1871, Marx still had no idea about what precise political form workers' power would take. Then, on 17 April, he wrote to Louis Kugelmann suggesting that a 'new point of departure of world-wide importance' was underway.[7] He was referring to the Paris Commune which had been proclaimed a few weeks earlier on 28 March. It had an enormous impact on Marx as it demonstrated through practical experience a possible model that could be followed. Twenty years later Engels summarised their mutual feeling:

> Of late, the Social-Democratic philistine has once more been filled with wholesome terror at the words: Dictatorship of the Proletariat. Well and good, gentlemen, do you want to know what this dictatorship looks like? Look at the Paris Commune. That was the Dictatorship of the Proletariat.[8]

The Paris Commune arose out of the defeat of Louis Bonaparte's Second Empire during the Franco-Prussian war and his capture at Sedan in 1870. Prussia demanded large indemnities and stationed its troops around Paris to ensure they were paid. The newly formed provisional Government of National Defence were anxious to settle matters quickly and so wanted to disarm Paris. The prime minister, Louis-Adolphe Thiers, ordered the handover of artillery belonging to the National Guard, which had been paid for by public subscription, but this symbolic act enraged the population who mobilised to prevent it. A spontaneous revolution followed, but one that grew out of a deep, structural crisis which followed the demise of Bonapartism.

The Paris Commune lasted just two months, but this brief revolt was accompanied by a number of remarkable measures which Marx celebrated in *The Civil War in France*. Foreigners were elected to office because it was declared that 'the flag of the Commune is the flag of the World Republic'.[9] Full separation of Church and State was decreed and, as Marx put it, 'the priests were sent back to the recesses of private life, to feed upon the alms of the faithful in imitation of their predecessors, the apostles'.[10] All debt obligations for three years were postponed and the interest written off. Pawnshops were closed because they acted as parasites on working-class poverty. Workplaces, which had been shut by employers, were to be reopened as cooperatives after plans were drawn up by their former employees. Night work and the hated workers' registration cards were abolished. The great symbol of French chauvinism, the Victory Column on the Place Vendôme, which had been cast from guns captured by Napoleon after the war of 1809, was demolished.

However while these were remarkable decrees, Marx was more interested in the specific forms through which workers might exercise political power. *The Civil War in France* was written to generalise this experience beyond the specificity nineteenth-century Paris. We may, therefore, legitimately use this book to outline political forms of a post-revolutionary state in the twenty-first century. This will mean adding to and adapting some of the features Marx considered to be significant.

CONTROL OVER ELECTED REPRESENTATIVES AND PAYMENT OF AVERAGE WAGE

The Commune introduced two key measures to deal with an issue that has confounded working-class politics ever since: how to keep control over elected representatives. It decreed, first, that electors would gain a right of recall over their representatives. The representatives would be bound by formal instructions, and should they at any point defy their mandates, they could be recalled and replaced with another. Second, elected representatives were to be paid the average worker's wage. The excuse that high wages were necessary to get the 'best and brightest' was abolished and replaced with a non-hierarchical principle that guarded against the corruption of office. With a touch of irony, Marx drew a comparison with how businesses organised their affairs:

> Instead of deciding once in three or six years which member of the ruling class was to misrepresent the people in Parliament, universal suffrage was to serve the people constituted in Communes, as individual suffrage serves every other employer in search of workmen and managers in his business. And it is well known that companies, like individuals, in matters of real business know how to put the right man in the right place, and, if they for once make a mistake, to redress it promptly.[11]

These two principles are even more relevant today as there has been a decline in popular sovereignty in Western democracies. Colin Crouch has characterised the current era as a 'post-democracy' where 'politics and government are increasingly slipping back into the control of privileged elites in the manner characteristic of pre-democratic times'.[12] There is a crisis of representation because political parties periodically deceive the electorate and do not fulfil their promises. Western democracy is increasingly seen as a 'managed democracy' where the formalities of elections are maintained but where the electorate has little input into decision-making.[13] There were popular demonstrations involving hundreds of thousands of people in countries all over the world against George Bush's war on Iraq, but political elites continued to support that war, either overtly or covertly. There is a consensus on core politics between parties and so 'party–voter distances have been stretched, while party–party differences have lessened'.[14]

The two democratic principles of the right to recall and payment of the average wage could help to break this trend but, given the scale of the problem, they would have to be accompanied by other measures. To establish real democracy there would have to be an outright ban, backed by prison sentences for those who transgress, on all attempts to influence political decisions through the use of money. At present corporate lobbying has become an insidious way of undermining popular decision-making. In the 1980s, American financial corporations, for example, spent an estimated €5.1 billion lobbying for the removal of the Glass–Steagall Act.[15] This Act restricted the speculative activity of banks and its removal helped to generate the casino economy which came crashing down in 2008. In a socialist society, all funding of political parties from private sources would cease as these turn elections into a contest over who has the biggest 'war chest' to produce glossy propaganda. Yet even these measures cannot rectify the problem unless an even greater issue is tackled: the unelected arm of the state.

ELECTION OF STATE OFFICIALS AND DE-BUREAUCRATISATION

Marx argued that state officials should be elected and subject to recall. He also attacked the 'sham independence of judges',[16] which masked subservience to political masters and suggested that 'like the rest of public servants, magistrates were to be elective, responsible and revocable'.[17] The proposals were designed to deal with a deep contradiction which lies at the heart of Western democracy. Representative democracy – even with the limitations described above – is confined to a small space within the state apparatus. The parliament is surrounded by a huge administrative state which, as even the liberal academic Norberto Bobbio acknowledged, 'obeys a completely different logic of power, that descends from above rather than ascends from below, that is secret rather than public, based on hierarchy rather than autonomy'.[18] This overwhelms the small spaces of representative democracy which become increasingly 'fictitious as centres of power'.[19] The parliament functions as a stage where the citizen-consumer watches a political drama and debate but real, concrete power is exercised through the administrative apparatus that surrounds government ministers. Increasingly, the unelected, permanent political elite are plugged into international networks which shape their decision-making and make them even more remote from those they purport to serve.

Control of the unelected state is often in the hands of the sons and daughters of the wealthy – or at least, those who have been moulded to serve them. In France, this is virtually institutionalised through the appointment of the *enarques* (those who have attended the elite Ecole Nationale D'Administration) to key positions. Elsewhere, selection is based on access to postgraduate education, attendance at elite institutions or involvement in political networks. Even where recruitment is not directly drawn from the wealthy, top state officials are recruited on the basis of their proven loyalty to serving their needs.

Marx's argument for the democratisation of public administration, therefore, makes even more sense today. Top officials who are responsible for coordinating key agencies of public administration, such as education or transport, should be elected. Provision should certainly be made for transparency about candidate qualification but these should by no means be confined to formal educational credentials and the rule about the average wage would also apply. Instead of CEO-type figures who have absorbed the ethos of business decision-making, a socialist administration would recruit people who are imbued with a public spirit; are willing to engage in self-sacrifice through attending hosts of meetings; and are motivated by a desire to encourage participation from those they work with.

Even these more radical proposals, however, are quite limited for modern society because the bureaucratic apparatus has grown enormously since the days of the Paris Commune. Today the lives of most people are dominated by their interaction with two deeply hierarchical spaces – the public sector and large corporations. Simply electing people to the top of each of these areas will not break the bureaucratic culture.

The de-bureaucratisation of public administration can only be achieved by unleashing the creative energies of those who work there because a bureaucratic hierarchy functions through control of knowledge, inducing passivity and cynicism in those below. A post-revolutionary state would reverse this relationship. Workers in public administration would enjoy forms of self-management in order to meet the targets and goals set by society at large. Instead of bureaucratic routinism, a premium would be placed on discussion and ideas within agencies and democratic engagement with elected councils of users. Like all other workers, public administration workers would enjoy the right to have regular workplace meetings which would decide how to carry out their functions. The decisions of coordinators or managers, who were elected at such meetings, would be made transparent and answerable to the wider assembly. The cult of secrecy, which is now overladen with formal written codes and informal secretive verbal codes, would be abolished.

Marx's proposal for the election of judges requires particular attention as it challenges the very foundations of liberalism. Marx's primary target is 'the sham independence' that disguises a distinct class bias. Judges in modern capitalist societies are typically appointed by government parties and are drawn from the upper social class. They implement a law that places overwhelming emphasis on protecting the rights of property and this gives the rich an additional channel through which to promote their interests beyond their influence in the state bureaucracy. Conversely, the justice system is typically mobilised against workers who take industrial action through the use of injunctions. A post-revolutionary state would have to reverse this pattern by recruiting judges from a working-class background and requiring them to implement a corpus of law that reflects the interests of this class. As a reflection of that different class basis, they would be elected and recallable.

It does not follow from this, however, that populist 'hanging judges' would rule the roost. For one thing, the culture of a post-revolutionary state would not be shaped by the same 'politics of fear' whipped up by the present-day corporate media. A more equal society would also remove the main reason for imprisonment in modern society – transgression against private property. Individual conflicts of interest would certainly persist and some will require adjudication, but there is no reason why judges would not be required to exercise genuine independence on these matters. The right to elect judges and recall them should, therefore, not be equated with a popular vote on individual judgments. It is rather a mechanism to ensure that, over a longer time frame, justice is linked to the greater democratisation of social life.

ABOLITION OF SPECIAL FORCES OF REPRESSION AND THE CREATION OF DEMOCRATISED, COLLECTIVE AGENCIES OF FORCE

Marx acknowledged that a post-revolutionary state could not immediately enter a realm of human freedom and that force would continue to play a role in society. The key issue, however, was the relative mix of force and freedom and who the threat of force was primarily directed at. Marx noted that the first decree of the Paris Commune was the suppression of the standing army and that the police was 'stripped of its political attributes and turned into a responsible and at all times revocable agent of the Commune'.[20]

These measures are even more relevant today because, in a capitalist society, the threat of force is primarily directed at the poor and the working class. One of the first police forces was formed in Ireland to help seize tithes from a Catholic population for the Anglican clergy. Later, in 1829, the Metropolitan Police Act was passed to create a uniformed police force in London to deal with working-class riots and the intrusion of the 'blue locusts' into local communities was often met with fierce resistance.[21] The benign image of the local bobby, who provides a 'service' rather than being part of a 'force', was consciously constructed over a long period to help disarm opposition.[22] However, behind the image, the police are still shaped by the class society they serve.

Invariably, they are separated from local communities and develop a defensive solidarity within their ranks to protect themselves. Most police action takes place beyond public scrutiny and some 'forced community isolation' is deemed necessary for police officers.[23] This gives rise to a feeling that they are in conflict with those they are supposed to serve and that they need to 'coerce respect from the public'.[24] In addition, the sheer boredom of most police work leads to a search for 'interest, excitement or sensation' in their encounters with the wider population.[25] This often leads to the harassment of local youth or ethnic minorities who, according to the folk sociology prevalent in police ranks, are deemed to be prone to criminality. These features of police life lead to a distinct 'cop culture' characterised by high levels of sexism, racism and disproportionate support for right-wing politics.[26] Additionally, the law is constructed as a resource which gives the police huge discretion in its implementation. As Dorren McBarnet points out, police discretion provides ample room to get guilty verdicts in lower courts while more open outcomes are possible in higher courts where elites plead their cases.[27] The result is a two-tier system of justice, with the mechanisms of social control being used to create a burgeoning prison population.

As well as these routine features of police life, there are specialised units whose sole purpose is to break political opposition to the system. The political police in Special Branch units spy on left-wing organisations and sometimes infiltrate them to create divisions. The riot squad ('public order units') is deployed to break up large-scale mobilisation and strike fear into demonstrators. Increasingly, large-scale surveillance of the population is undertaken through the use of the US Patriot Act, the EU directive on Data Retention or the so-called ECHELON system, which routinely filters all telecommunication traffic passing through the UK for key words that indicate subversive thoughts.

These patterns, it should be stressed, do not arise primarily from the proclivities of individual police officers but from their structural role in a capitalist society. A post-revolutionary state could break up this structure and remodel the use of force so that it was primarily directed at the 'white-collar crimes' of the privileged. At a minimal level, the specialised units of political police, riot squads and mass surveillance would be abolished. The distinct features of secrecy and 'forced community isolation' of the current police and army would also be changed. There would be no need to isolate soldiers in barracks where drilling is designed to inculcate unquestioned discipline and square-bashing; saluting of officers and bans on political discussion would almost certainly be abolished. Beyond that, the very idea of a standing army or a distinct police force might eventually come under question. Options range from arming the civilian population to greater use of volunteer units for local self-policing. These could be linked by organised networks and by a small core staff at a central level.

CHEAP GOVERNMENT AND A FREE MEDIA

Marx argued that the Commune 'made that catchword of bourgeois, cheap government, a reality'.[28] This was originally a progressive demand which was directed at the luxury spending of the aristocracy. Subsequently, the cry of 'cheap government' has been given a more reactionary twist by neo-liberals who try to focus the frustrations of society on taxes. Yet if by 'cheap government' is meant a reduction of wasteful spending on bureaucracy, then a post-revolutionary society would make that a reality through a host of measures: cutting the salaries of 'dignitaries'; eliminating public relations 'branding'; dispensing with organisational consultants who charge exorbitant hourly fees; ending the practice of bureaucratic monitoring through benchmarking 'outputs'; eliminating vast levels of paperwork; and most of all, by a reduction in managerialism.

The other catchword, a 'free press', could also be made a reality. Marx wrote in an era when state censorship was the main means of impeding the free expression of ideas but today the central issue is the corporate control of the media. Under capitalism, the greater your wealth, the better your chance to influence the opinions of others. Conversely, the poorer you are, the more your views are marginalised. Rupert Murdoch is able to influence millions because he is worth €9 billion, but thousands of trade unionists do not even get access to the airwaves because they don't have money. So powerful has Murdoch become that one former aide to Tony Blair described him as 'effectively a member of Blair's cabinet'.[29]

A post-revolutionary state would deprive millionaires of the right to own the media and no one would be allowed influence in society by virtue of their wealth. The print media and television networks would be taken into public ownership and thrown open to a variety of independent voices. Instead of a top-down media screaming at a nation of consumers, greater emphasis would be placed on interactive discussion and debate. Access to publicly owned media networks and printing presses could be allocated according to democratic criteria. Each group or creative network could apply to take on media production for a period and would adhere to criteria which open it out to the different views in society.

BEYOND PARLIAMENTARIANISM – DEMOCRACY IN EVERYDAY LIFE

Marx noted that 'the commune was to be a working body, not a parliamentary body, executive and legislative at the same time'.[30] The aim he suggested was 'self-government by the producers'.[31]

Universal suffrage was only forced on the ruling elite through workers' struggles. In Belgium, for example, workers staged two general strikes in 1893 and 1902, while in Britain the Chartists and the Reform Movement fought for the right to vote. Socialists have, therefore, been to the fore in advancing democratic rights under capitalism and in defending those rights against dictatorship and fascism. This, however, does not imply that parliament remains a suitable vehicle for the radical form of democracy implied in a workers' state.

First, parliamentary democracy is based on the separation of economic and political decision-making. Formally, parliament passes laws to govern a country and enacts only 'accessory laws'[32] to regulate the conditions under which production takes places, such as on health and safety. But this leaves the economy in private hands. The organisation of production and services affects our lives in countless ways, yet these are relegated to an economic sphere controlled by unelected large corporations. This separation between political and economic decision-making is now untenable because, without economic democracy, the formal power of a parliament to govern a country is diminished. A workers' state, therefore, requires an extension of democracy into all aspects of the economy.

Second, parliamentary democracy is based on the separation between a tiny number of active decision-makers and a passive, 'apathetic' mass. The early theorists of democracy foretold an active citizenry who scrutinised decision-making and made informed choices via their represesentatives. Modern capitalism, however, discourages any such involvement and promotes a suspicion of 'activists' who break the norms of social peace. The 'apathy' that characterises most Western societies is not a natural condition that arises from disinterest but is induced by the structures of a society which daily demonstrate to people that they cannot exercise control over their lives. 'Apathy' is a rational – if somewhat weak – response to this state of affairs and is a form of withdrawal from political structures that offer no hope. Parliamentarians are supposed to compensate for this apathy by developing a special expertise on law-making but even this turns out to be a fiction. Most parliamentarians transform themselves into engineers of public opinion, seeking, through sound-bites and press circuits, to create a political personality that garners electoral support. Actual policy-making is increasingly organised in specialised think-tanks and policy research staffs and is undertaken by a smaller number of parliamentarians who take on the role of policy-makers. If workers are to take genuine control of their society, they need to break the dichotomy of active decision-maker/passive consumer.

Third, the electorate in a parliamentary democracy is organised in discrete geographical constituencies that have no real social connections. Originally, the burghers of a free medieval town were elected from geographical areas which reflected organic social organisation. Even the Paris Commune was based on municipal councillors from geographical wards but this reflected more real social networks between people at the time. In modern society, however, social organisation does not map easily with the geographical electoral constituencies because it typically unites people with opposing class interests. The typical electoral constituency encompasses salubrious upper-class neighbourhoods as well as poor, densely populated housing estates and the elected deputy is supposed to represent the interests of both. The lack of social cohesion means that electors gain little leverage over their representative as they cannot come together to discuss issues beyond those that affect their direct local area. A more radical form of democracy, therefore, implies going beyond geographical constituencies.

Fourth, parliaments are not responsive to the changing moods and opinions of society. Typically, they are elected for a four- or five-year term and even when the government loses support they cannot be removed until their term ends. Deputies are also supposed to enjoy autonomy from popular pressure and to make up their own minds. In reality, they belong to top-down parties whose leaderships are committed to common core policies for running the state. These party machines function in a deeply hierarchical manner, with the party leader personally choosing ministers for governmental office. No public minutes are produced of cabinet decisions and a party whip ensures that the majority of deputies are used as voting fodder for the political elite. If workers are to control society, they will need institutions which reflect bottom-up debates that occur in real time.

Marx never worked out a political alternative that went beyond parliamentarianism and confined himself to the general principle that it should be a 'working body' that had both legislative and executive functions.[33] In other words, it should not only decide laws but organise how they were implemented. This implied a reliance on the creative energies of many thousands of workers rather than a bureaucracy. But when Marx was writing *The Civil War in France*, workers were organised into small workshops that averaged between 20 and 30 employees. The short-lived nature of the Commune and the weakness of working-class organisation meant that a developed institutional alternative did not emerge. The later experience of the workers' movement in revolt, however, filled this missing gap.

Workers' councils have typically been formed during the highest level of struggles against capitalism and they also provide a model for how a new society can be organised. They arise in the course of general strikes, occupations or mass resistance and have their roots in forms of direct democracy where workers come together in mass meetings to elect delegates who are accountable to those meetings and are recallable. They have arisen in a number countries at different times and have taken various organisational forms. In Russia, in 1905 and 1917, they were known as soviets; in Budapest in 1956, they were grouped around the Central Workers' Council; in Chile in 1973, they were known as *cordones*; in Iran in 1979, workers formed *shoras*.

Workers' councils only arise spontaneously from the needs of struggle and cannot be conjured into existence by a party or a group of intellectuals. They are not dependent on a pre-existing socialist consciousness but sometimes expand dramatically from the smallest of economic struggles. In 1905 in Russia, for example, they started with a typographers' strike over punctuation marks and, as Trotsky put it, 'ended by felling absolutism'.[34] They reflect a shared experience of workers in the labour process and tend to arrive at collective decisions in quick and sometimes unanimous ways that reflect the needs of struggle. During the Hungarian uprising in 1956, one delegate, Ferenc Toke, observed that during a key meeting, 'it was noticeable, that everybody, although they came from different factories, wanted exactly the same thing as if they agreed their view in advance'.[35] As organs of direct democracy, workers' councils unite the working class in direct struggle.

Such organisations can also form the political structure of a post-revolutionary society. Instead of geographical constituencies, workplaces, made up of both blue- and white-collar workers, form a natural forum for collective discussion because they are able to convene meetings, pass resolutions and send direct mandates to delegates who go on to higher bodies. If they were linked with councils for non-worker delegates such as pensioners, peasants, students and unwaged parents, they could form the core element of a new democracy. By establishing a space for collective discussion, they could send directly mandated representatives to councils which govern society. These councils, in turn, could more easily reflect the changing opinions of workers directly. They would also naturally overcome the division between economic and political decision-making and extend democracy into all aspects of daily lives. Crucially, they would involve the mass of people in self-government by allowing them to take real decisions that lead to greater control over their lives and so reduce the structural basis of apathy.

The standard argument against direct democracy raised by political theorists such as Robert Michels is that while it worked in Ancient Greece, it could not possibly function in a modern urban society. Unlike the Athenian *polis*, modern city dwellers cannot assemble because they would not all fit into even the largest football stadium.[36] But there is no need to. If a delegate structure is rooted in an electorate with significant economic and political power, representatives can be made subject to popular mandates. Delegates representing hundreds or thousands of workers could be mandated from offices and factories. Smaller workplaces could combine to gain their quota of delegates. If each delegate had to periodically report back and was subject to recall, then direct democracy could be fused with genuine representation. Such structures allow for mass involvement in decision-making and create the foundation which combines legislative and executive decision making.

There is no dewy-eyed sentimentality in Marx's writings on the Paris Commune. The workers, he wrote, did not expect miracles and had 'no ready-made utopias' or 'ideals to realize'.[37] Their embryonic workers' state was only 'a lever for uprooting the economic foundations upon which rests the existence of classes and, therefore, of class rule'.[38] The only way this could occur was 'to set free elements of the new society with which the old collapsing bourgeois society is pregnant'.[39] It is to those elements we must now turn to see how the economic foundations of a new society can be laid.

11
The Economics of Socialism

In April 2010 the giant BP oil company was under pressure because it was paying $500,000 a day for a drilling a rig that replaced one damaged in a hurricane. A decision was made to cut costs and use a cheaper and riskier method of casing the steel tubes in the well. One engineer described the operation as 'a nightmare' but another BP official, Brett Cocales, wrote in an email: 'But, who cares, it's done, end of story, will probably be fine and we'll get a good cement job ... [it] is right on the risk/reward equation'.[1] Four days later the well exploded, killing eleven workers and sending oil gushing into the Gulf of Mexico to cause the US's greatest environmental disaster ever. The Deepwater Horizon spill was an accident waiting to happen. But who, exactly, owns BP and who makes the decisions in it?

Across the world 80,000 people cooperate in the activities that go under the label BP. The owners of the corporation, however, do not engage in any of this work but are predominantly financiers. The biggest chunk of BP is owned by JP Morgan and a hedge fund, Blackrock, Inc. Other owners include the Kuwaiti Investment Authority, which is run by the Al Sabah royal family; Axa; Bank of New York Mellon Corporation; and other hedge funds such as State Street, Legal and General and the Capital Group. These are shadowy names that hide the faces of rich people who appoint a board of directors to run the corporation. BP has just six executive directors who are all male and white. They were led by their CEO, Tony Hayward, who was paid a salary of $4.7 million in 2009.

PUBLIC OWNERSHIP

All major corporations are run in a similar manner and one of the first steps in socialism will be to take control of them. Instead of allowing the collective work of 80,000 people to be directed by a few private individuals, they will be taken into public ownership. This process would start immediately after a revolution and 'common ownership by the nation of all the means of production' would then gradually expand.[2] Corporations that control manufacturing production or are large service providers would be nationalised. So too would the banking industry, the major supermarket chains and all corporations that have seized hold of natural resources. Of particular importance would be the retaking of public utilities privatised during the last three decades of neoliberalism. These include the railways, electricity generation, water, bus services, waste collection and all hospitals, schools and universities. Such nationalisation would in all likelihood take place without compensation to the original owners. As corporations are brought into public ownership, their functions would be integrated and competition between them eliminated.

The justification for this dramatic action can easily be advanced. Productive activity requires the cooperation of large numbers of workers yet their social energy is robbed by a tiny minority who do not work. This contradiction between 'socialised production and capitalist appropriation'[3] is no longer appropriate because it gives a corporate elite too much power. They will use their huge concentration of wealth to bend society to their will. One oil industry lobbyist, Harold Scroggins, put this rather succinctly: 'We came to a decision some time ago that the only way we could change the political fortunes of the petroleum industry was to change Congress.'[4] Eventually, concentrated economic power must lead to a reduction of even the minimal democratic spaces that exist within capitalism. As a result, citizens are reduced to consumers whose political choices are manipulated by large conglomerates.

The standard economic arguments raised against public ownership have become particularly weak in the wake of the banking collapse and the BP scandal. It is claimed, for example, that public ownership must be inefficient because it would be guided by rent-seeking political forces and would not be subject to competition (rent-seeking is a jargon term which means seeking to benefit oneself). Typically, these arguments contrast an idealised market model with bureaucratic state ownership but this has become an artificial dichotomy. Actually existing capitalism is no longer based on small firms that are price-takers in a 'free' market. Many corporations have become monopolies or oligopolies and fix prices, entrap customers or use the asymmetry of information to sell less than perfect products.

The claim that public enterprises would be run by rent-seekers who have no interest in efficiency does not apply to Marx's model because he was not advocating nationalisation *within* capitalism but rather public ownership *to break* it. Present-day state companies are often inefficient both because of their bureaucratic culture and because they are under pressure to subsidise private industry. An EU directive, for example, states that all public–private partnerships must ensure that there are 'important safeguards for private investors, in particular the stability of long term cash-flows from public finances'.[5] Marx's argument for nationalisation makes the opposite assumption: that the current political elite who run the state and who are tied to private capital will be broken up. Public ownership would then become ownership by the people at large, exercised through elected delegates who are directly answerable to their electorate. The funding and track record of public entities would be made far more transparent to the wider population than they are today. As patronage and inflated salaries are removed, it is difficult to see why individual rent-seeking might occur.

Although mistakes can never be ruled out in any system, Marx's advocacy of public ownership would lead to increased efficiency in a host of ways.

Common ownership of the means of production would do away with branding and duplication. Branding is a strategy to get consumers, who have become oversaturated with advertising, to buy goods by attempting to create a feeling of emotional transcendence associated with particular products. Scott Bedbury, Starbucks' vice president of marketing, explained the strategy: 'consumers don't truly believe there's a huge difference between products' and that is why the brand must 'establish emotional ties' with their customers, such as through 'the Starbucks Experience'.[6] This leads to an absurd waste of resources and human creativity as vast numbers of people are hired to create imagery for such fleeting sensations. Global advertising reached $613 billion in 2008 and an increasing percentage of it is directed at children.[7] While information would be freely available on products and services, socialism would do away with 'the art of arresting the human intelligence just long enough to get money from it'.[8] More generally, common ownership would reduce unnecessary duplication as it would no longer be necessary to have rival systems of production because integration would allow for a better division of labour and more efficiency. Instead of producing rival washing machines, for example, factories could share information of the best product and organise their facilities to produce a few versions.

Public ownership would also lead to a higher quality of product and service. In capitalist society, there is an economic incentive to reduce the lifecycle of goods because markets cannot expand if computers, MP3 players or televisions are onetime purchases. One academic study even noted that 'Several economists have argued that product longevity may be socially disadvantageous'.[9] The industrial designer Brook Stevens put it this way:

> We make good products, we induce people to buy them, and then next year we deliberately introduce something else that will make those products old fashioned, out of date, obsolete ... It isn't organised waste. It's a sound contribution to the American economy.[10]

Corporations employ a tactic of 'contrived durability' by using technologies that artificially shorten the lifecycle of their products. The batteries of Apple iPods, for example, are hard to remove, forcing customers to make an expensive service call or buy a new product, while cars are built to last a decade or less. Another strategy is 'planned obsolescence' whereby corporations introduce newer variations of the same product and prevent customers upgrading. New software is regularly produced which is deliberately made incompatible with older versions. Textbooks are continually changed instead of selling 'add-ons' to older versions. These strategies make a mockery of rhetoric about 'sustainability' as they add to waste mountains. Public ownership would, therefore, be more efficient because there would be no need to create products that do not last. Instead, there would be cooperation to make the best products with available technology and later improvements would be made compatible with the old.

Public ownership would also eliminate the problem of externalities. An externality is defined as a cost that is offloaded onto others who do not take part in a market transaction. The owners of factory farms, for example, purchase large quantities of antibiotics to reduce disease in their cattle, but the real cost of these transactions is borne by consumers whose immune system is reduced by the overuse of antibiotics in the food chain. When these consumers need more hospital care, society picks up the tab rather than the drug producers or the farmers. Similarly, the real cost of the car is not set by market prices because its externalities are offloaded onto society. The cost of healing people who are injured in car crashes or who suffer from asthma from exhaust fumes; the waste of time brought about by traffic jams; the effects of air pollution – all of these are borne by society rather than by the car manufacturer. To a greater or lesser extent, every capitalist firm will try to offload some of the costs of production onto society. As Robert Monks explained:

> The corporation is an externalizing machine in the same way that the shark is a killing machine. Each one is designed in a very efficient way, to accomplish particular objectives ... There isn't any question of malevolence.[11]

But when there is common ownership, there is no need to hide the real costs. Instead, all costs would be accounted for and a real effort would be made to minimise the effects on the physical and social environment.

The extra efficiency that comes about, however, does not mean that common ownership of every unit of the economy is necessary. There is no reason why small enterprises such as bicycle shops, internet cafés or restaurants need to be taken into public ownership. Nor is it likely that Marx's original advocacy of land nationalisation could take effect – at least for some time.[12] Marx assumed that capitalist agriculture would eliminate or reduce private smallholdings and that a large class of agricultural labourers would emerge in the countryside, as distinct from peasant proprietors. However, these assumptions proved wrong and, for a variety of reasons, small farm-holdings have persisted. As socialism assumes the consent of the vast majority of society, nationalisation of small businesses and farm-holdings is unlikely.

In fact, the reverse might occur for a while because, as Cliff has pointed out, the private farm might gain a new lease of life under the socialist regime.[13] Farmers would not face high mortgage rates from banks; they would enjoy access to the publicly owned trading networks that replaced supermarket chains; they would be guaranteed a demand for their products rather than being subject to the fluctuations of a global market; and they would gain free access to all scientific advances in agriculture. Small shopkeepers would gain similar advantages from a socialist society that had broken the power of large retail chains and reduced taxes through genuine cheap government.

Nationalisation, therefore, only applies to large corporations in each economic sector and only in the longer term would public ownership spread outwards from there by consent. The great advantage the new mode of production offers is the possibility of more freedom because of its higher level of productivity. If the socialist sector of the economy could reduce the working week to, say, 30 hours, this becomes an enormous attraction for those involved in petty capitalism. A shopkeeper or farmer works extremely long hours and often deprives the family of holidays which explains why often their children flee to take on paid employment. Those who hold on do so in the belief that it guarantees some security and a slightly better living standard than that held by workers. If this same security and rising living standards were available elsewhere, a new impetus would be created for forms of cooperative ownership in these sectors.

WORKERS' SELF-MANAGEMENT

The pre-eminent American political scientist Robert Dahl once pointed to an illuminating issue:

> *If* democracy is justified in governing the state then it must *also* be justified in governing economic enterprises; and to say it is *not* justified in governing economic enterprises is to imply that it is not justified in governing the state.[14]

Dahl was no radical but it was a damning indictment of the contradictions in democracy under capitalism. Officially, the people can decide on the future of their country through a democratic process but when they go to work they cannot have the slightest say. They are subject to the tyranny of the boss.

One justification for tyranny is that work must be organised along the lines of an army. Managers and supervisors act as the generals and non-commissioned officers to impose discipline and get the work done. The implication is that efficiency comes from a division between mental and manual labour. Some are paid to think, plan and conceptualise, and others are reduced to 'detail' workers who work on a small part of the work process. Yet this apparently natural law of efficiency did not apply to societies before capitalism. Peasants, for example, had to both think and plan their work – and then physically carry it out. There was a social division of labour as work was divided between different occupations but carpentry, for example, was not broken down into minute parts to be supervised by someone who was exclusively engaged in planning. The division between mental and manual labour – or, more accurately, the division between a tiny managerial elite who plan and workers who carry out orders – is the dominant feature of capitalism.

Historically, capitalism socialised production by bringing together disparate producers and coordinating their efforts. But it then subordinated their combined work to profit and took control out of the hands of the producers. The knowledge, will and judgement of workers could be used to direct production but instead, as Marx showed:

> The possibility of an intelligent direction of production expands in one direction because it vanished in many others. What is lost by the specialised workers is concentrated in the capital which confronts them. It is a result of the division of labour in manufacture that the worker is brought face to face with the intellectual potentialities of the material process of production, as the property of another and as a power which rules over him.
>
> This process of separation begins in simple co-operation, where the capitalist represents to the individual workers, the unity and the will of the whole body of social labour. It is developed in manufacture, which mutilates the worker, turning him into a fragment of himself. It is completed in large-scale industry, which makes science a potentiality for production which is distinct from labour and presses it into the service of capital.[15]

The word manage comes from the Latin *manus* and originally meant to train a horse in its paces, to cause it to do the exercise of *manege*.[16] Capitalism needed its own science of management because workers and capitalists only enter into contracts because each cannot avoid the other. The capitalist needs workers for profits: the worker needs the capitalist to earn a wage. This contractual relationship does not guarantee a sufficient work effort to create surplus value and a new science of managerial control had to be created to bring this about. At first Taylorism sought to organise the labour process so that all planning lay in the hands of management. But corporations also found that workers have vast levels of implicit knowledge about how best to do their jobs and they wanted to tap into this resource. This explains why Taylorism is sometimes combined with, or replaced by, another managerial strategy known as 'mock empowerment'.

Today workers are often promised 'job enrichment' and 'employee involvement' provided they go 'beyond the contract' and give more of their energy to meeting the goals set by management.[17] Management's primary aim is to draw on the latent skills of workers without losing control. Mock empowerment is often linked to work teams that exert coercive control over individual members. Here the social energy of working together is imprisoned within a tight framework that supports management's goals.[18] The result is often the growth of a corporate bureaucracy whose primary purpose is to monitor target outputs and set up internal markets so that work teams are forced to compete against each other.

Against both old-style Taylorism and fake empowerment programmes, Marx advocated the 'self-government of the producers'.[19] He recognised that there were two sorts of productive power: the instruments of production and labour power, but that 'of all the instruments of production, the greatest power is the revolutionary class itself'.[20] In other words, the principal way to raise productivity was to release the creative energies of workers. Instead of a tiny managerial elite planning how work was to be organised, all workers should be involved. Resources that were wasted on a managerial hierarchy could also be done away with. In its place, Marx argued for workers' self-management.

Marx did not draw up a detailed plan but if we follow his method and look at the actual struggles we can get some idea. Workers constantly resist management attempts to subjugate their labour to their designs. Battle-lines are drawn over what Carter Goodrich called the 'frontier of control' where management press for more 'flexibility', while workers seek to maintain some autonomy over the pace of work and allocation of duties.[21] These struggles for what might be termed 'job control' are a feature of trade union life and contain the germ of more serious rebellions.[22] Sometimes in the course of heightened struggles, they escalate to more dramatic forms of 'worker control'. In Argentina between 2001 and 2002, and in Venezuela today, workers found that their employers tried to asset-strip plants to safeguard their own wealth. Struggles erupted to resist them, and by 2003, there were 161 occupied factories in Argentina, while in Chavez's Venezuela a continual battle is under way to extend workers' control in a number of celebrated disputes.[23] Typically, a type of dual power exists in these occupations: a factory is formally owned by a capitalist or has been nationalised by the state, but the workers seek to impose their way of organising production on the authorities. They demand that the accounts books be opened to establish the true financial situation of the firm; they take control over hiring and firing; and, in more developed cases, they take control of the organisation of production itself.

Workers face two major obstacles in their struggle for freedom: the managerial team appointed by capitalists and the power of market forces. Even if the immediate boss is thrown out, the pressure to restore a hierarchy to dovetail production with the 'needs of the market' remains. Workers' self-management, therefore, can only expand alongside the battle to subordinate the wider economy to the needs of the people. But how might it work internally?

Each workplace would have a regular assembly, meeting perhaps once a month, and would elect its own executive to organise the day-to-day running of the concern. This executive might be composed of delegates from different sections or elected on an all-workplace basis. It would also draw up a production plan for the wider assembly to consider. Such a plan would take the output targets, which have been assigned to the workplace by the wider society, and consider how to achieve them. Workers would make decisions on how pay is organised and distributed; what investment to make in new technology; how the production process is organised. Once the general plan is agreed, different sections might elect coordinators to ensure that production flows smoothly. These coordinators would not receive a higher wage or have privileges – and there might be a rotation of the position. No matter how good any plan is, it would need adaption and so meetings of work units would take place regularly to create new iterations for their individual areas. At every level, decision-making would be driven by bottom-up democracy rather than a top-down hierarchy.

Workers' self-management would lead to an increase in productivity for a number of reasons. First, it would eliminate the waste associated with a large and overpaid managerial layer. What was formerly known as management accountancy would be reduced to tracking inputs and outputs, rather than instilling competition between workers. Second, workers' self-management would unleash the creative energies of those who are currently relegated, to the 'not paid to think' category. Current workplaces operate on the assumption that a 'senior management team' of, say, twelve people have better insights into running an organisation of, say, 2,000 than the other 1,988. But this could not possibly be so. No matter how much 'brainpower' they claim to possess, there must be some ideas management have overlooked. Third, it would create an incentive for greater effort because people were working for themselves. It would also create a genuine acceptance of changes because these would lead to a shortening of the working week, easier work or extra pay and would not be contributing to profit. Finally, workers' self-management would enormously improve communication. In a top-down model, those at the bottom have every reason to hide information as they have no voice in how it will be used. Workers' self-management abolishes a top and a bottom and so removes that inhibition.

However, such a system also faces problems. One immediate issue is the role of higher paid specialists such as accountants or engineers. While their skills are often distorted by capitalist relations, it is still necessary to use real cost accounting or modify technology. The educational level of many manual workers and the level of specialisation mean that they do not have these skills. So what is to be done?

One solution was described by the American journalist John Reed, when he visited factories after the Russian Revolution of 1917. He listened in on a discussion about specialists:

> Finally there was a committee meeting at one of the factories, where a workman rose and said: 'Comrades, why do we worry? The question of technical experts is not a difficult one. Remember *the* boss wasn't a technical expert; *the boss* didn't know engineering or chemistry or bookkeeping. All he did was to own. When he wanted technical help, he *hired* men to do it for him. Well, now we are the boss. Let's *hire* engineers, bookkeepers, and so forth – to work for us![24]

Hiring such specialists, who are out of sympathy with the idea of workers' self-management, might however involve some practical concessions. The specialists might demand extra pay or easier work arrangements, and given a choice between production ceasing and making these concessions, it might be wiser to take the second course.

In an interesting discussion conducted on this issue at a Latin American Congress of Sociology in 1972 during the workers' upsurge in Allende's Chile, Michel Raptis suggested a longer-term solution.[25] In a society evolving towards socialism permanent education would become a viable possibility. The opening up of education to manual workers would be valuable in itself in terms of developing human capacity, but it would also be a factor vitalising the economy and increasing productivity. A socialist society would, therefore, establish a new division of time: one for direct productive work where all would contribute and a time devoted to educational labour. While access to higher education would be free and would continue through lifelong learning and work sabbaticals, educational credentials would not command higher monetary rewards. So medical education, for example, would be opened up to the children of workers for free but the enormous salaries paid to medical consultants would be abolished. Similarly, more workers could become accountants or engineers but this would not carry a higher monetary reward.

Another problem area for workers' self-management is individual labour discipline. In every workplace, there are those who want a free ride from the efforts of others and it is doubtful that this will disappear immediately after a revolution. Tony Cliff, however, provided an interesting approach to the issue:

> Under capitalism this discipline confronts the worker as an external coercive power, as the power which capital has over him. Under socialism discipline will be the result of consciousness; it will become the habit of a free people. In the transition period it will be the outcome of the unity of the two elements – consciousness and coercion.[26]

A revolution lays the basis for a huge change in culture and personal motivation by promoting the values of solidarity and cooperation. Concerted efforts at national and workplace level could be made to instil those values and leave behind the 'dog-eat-dog' value system of capitalism, and this creates the possibility for discipline to arise from consciousness rather than external necessity. Yet, in the meantime, certain elements of coercion will also apply. At a workplace level, there might be discussion on collective disciplinary codes and agreed sanctions for those who fail to take part in production. In the *Critique of the Gotha Programme*, Marx acknowledged that in the first phase of a transition out of capitalism, the notion of equal rights for equal work would prevail. The individual worker

> gets back from society – after the deduction - what he has given it. What he has given it is his individual quantum of labour ... . Society gives him a certificate stating he has done such and such amount of work (after the labour done for the communal fund has been deducted) and with this certificate he can withdraw from the social supply of means of consumption as much as costs an equivalent amount of labour. The same amount of labour he has given to society in one form, he receives back in another.[27]

This involves both a degree of compulsion, as consumption is tied to work participation, and a degree of inequality that hides behind formal equality. The workers who receive equal rewards for equal work are, of course, not equal individuals because one has more social needs than another. Marx was simply being honest, asserting that real change had to be practical and that hangovers from capitalism should not be masked by flowery rhetoric. He therefore distinguished between a phase of transition and the realm of freedom.

However, this new mix of conscious discipline and some compulsion is a huge step forward from capitalist control. No longer can a worker be sacked for insubordination, 'attitude' or failing to kowtow to supervisors. Instead they now have a real role in shaping their working lives. Dahl's conundrum about official claims for political democracy and the lack of economic democracy has been resolved.

PLANNING

However, even if there is public ownership of large corporations and workers' self-management, the tyranny of 'market forces' would still need to be broken. This God-like anonymous power, which dominates the lives of modern humanity, is a code word for the alienation of our collective labour.

As we have seen, 'market forces' are large units of capital which seek to expand through producing exchange values. The more goods and services that are produced at the cheapest cost, the higher the profits and the governing rule of this economy is the 'law of value'. Commodities will sell if they contain abstract, socially necessary labour that is the equivalent to the average level prevailing in the economy. But this average is only established after production has commenced by a brutal, wasteful process of coordination via the market. In 1998, for example, Shell wrote off €4.5 billion of investment it had made in refineries and chemical plants because oil prices had fallen after it made its original decision. These write-offs only add to further pressure to comply with what Raya Dunayevskaya called the min-max rule – 'minimum costs and maximum production'.[28]

Unless we can be rid of market forces, older forms of top-down control will revive even if there is workers' self-management and public ownership. Someone will re-emerge to enforce the min-max rule and even if that person is called a comrade, a coordinator and a wonderful human, no matter what – the 'old crap' will come back. Market forces persist because they are a way of coordinating the myriad of economic activities and of allocating resources. However, they are also a 'no confidence vote on the social capacities of human species' because[29] that coordination operates behind our backs, through blind laws of an 'invisible hand' over which we have no control. As an alternative, Marx and Engels advocated that 'the social anarchy of production gives way to a social regulation of production upon a definite plan, according to the needs of the community and of each individual'.[30]

But how can this happen? Support for the free market is instilled into every child in the Western world. The free market is supposed to bring choice, democracy and efficiency and is seen as the only way to run a modern economy. It has become the paradigm that frames our understanding of economics. Challenging that paradigm means 'thinking outside the box', but that immediately leaves one open to the charge of being utopian or 'unrealistic'. Nevertheless, if we suspend this contrived scepticism about big alternatives, then planning has a number of advantages over market forces.

First, it creates greater democratic control over investment and allows people collectively to set goals for an economy that reflects human values. Specifically, it allows us to deal with growing threats to the planet itself. In contrast, when investment is driven by the logic of competitive accumulation, it can only lead to destructive effects on humanity.

In 2005 the Millennium Ecosystem Assessment found that 60 per cent of the world's ecosystem services were being degraded or used unsustainably.[31] These included the provision of fresh water, food from fisheries, waste treatment and climate regulation. Global warming is also accelerating and the leading expert, Jim Hanson, has suggested that if humanity wishes to preserve a planet similar to that on which civilisation developed and to which life on earth is adapted, it will have to reduce carbon emissions from its current 385 parts per million to 350 ppm.[32] Yet this is impossible if the key investment decisions are not controlled collectively. Attempts to deal with the issue by market mechanisms have proved an unmitigated disaster.

The EU, for example, introduced a cap and trade system where corporations were allocated a carbon pollution allowance and had to buy extra credits if they went beyond this. The theory was that by turning pollution into a commodity that could be traded, corporations would be forced to adjust their behaviour when the prices rose. Yet the opposite occurred. Over the period 2005–7, emissions *increased* by 1 per cent.[33] EU performance over the first Kyoto commitment period (2008–12) was no different from the

US performance, despite the fact that the US had no emissions trading scheme. The creation of a new carbon market simply led to an explosion in speculation and there are now about 80 carbon investment funds speculating on carbon caps. As one critic, Larry Lohman, put it:

> As a new asset class, carbon has proved a magnet for hedge funds, energy traders, private equity funds, and large global investments banks such as Barclays, Citigroup, Goldman-Sachs, Credit Suisse, BNP Paribas and Merrill Lynch as well as index providers and European exchange traded commodity sponsors.[34]

This simply illustrates that democratic planning rather than the market is required to save the planet. With planning, information on the best technology that could cut carbon emission would be shared. Dependency on fossils fuels would be reduced in a coordinated way and investment in sustainable forms of energy developed. The treadmill system of ever-increasing the throughputs of energy and raw materials to stay ahead of rivals would end.

Second, planning reduces the uncertainty that arises in economic decision-making. Two kinds of uncertainty can be distinguished: one is primary uncertainty arising from unforeseen events such as the eruption of a volcano or a host of unknowable events; the second is market uncertainty which occurs because atomised decision-makers do not know what intermediary suppliers, rivals and people who consume their goods are doing. Planning cannot eliminate the first but it can substantially reduce the second.

Decision-making in the market is like a large prisoner's dilemma. In the classic prisoner's dilemma, suspects are brought to different police stations and offered inducements to confess or face the sanction of a higher sentence if the other gives evidence against them. Because one cannot know how the other will respond, they are more likely to confess rather than risk the higher sentence. Both end up with worse options because they are not able to coordinate their responses. Planning reduces this uncertainty by allowing coordination between different economic units that are affected by each other's decisions.

Third, planning reduces waste that is caused by defensive strategies undertaken by large corporations to override market uncertainty. The 'too big to fail ethos' of giant corporations means they spend an increasing proportion of their revenue on unproductive expenditures designed to protect their market share.

Car companies pay high sums to distribution networks to stock their brand; arms manufacturers pay huge bribes to state officials to buy their lethal products; vast sums flow into derivative markets that were originally designed to 'hedge' against unforeseen market changes. Technology is designed not just for efficiency but as a mechanism to lock in customers. Microsoft products are often of a poor quality but the corporation had the foresight to develop an operating system that makes their use easier than some open source programmes.[35] By reducing market uncertainty, planning also does away with the need for these unproductive expenditures.

The shift from running an economy through blind, atomised forces to using a democratically decided plan can only occur gradually and, for a period, some market mechanisms would survive. Pat Devine has introduced an important distinction between market exchanges and market forces. *Market exchange* involves the exchange of goods and services through pricing mechanisms. *Market forces* refer to changes in patterns of investment, for example, occurring through uncoordinated decisions motivated by self-interest.[36] After a revolution, the latter would decline rapidly but the former would continue for some time as a discipline that coexists with democratic decision-making. This is because a new socialist economy builds on the foundations of the old but changes its priorities in fundamental ways. There could be no question of a complete destruction to 'start from scratch'.

Planning already occurs to a considerable extent in modern capitalism as an increasing level of economic activity takes place inside one giant firm rather than on an open market. The allocation of resources within these corporations and the transfer of goods from one manufacturing unit to another are not based on market principles but are organised through central planning. Elaborate technical forms of planning also develop through global supply chains. Using advances in military logistics, corporations like Dell embed themselves in a global chain of far-flung production networks. Their planned use of complex networks is made possible through new forms of information technology.[37] Giant retail outlets also engage in extensive planning to keep their shelves stocked with the right amount of miscellaneous goods that customers want. This is only possible because they have huge databases that compile information on consumer patterns.

This type of planning is dictated in a top-down manner by boards of directors who have little interest in the welfare of their staff. Moreover, these forms of planning are disrupted by the overall irrationality of the system. No matter how systematic a corporation has been in integrating its productive units, it can descend into chaos because there is a run on its share price. Everything is subordinated to beating rivals and so the purpose of the elaborate planning in a global supply chain is to exert a fierce pressure to cut costs through destructive forms of competition.[38]

Nevertheless, the information generated by these forms of planning and even the stable prices established by market mechanisms provide the technical data to build on for socialist planning. Unlike market economies or the old command economies of the former communist regimes, the goal of socialist planning is to make the economy serve human goals. Its aim is to take control of our alienated, collective labour, and common ownership of the means of production is the sole mechanism to achieve this. It can only work through a profound extension of democracy that combines 'centrally taken decisions where necessary with decentralised decision-making wherever possible'.[39]

At a central level, a post-revolutionary society needs periodically to decide by democratic means a number of key issues that will provide the framework for its economy. The types of decision which can be made democratically by delegates who are elected at national level include:

- *What items can be decommodified and made freely available?* Health, education, water and waste collection might be designated as a free public service funded by taxes on the labour of all. Public transport might also be made freely available or at a greatly subsidised rates to reduce car dependency. But other candidates for decommodification would require considerable debate.

- *What is the balance between the investment and consumption funds?* In current society this is dictated by the level of exploitation and prevailing profit rates. In a socialist society, people need to decide democratically on proportions between investment and consumption. Linked to that they need to debate how much of the social surplus is retained for innovation.

- *What is the length of the working week?* Talk about consumer choice often ignores the implications for the length of the working week. In a post-revolutionary society, people need to decide democratically on the length of the working week as this has implications for their overall economic plan. A shorter working week of, say, 30 hours means fewer consumer goods while one of 40 might mean more.

- *What are the minimum and maximum incomes?* A minimum income is accepted in most capitalist economies but there is no maximum. The average pay of a CEO in the US is now 275 times that of the average pay of a worker.[40] This pay gap is unacceptable and a maximum income, say, four or five times the minimum wage, needs to be established. This implies that in the early phase of socialism income differentials will continue – but at a much reduced rate.

- *What policies should be adopted to reduce pollution, cut carbon emissions and conserve energy?* These are the collective problems that face modern society. In a post-revolutionary society, delegates need to debate strategic options for dealing with these problems and that will involve real choices between alternatives. Such options may be supported by technical data, but ultimately they involve decisions about how best to organise production. Decisions, for example, need to be made about the use of fossil fuels, frequency of car use and levels of investment in renewable energy.

- *How should investment be allocated across sectors and regions?* This will involve considerable debate. While there is a technical dimension because investment decisions have knock-on and cumulative effects, the various models should be made available to elected lay delegates so that they can decide. In a post-revolutionary society, political parties or looser network associations might also form around these types of debates.

Decisions on these broad topics will have to lead to a coherent and integrated plan. One can imagine an assembly of delegates debating the broad parameters and then referring the debate to a planning commission which has greater technical expertise on input–output modelling. The crucial thing, however, is to subordinate technical decision-making to real democratic choice on social objectives. A planning commission would have to be transparent about the implications of different models and would have to engage in repeated discussion with elected delegates. Alternative planning commissions might emerge to present different options and these debates would also be broadcast to a wider population, who could mandate their delegates.

Once the main targets for different sectors have been decided, worker delegates from each industry or service would decide on how investment should be allocated between each production unit. The design and quality of goods and services will also need to be discussed with consumer councils for these areas. So instead of vast sums being spent on advertising products that have already been produced, there could be a real democratic input beforehand. There is no reason, for example, why different designs of clothing or shoes cannot be hosted on websites and indications given on preferences.

Sectoral councils also need to decide on criteria for how investment which is provided from a central authority will be allocated and discuss what happens to units which underperform. Here, some element of market discipline will supplement democratic criteria for a period. If sales figures from one shoe factory are low and market research – which is now shared between all units – indicates that it has to do with poor quality, then a remedy needs to be put in place. But should that fail, decisions need to be made on reduced capacity and a relocation of staff to other areas unless there are overwhelming social reasons why the facility should be maintained.

After these sectoral discussions, the decentring of decision-making needs to continue down to workplace level. Individual workplaces will be allocated output targets, but they need to decide how best to achieve them. The most efficient and democratic way to achieve these is by means of workers' self-management.

This short version of a model of central and decentred planning meets many of the objections raised by writers like Alex Nove. Nove claims that a central authority could not efficiently plan for the complexities of the modern integrated economy.[41] This is a somewhat odd objection because multinational corporations and global supply chain management companies already engage in complex planning for economies that are the size of countries. However, in the above model, there is no need for a central authority to make decisions on millions of items as many decisions are decentred. A related argument from the Austrian school of neoliberal economics suggests that the 'tactic knowledge' and subjective preferences of consumers would not be available to the planners.[42] However, if the basis of socialist planning is a radical extension of democracy, then why would workers and consumers *not* articulate their 'tactic knowledge' and subjective preferences? What possible reason have they for holding back when they know they can make a difference? Nove also claims that socialist planning cannot adequately deal with qualitative aspects of goods or services because these are hard to define.[43] However, existing capitalist corporations employ specialised units of quality control because they assume they know what 'good quality' is. Why, therefore, could sectoral councils and self-managed workplaces not arrive at even better decisions on quality?

There are no perfect utopias and undoubtedly many mistakes will be made when society takes control over the economy. Yet it can be done. Just as spurious arguments were used in the past to suggest that the 'plain people' could not possibly vote on the politics of their country, similar arguments are advanced today to claim that they could not run an economy. This is despite the fact that modern economies are based on the coordination, cooperation and integration of the work efforts of millions around the globe. It is only a dark superstition that assumes that these same people cannot make democratic decisions about their own efforts.

12
Into the Beyond

Is that it, then? Is Marx's conclusion that we simply need public ownership, workers' control and socialist planning just another alternative economic programme?

In one sense Marx was an intrepid 'economic investigator' who 'remained throughout his life a sworn enemy of all imaginary constructions'.[1] He loathed fantastic schemes and studied economics because it gave access to certain laws that could not be magically blown away. Today, for example, all manner of conspiracy theories abound about fiat or paper money. The Federal Reserve is said to be run by the Bilderberg Group, the freemasons or the Trilateral Commission and they supposedly conspire to create illusionary money to trap us into debt. If only there was a return to gold-based currency, this would stop. Unfortunately, weakness breeds these types of fantastic schemes and the more atomised people are, the greater the illusions.

Capitalism, Marx repeatedly argued, was not primarily based on tricks or fraud although they were often used by the rich and powerful. Its brutality arose from the fact that the products of our own labour take on a life of their own and operate according to their own laws. Whether money appears as paper, gold or embossed silver makes little difference; it represents the congealed labour of an alienated humanity. Marx, therefore, studied economics only to discover the contradictions in the system that reduced humanity to 'economic man'. But the mere fact that he focused on this did not mean that human potential was restricted to production, exchange and distribution. It was capitalism, not Marx, who had created 'economic man'.

Liberation from 'economic man' can only be finally achieved through communism. The manner in which the word 'communism' has been sullied through its association with Stalinist tyranny means that it often grates on the modern ear and so it is best to think of it through another term used by Marx: the 'realm of freedom'. The transition between a post-revolutionary society and this realm of freedom is gradual. There is no 'end of history' and a socialist society will go through different phases which open up new possibilities. There is an open acknowledgement that this transitional society is imperfect and does not resemble a utopia. This acknowledgement is in marked contrast to a bourgeois society which hides its contradictions behind an elaborate rhetoric of 'freedom' or 'equality of opportunity'. Workers who run society have no need for such hypocrisy and can look reality in the face because they know they can change it. The possibilities depend on both the level of the productive forces and the quality of democracy, education and cultural attainment.[2]

The level of development of the productive forces is not about building steel plants or dotting the landscape with ever more factories or showing rising figures for GDP. This caricature arose from the way Stalinism mimicked Marxism in words. The more it frog-marched society through a forced industrialisation programme, the more it talked hypocritically about a classless society and claimed advances in production. Genuine development of the productive forces means, first, repairing the huge damage that has been done to the planet and, second, doing so in ways that reduce working time and improve the quality of work. This is an enormous task that will require the creative energy of millions.

To repair the planet we will have to shift from reliance on fossil fuels to wind power, wave power and other forms of sustainable energy. We will have to move to an economy that reduces waste through recycling. We will have to stop the overuse of harmful crop sprays, animal antibiotics and carcinogenic forms of food processing. Even while doing that and more, we will have to develop the new technologies which are guided by different priorities. The more automation of hard physical manual labour the better. The greater the level of autonomous decision-making for the worker even better. And crucially, the fewer hours required to be spent at work the more time there is for other creative aspects of the human personality.

Marx outlined two desirable objectives for work in a socialist society. One is an end to the 'enslaving subjugation of the individual to the division of labour'[3] and, of particular importance, the other is removing the division between mental and manual labour. Supporters of capitalism assume that work will always be a punishment visited on humankind for our sins or because we are naturally lazy. But they have to assume this in order to justify the dehumanisation caused by their own system. As Marx put it, they have no inkling that people need 'a normal portion of work and a suspension of tranquillity' or that 'overcoming obstacles is itself a liberating activity'.[4] In a socialist society, therefore, every effort will be made to link work to human creativity so that it is not only a means to an end but an activity desired in itself.

Second, however, life is not just about work and Marx argued that we need a reduction in the hours worked. If work can be reduced to 25 hours or 20 hours, there is clearly more time for education and wider cultural development. This becomes possible if resources are not wasted on profit, managerialism and competition. The reduction in working hours will allow the achievements in culture to be spread throughout society so that they are no longer the property of a privileged elite. If there was a rational organisation of society, Engels argued, that could give

> each individual sufficient leisure so that what is really worth preserving in historically inherited culture – science, art, forms of intercourse – may not only be preserved but converted from a monopoly of the ruling class into the common property of the whole of society, and may be further developed.[5]

The other requirement for moving from a realm of necessity to a realm of freedom is that productivity increases to such a degree that 'all the springs of co-operative wealth flow more abundantly'[6] and there is more than enough to be spread around. In other words, productivity outpaces human need. This is a more complex concept because the great dialectic of human history is that human needs expand alongside the ability to meet them. Marx explained:

> Just as savage man must wrestle with nature to satisfy his needs, to maintain and reproduce his life, so must civilised man, and he must do so in all forms of society and under all possible modes of production. This realm of natural necessity expands with his development, because his needs do too; but the productive forces to satisfy these expand at the same time.
>
> Freedom, in this sphere, can consist only in this, that socialised man, the associated producers, govern the human metabolism with nature in a rational way; bring it under their collective control instead of being dominated by it as a blind power; accomplishing it with least expenditure of energy and in conditions most worthy and appropriate for their human nature.[7]

The key point here is that the 'associated producers' govern this relationship in a rational way. When Marx suggests that it is possible that the productive forces can increase fast enough to outstrip expanding human needs, he is not referring to imaginary needs where we fantasise about the most idyllic kitchen designs or high-performance cars. He means reasonable needs that grow with the development of society, but do so within certain cultural limits. One might argue, for example, that access to the internet and new forms of communication are a reasonable need in the twenty-first century when once they were fantasies. Within this complex of socially shaped needs, there are primary needs for food, clothing, shelter, heating and light and these must be met before more culturally determined needs. The greatest indictment of capitalism is that it does not provide for these needs for about one third of humanity even though we produce enough food and energy to do so. If socialism achieved nothing more than feeding the world's hungry, that alone would justify revolution.

It should go further, however, and eventually aim to provide food, lighting, clothing, heat and shelter as free goods. If that happened, then the possibilities for human development dramatically increase. The very idea of free food or lighting is a scandal to minds trained to think in terms of profit. 'How could it be done? Would everyone not just help themselves?' is the cry to the wild-eyed dreamer. But global food supply already exceeds per capita caloric needs by 20 per cent yet food riots occur because it is not distributed to the hungry.[8] There is currently so much waste food that in a different society nutritious food could be provided for free – or certainly very cheaply – in communal restaurants. That in itself would also help eliminate waste that arises with individual household consumption and give people a choice of eating at home or eating out. The fact that food is available for free does not necessarily mean that people will gorge themselves. After all in those countries where water is free people do not spend their time at the taps drinking for fear it will be their last drop. The problem of obesity has much more complex causes than mere availability and has more to do with pushing food for profit – via advertising or constant display, for example – and cultures of boredom and sedentary living.

If society could eventually both reduce the working week and still meet reasonable needs, then the realm of freedom could begin. Realistically, this could not happen until generations have passed after the overthrow of capitalism and it is difficult even to imagine it for those living in the present age. Marx, therefore, did not dwell on it in any detail because he disliked utopian thinking and wished to focus on the overthrow of the current order. Nevertheless, his scattered remarks indicate the deeply humanist vision behind Marx's politics and economics.

Freedom for Marx meant much more than the abstract concept of 'individual liberty'. Historically, society moved from relations of personal dependence where the majority were reliant on masters or lords to personal independence in the capitalist era. But while this era of individual liberty was progressive, it came at the cost of an even greater external control. Marx summarised the issue as follows:

> In the imagination individuals seem freer under the domination of the bourgeoisie than before, because their conditions of life seem accidental; in reality, of course, they are less free, because they are subject to the violence of things.[9]

The realm of freedom means overcoming the artificial divide between the individual and society which capitalist society fomented. Instead of just being free in our personal lives, we should strive for freedom in both our personal and public lives. The ideal, therefore, is the *social individual*, whose individuality flourishes because he or she participates in a free society. This individuality grows because a free society would enhance the human imagination by providing far more stimulation and creativity than the current order. This also means a far greater diversity between individual people than currently exists.

Freedom also meant the withering away of the state and the nation. A state was necessary in a transitional period, but as the networks of the former capitalist class are finally broken up and they rejoin society as individuals, there is no need for a state. Engels put it like this:

> As soon as there is no longer any social class to be held in subjection; as soon as class rule, and the individual struggle for existence based upon our present anarchy in production, with the collisions and excesses arising from these, are removed, nothing more remains to be repressed, and a special repressive force, a state, is no longer necessary. The first act by virtue of which the state really constitutes itself the representative of the whole of society – the taking possession of the means of production in the name of society – this is, at the same time, its last independent act as a state. State interference in social relations becomes, in

one domain after another, superfluous, and then dies out of itself; the government of persons is replaced by the administration of things, and by the conduct of processes of production. The state is not 'abolished'. *It dies out.*[10]

Marx and Engels also thought that the nation itself would wither away as barriers between people were dismantled in a socialist society. In the *Communist Manifesto* they argued that workers had to win political supremacy and 'rise to be the leading class of the nation'.[11] But a victorious revolution in one country would have to spread across the world and as it did so, it would undermine the very basis of a nation state.

National differences, and antagonism between peoples are daily more and more vanishing, owing to the development of the bourgeoisie, to freedom of commerce, to the world market, to uniformity in the mode of production and in the conditions of life corresponding thereto.
The supremacy of the proletariat will cause them to vanish still faster ... In proportion as the antagonism between classes within the nation vanishes, the hostility of one nation to another will come to an end.[12]

This does not imply that cultural diversity will vanish or that people will not be able to speak the language they wish. Just as individuality will flourish in a new realm of freedom, all manner of music and literature that were shaped by particular 'national' experiences will flourish. But passports, immigration controls, petty bureaucracies that try to stoke up national difference to defend their own privileges – all of these will hopefully vanish. The withering away of the state and the nation does not, however, mean there is no public power. The greater diversity among people that grows with a flourishing of individuality will lead to new forms of non-class conflict that may require mediation or arbitration.[13] However, there will be no need for this social function to be provided by an extensive apparatus.

Finally, Marx's vision included the creation of a new human sensibility because the realm of freedom was about 'the development of human powers as an end in itself'.[14] Surviving forms of racism, sexism and homophobia would be abolished and exhibits of these activities would be on view in the Museum of Capitalism. Cultural knowledge and sensitivity, which once had been the monopoly of elites, could be made the property of society at large. But above all, the stunting of the human personality by private property could finally end. Marx argued:

> Private property has made us so stupid and one sided that an object is only *ours* when we have it – when it is used for us as capital or when it is possessed, eaten, drunk, worn, inhabited etc. – in short, when it is *used* by us.[15]

The human personality is not limited to defining our relationship to other people and to nature by how much can it be used by me. Marx thought instead that there could be a world where 'need or enjoyment has ... lost its egoistical nature and nature has lost its mere utility'.[16] That type of liberated human sensitivity lies well beyond the vision of those whose personalities have been stunted by capitalism. It will be for future generations to make and remake.

Notes

INTRODUCTION

1. M. Davis, 'Fear and money in Dubai', *New Left Review*, No. 41, September–October 2006, pp. 47–68.
2. www.thepalm.ae/jumeirah/about-us/introduction.
3. UNICEF, *The State of the World's Children 2008: Child Survival*, New York: UNICEF, 2007, p. 1.
4. United Nations, *Human Development Report 2006: Beyond Scarcity*, Basingstoke: Palgrave Macmillan, 2006, p. 5.
5. United Nations, *Millennium Development Goals Report 2007*, New York: United Nations, 2007, p. 45.
6. Ibid., p. 44.
7. M. Ravallion, S. Chwen, and P. Sangraula, 'Dollar a day revisited', *World Bank Economic Review*, Vol. 32, No. 2, June 2009.
8. K. Marx, *Economic and Philosophic Manuscripts*, Moscow: Progress Publishers, 1977, p. 65.
9. J. Davies, *Personal Wealth from a Global Perspective*, Oxford: Oxford University Press, 2009.
10. Forbes Rich List, 2009.
11. J. J. Rousseau, 'Discourse on the Origin of Inequality among Men', in M. Cohen and N. Ferman (eds.), *Princeton Readings in Political Thought: Essential Readings Since Plato*, Princeton, NJ: Princeton University Press, 1996, p. 313.
12. Marx, *Capital*, Volume 1, Harmondsworth, Penguin, 1976, p. 406.
13. Ibid., p. 342.
14. K. Marx, 'Theses on Feuerbach', in C. Arthur, *The German Ideology: Part One*, London: Lawrence & Wishart, 1974, p. 123.

1 REBEL WITH A CAUSE

1. S. S. Prawer, *Karl Marx and World Literature*, Oxford: Clarendon Press, 1976, p. 19.
2. F. Wheen, *Karl Marx*, London: Fourth Estate, 1999, p. 13.
3. Ibid., p. 32.
4. M. Kitchen, *A History of Modern Germany*, Oxford: Blackwell, 2006, pp. 17–18.
5. D. Blackbourn, *History of Germany: the Long Nineteenth Century*, Oxford: Blackwell, 2003, p. 92.
6. Quoted in H. Marcuse, *Reason and Revolution*, Oxford: Oxford University Press, 1941, p. 229.
7. G. Lukács, *The Young Hegel*, London: Merlin, 1938.
8. C. Taylor, *Hegel*, Cambridge: Cambridge University Press, 1975, p. 54.
9. G. Hegel, *The Philosophy of History*, Kitchener: Batoche Books, 2001, p. 33.

10. S. Hook, *From Hegel to Marx*, New York: Colombia University Press, 1994, p. 81.
11. Taylor, *Hegel*, p. 103.
12. R. K. Williamson, *An Introduction to Hegel's Philosophy of Religion*, New York: State of New York University Press, 1984, p. 258.
13. Ibid.
14. Hook, *From Hegel to Marx*, p. 36.
15. Ibid., p. 42.
16. K. Westphal, 'The basic context and Structure of Hegel's philosophy of right', in F. Beiser (ed.), *The Cambridge Companion to Hegel*, Cambridge: Cambridge University Press, 1993, p. 239.
17. C. Taylor, *Hegel*, Cambridge: Cambridge University Press, 1975, p. 422.
18. M. Rubel, *Marx: Life and Works*, London, Macmillan, 1980, p. 2.
19. K. Marx and F. Engels, *The Holy Family*, in *Marx–Engels Collected Works*, Volume 10, Moscow: Progress Publishers, 1975.
20. D. McClellan, *The Young Hegelians and Karl Marx*, London: Macmillan, 1969, p. 27.
21. K. Marx, 'Freedom in general', *Rheinische Zeitung*, 139, Supplement, 19 May 1842, www.marxists.org/archive/marx/works/1842/free-press/ch06.htm.
22. K. Marx, 'On the Assembly of Estates', *Rheinische Zeitung*, 130, Supplement, 10 May 1842, www.marxists.org/archive/marx/works/1842/free-press/ch03.htm.
23. K. Marx, 'Critique of Hegel's doctrine of the state', in K. Marx, *Early Writings*, Harmondsworth: Penguin, 1975, pp. 107–8.
24. Ibid., p. 114.
25. K. Marx, Preface to *A Contribution to the Critique of Political Economy*, Moscow, Progress Publishers, 1970, p. 19.
26. A. Gilbert, *Marx's Politics: Communists and Citizens* Oxford: Martin Robertson, 1981, p. 37.
27. K. Marx, 'Critical notes on the article "The King of Prussia and Social Reform"', in *Early Writings*, p. 403.
28. Ibid., p. 412.
29. M. Lowy, *The Theory of Revolution in the Young Marx*, Chicago: Haymarket Books, 2005. p. 74.
30. J. Charlton, *The Chartists: The First National Workers' Movement*, London: Pluto Press, 1997.
31. Quoted in T. Hunt, *The Frock-coated Communist: The Revolutionary Life of Friedrich Engels*, London: Allen Lane, 2009, p. 120.
32. Marx to Ruge, Kreuznach, September 1843, www.marxists.org/archive/marx/works/1843/letters/43_09.htm.
33. Gilbert, *Marx's Politics*, p. 68.
34. H. Draper, *Karl Marx's Theory of Revolution: Volume. 4, Critique of Other Socialisms* New York: Monthly Review, 1990, p. 29.
35. K. Marx and F. Engels, *The Communist Manifesto*, in *The Revolutions of 1848*, Harmondsworth: Penguin, 1973, p. 67.
36. A. Nimtz, *Marx and Engels: Their Contribution to the Democratic Breakthrough*, New York: State University of New York Press, 2000, p. 70.
37. 'Demands of the Communist Party of Germany', in *Marx–Engels Collected Works*, Volume 7, Moscow: Progress Publishers, 1977, p. 3.
38. K. Marx, 'Address to the Central Committee (March 1850)', in Marx, *The Revolutions of 1848*, Harmondsworth: Penguin, 1973, pp. 323–4.

39. W. Blumenberg, *Karl Marx: An Illustrated History*, London: Verso, 1998, p. 93.
40. A. Callinicos, *The Revolutionary Ideas of Karl Marx*, London: Bookmarks, 2004, p. 27.
41. W. Blumenberg, *Karl Marx: An Illustrated History*, London: Verso, 1998, p. 104.
42. 'Provisional Rules of the International', in K. Marx, *The First International and After: Political Writings*, Volume 3, Harmondsworth: Penguin, 1974, p. 82.
43. P. Foot, *The Vote: How it was Won and How it was Undermined*, London: Penguin-Viking, 2005, pp. 135–59.
44. I. Berlin, *Karl Marx*, Oxford: Oxford University Press, 1996, p. 189.
45. Friedrich Engels, speech at the grave of Karl Marx, 17 March 1883.

2   A FOR PROFIT SOCIETY

1. K. Marx, *Capital*, Volume 1, Harmondsworth: Penguin, 1976, p. 874.
2. Ibid., p. 915.
3. Ibid., p. 928.
4. Ibid., p. 933.
5. M. Beaud, *A History of Capitalism*, London: Macmillan, 1981, p. 31.
6. R. Buell. *The Native Problem in Africa*, New York: Macmillan, 1928, p. 331.
7. FBI, *Crime in the United States 2005*, New York: FBI, 2005.
8. E. P. Thompson, 'Time, work discipline and industrial capitalism', *Past and Present*, Vol. 38, No. 1, 1967, pp. 56–97.
9. Ibid.
10. P. Linebaugh, *The London Hanged: Crime and Civil Society in the Eighteenth Century,* London: Verso, 2003.
11. Marx, *Capital*, Volume 1, p. 125.
12. F. Engels, Preface to *Capital*, Volume 3, Harmondsworth: Penguin, 1981, p. 103.
13. P. Sweezy, *The Theory of Capitalist Development*, New York: Monthly Review, 1970, p. 24.
14. Marx, *Capital*, Volume 1, p. 132.
15. Ibid., p. 254.
16. J. Schor, *Born to Buy,* New York: Scribner, 2004, p. 20.
17. Quoted in E. Mandel, *The Formation of The Economic Thought of Karl Marx*, London: Verso, 1971, p. 41.
18. Sweezy, *The Theory of Capitalist Development*, p. 31.
19. D. Foley, *Understanding Capital: Marx's Economic Theory,* Harvard, MA: Harvard University Press, 1986, p. 16.
20. K. Marx, *Grundrisse*, Harmondsworth: Penguin, 1973, p. 157.
21. Marx, *Capital*, Volume 1, p. 280.
22. Ibid., pp. 279–80.
23. K. Marx and F. Engels, *Manifesto of the Communist Party*, in Karl Marx, *The Revolutions of 1848: Political Writings*, Volume 1, Harmondsworth: Penguin, 1973, p. 72.
24. Marx, *Capital*, Volume 1, pp. 739 and 742.

3   ALIENATION

1. R. Wilkinson and K. Pickett, *The Spirit Level: Why Equality is Better for Everyone,* London: Penguin, 2009.

2. O. James, *The Selfish Capitalist: Origins of Affluenza,* London: Vermillion, 2008, p. 40.

3. N. Wolff, *The Beauty Myth: How Images of Beauty are Used against Women,* London: Vintage, 1990.

4. K. Lau, *New Age Capitalism: Making Money East of Eden,* Pennsylvania: University of Pennsylvania Press, 2000, p. 7.

5. F. Engels, *Ludwig Feuerbach and the End of Classical German Philosophy,* Moscow: Progress Publishers, 1946, Part 3.

6. L. Feuerbach, *The Essence of Christianity,* New York: Cosimo, 2008, p. xiv.

7. Quoted in S. Hook, *From Hegel to Marx: Studies in the Intellectual Development of Karl Marx,* New York: Colombia University Press, 1994, p. 247.

8. Ibid., p. 247.

9. Feuerbach, *The Essence of Christianity,* p. 270.

10. K. Marx, *Theses on Feuerbach,* in K. Marx and F. Engels, *The German Ideology,* London: Lawrence & Wishart, 1974 p. 122.

11. Ibid., p. 122.

12. Ibid.

13. K. Marx and F. Engels, *The German Ideology,* London: Lawrence & Wishart, 1974, pp. 50-1.

14. Ibid., p. 47.

15. Marx, *Theses on Feuerbach,* p. 121.

16. F. Engels, *The Part Played by Labour in the Transition from Ape to Man,* Moscow: Progress Publishers, 1934.

17. E. Fischer, *The Necessity of Art,* Harmondsworth: Penguin, 1978, p. 23.

18. B. McKibben, *The End of Nature,* New York: Random House, 2005.

19. K. Marx, *The Economic and Philosophic Manuscripts,* Moscow: Progress Publishers, 1977, p. 68.

20. I. Meszaros, *Marx's Theory of Alienation,* London: Merlin Press, 1972, p. 162.

21. K. Marx, *Capital,* Volume 1, Harmondsworth: Penguin, 1976, p. 284.

22. Marx, *Economic and Philosophical Manuscripts,* p. 68.

23. H. Marcuse, *Reason and Revolution,* London: Routledge, 1977, p. 275.

24. Marx, *Economic and Philosophical Manuscripts,* p. 66.

25. Ibid., pp. 65-6.

26. Ibid., p. 66.

27. Ibid., p. 66.

28. P. Taylor and P. Bain, '"An assembly-line in the head": Work and employee relations in the call centre', *Industrial Relations Journal,* Vol. 30, No. 2, 1999, pp. 101-17.

29. Quoted in G. Ritzer, *The McDonaldization of Society,* Newbury Park, CA: Pine Forge Press, 1993, p. 119.

30. H. Braverman, *Labor and Monopoly Capital,* New York: Monthly Review Press, 1974, p. 119.

31. Ritzer, *The McDonaldization of Society,* p. 119.

32. P. Basso, *Modern Times, Ancient Hours,* London: Verso, 1998, p. 61.

33. F. Green, *Demanding Work: The Paradox of Job Quality in the Affluent Economy,* Princeton, NJ: Princeton University Press, 2006, p. 1.

34. F. Braudel, *Civilisation and Capitalism, 15th to 18th Century. Volume 1: The Structure of Everyday Life,* Berkeley, CA: University of California Press, 1992, p. 61.

35. E. Le Roy Ladurie, *The French Peasantry 1450–1660*, Berkeley, CA: University of California Press 1987, p. 79.
36. D. Noble, *Forces of Production: A Social History of Industrial Automation*, New York: Knopf, 1984.
37. Marx, *Capital*, Volume I, p. 425.
38. Marx, *Economic and Philosophic Manuscripts*, p. 23.
39. Ibid., p. 20.
40. Ibid.
41. Marx, *Economic and Philosophic Manuscripts*, p. 70.
42. C. Bengs, 'Planning theory of the naive', *European Journal of Spatial Development*, July 2005, pp. 1–12.
43. R. Williams, *Keywords: A Vocabulary of Culture and Society*, London: Fontana, 1983, p. 163.
44. A. de Tocqueville, *Democracy in America*, London: Fontana, 1994, p. 506.
45. D. Harvey, *A Brief History of Neoliberalism*, Oxford: Oxford University Press, 2005, p. 23.
46. Marx, *Economic and Philosophic Manuscripts*, p. 93.
47. Ibid., p. 70.
48. K. Marx, *Capital*, Volume 1.
49. K. Marx and F. Engels, *The Holy Family*, Moscow: Progress Publishers, 1975, p. 120.
50. D. Rushkoff, *Life Inc*, New York: Random House, 2009, p. 121.
51. Ibid., p. 99.
52. Marx, *Economic and Philosophic Manuscripts*, p. 102.
53. B. Ollman, *Alienation: Marx's Conception of Man in Capitalist Society*, Cambridge: Cambridge University Press, 1976, p. 150.
54. Marx, *Economic and Philosophic Manuscripts*, p. 100.
55. Marx, *Capital*, Volume 1, p. 65.
56. E. Burke, *Reflections on the Revolution in France*, London: John Sharpe, 1821, p. 83.
57. Ibid., p. 123.
58. Ibid.
59. Ibid., pp. 123-4.
60. Marx, *Economic and Philosophic Manuscripts*, p. 122.
61. Ibid., p. 36.
62. Ibid., p. 73.

4 SOCIAL CLASS

1. P. Kingston, *The Classless Society*, Chicago: Stanford University Press, 2000, p. 233.
2. W. Domhoff, 'Wealth, Income, Power', cafri.com.
3. E. Saez, 'Striking it richer: The evolution of top incomes in the United States', elsa.berkeley.edu/~saez/saez-UStopincomes-2007.pdf.
4. D. Johnson, 'The richest are leaving even the rich behind', *New York Times*, 5 June 2005.
5. R. Wilkinson and K. Pickett, *The Spirit Level: Why Equality is Better for Everyone*, Harmondsworth: Penguin, 2010, p. 84.

6. G. Singh and M. Siahpush, 'Widening socioeconomic inequalities in US life expectancy, 1980–2000', *International Journal of Epidemiology*, Vol. 35, No. 4, 2006, pp. 969–79.
7. Wilkinson and Pickett, *The Spirit Level*, p. 75.
8. K. Davis and W. E. Moore, 'Some principles of stratification', *American Sociological Review*, Vol. 10, No. 2, 1945, pp. 242–9.
9. F. Parkin, *Max Weber*, London: Routledge, 2002, p. 94.
10. G. E. M. de Ste Croix, *The Class Struggle in the Ancient World*, London: Duckworth, 1983, p. 43.
11. Ibid., pp. 43–4.
12. K. Marx, *The Communist Manifesto*, in *The Revolutions of 1848*, Harmondsworth: Penguin, 1973, p. 67.
13. Ibid.
14. F. Engels, *The Origin of the Family, Private Property and the State*, London: Lawrence & Wishart, 1972, p. 233.
15. Ibid., p. 159.
16. R. Lee, *The !Kung San: Men, Women, Work and Foraging Society*, Cambridge: Cambridge University Press, 1979, p. 118.
17. Quoted in C. Harman, *A People's History of the World*, London: Verso, 2008, p. 3.
18. P. Trouiller, O. Piero, E. Torreele, J. Orbinski, R. Laing and N. Ford, 'Drug development for neglected diseases: A deficient market and a public health failure', *The Lancet*, 9324, 22 June 2002, pp. 2188–94.
19. M. Angel, *The Truth about Drug Companies*, New York: Random House, 2004, p. 48.
20. H. Braverman, *Labor and Monopoly Capital*, New York: Monthly Review, 1974, p. 355.
21. K. Marx, *Capital*, Volume 3, Harmondsworth: Penguin, 1981, p. 1025.
22. Ibid.
23. H. Draper, *Karl Marx's Theory of Revolution. Volume 2: The Politics of Social Classes*, New York: Monthly Review Press, 1978, p. 478.
24. E. Hobsbawn, *Primitive Rebels: Studies in Archaic Social Movements in the 19th Century*, Manchester: Manchester University Press, 1959, p. 110.
25. R. Herrenstein and C. Murray, *The Bell Curve: Intelligence and Class Structure in American Life*, New York: Free Press, 1994, Chapter 9; E. Leacock Burke, *The Culture of Poverty: A Critique*, New York: Simon & Schuster, 1971.
26. M. Davis, *Planet of the Slums*, London: Verso, 2006, Chapter 8.
27. K. Marx, *Theories of Surplus Value*, Moscow: Progress Publishers, 1963, p. 158.
28. N. Poulanzas, *Classes in Contemporary Capitalism*, London: New Left Books, 1975.
29. Interview with Lawrence Otis Graham. 4 March 1999, www.pbs.org/newshour/gergen/march99/gergen_3-4.html.
30. P. Lissagray, *The History of the Paris Commune*, London: New Park, 1976, pp. 277–8.
31. Quoted in T. Cliff, *Class Struggle and Women's Liberation*, London: Bookmarks, 1984.
32. K. Marx, *Capital*, Volume 1, Harmondsworth: Penguin, 1976, p. 381.
33. A. Roy, 'Walking with comrades', *Outlook India*, 29 March 2010.
34. M. Gonzalez, *Che Guevara and the Cuban Revolution*, London: Bookmarks, 2004.

35. K. Marx, *The Eighteenth Brumaire of Louis Bonaparte*, in K. Marx, *Surveys from Exile*, Harmondsworth: Penguin, 1973, p. 240.
36. Ibid., p. 243.
37. N. Harris, *Mandate from Heaven: Marx and Mao in Modern China*, London: Quartet Books, 1979, Chapter 2.
38. Draper, *Karl Marx's Theory of Revolution*, p. 41.
39. Marx, *Capital*, Volume 1, p. 346.
40. D. Harvey, *The Enigma of Capital*, London: Profile Books, 2010, p. 58.
41. Ibid., p. 348.
42. J. Dalberg-Acton, *Essays on Freedom and Power*, Boston, MA: Beacon Press, 1949, p. 364.
43. D. Renton, *Fascism: Theory and Practice*, London: Pluto Press, 1999, p. 67.
44. K. Marx, *The Poverty of Philosophy*, New York: Prometheus Books, 1995, p. 187.
45. Ibid., p. 188.
46. K. Marx to Friedrich Bolte, 23 November 1871, in K. Marx and F. Engels, *Selected Correspondence*, Moscow: Progress Publishers 1965, p. 271.
47. T. Cliff and D. Gluckstein, *Marxism and Trade Union Struggle: The General Strike of 1926*, London: Bookmarks, 1986.
48. K. Marx, 'Minutes of the Central Committee Meeting of 15 September 1850', in K. Marx, *The Revolutions of 1848*, Harmondsworth: Penguin, 1973 p. 341.
49. Ibid.
50. J. K. Galbraith, *The Culture of Contentment*, London, Sinclair-Stevenson, 1992.
51. Braverman, *Labor and Monopoly Capital*, p. 297.
52. Quoted in A. Callinicos, 'The "new middle class" and socialists', *International Socialism Journal*, Vol. 2, No. 20, 1983.
53. D. Lockwood, *The Blackcoated Worker*, London: Allen & Unwin, 1958, p. 58.
54. Braverman, *Labor and Monopoly Capital*, p. 297.
55. Lockwood, *The Blackcoated Worker*, p. 79.
56. M. Power, *The Audit Society: Rituals of Verification*, Oxford: Oxford University Press, 1997.
57. E. O. Wright, *Class, Crisis and the State*, London: Verso, 1978, Chapter 2.
58. A. Callinicos and C. Harman, *The Changing Working Class*, London: Bookmarks, 1987.
59. Thomas Weiss, 'Revised estimates of the United States workforce, 1800–1860', in S. Engerman and R.Gallman (eds.), *Long Term Factors in American Economic Growth*, Chicago: University of Chicago, 1986, pp. 641–78.
60. D. Blackbourn, *History of Germany 1780–1918: The Long Nineteenth Century*, Oxford: Blackwell, 2003, p. 87.

5   GENDER AND RACE

1. D. Morley and K. Chen, *Stuart Hall: Critical Dialogues in Cultural Studies*, New York: Routledge, 1996, p. 418.
2. M. Hardt and A. Negri, *Multitude: War and Democracy in an Age of Empire*, Harmondsworth: Penguin, 2005.
3. K. Marx and F. Engels, *The Holy Family*, in *Marx–Engels Collected Works*, Volume 4, Moscow: Progress Publishers, 1975, p. 196.
4. F. Engels, *Principles of Communism*, in *Marx and Engels, Selected Works*, Moscow: Progress Publishers, 1969, p. 89.

5. 'Naked capitalists: There is no business like porn business', *New York Times*, 20 May 2001.

6. S. de Beauvoir, *The Second Sex*, London: Jonathan Cape, 1949, p. 89.

7. S. Brownmiller, *Against Our Will: Men, Women and Rape*, New York: Simon & Schuster, 1975, p. 15.

8. See C. Harman, 'Engels and the origin of human society', *International Socialism Journal*, Vol. 2, No. 65, Winter 1994.

9. F. Engels, *The Origins of the Family, Private Property and the State*, London: Lawrence & Wishart, 1972, pp. 113–14.

10. E. Leacock, *Myths of Males Dominance*: New York, Monthly Review Press 1981; E. Friedl, *Women and Men, an Anthropologist's View*, Long Grove, IL: Waveland Press 1975; K. Sachs, *Sisters and Wives*: Champaign, IL: University of Illinois Press, 1982; C. Gailey, *Kinship to Kingship: Gender Hierarchy and State Formation in the Tongan Islands*, Austin, TX: University of Texas Press, 1987.

11. E. Cantarella, *Pandora's Daughters: The Role and Status of Women in Greek and Roman Antiquity*, Baltimore, MD: Johns Hopkins University Press, 1987, p. 44.

12. V. Childe, *What Happened in History*, New York: Knopf, 1942.

13. Engels, *The Origins of the Family*, pp. 120–1.

14. Ibid., p. 129.

15. H. Wayne, *The Story of a Marriage. Volume 1: The Letters of Bronislaw Malinowski to Elsie Masson*, London, Routledge, 1995, p. 52.

16. Engels, *The Origins of the Family*, p. 121.

17. Ibid., p. 129.

18. Ibid., p. 125.

19. Cantarella, *Pandora's Daughters*, pp. 48–9.

20. Ibid., p. 134.

21. E.Shorter, *The Making of the Modern Family*, London: Collins, 1976.

22. K. Marx and F. Engels, *The Communist Manifesto*, in K. Marx, *The Revolutions of 1848*, Harmondsworth; Penguin, 1973, p. 83.

23. Engels, *The Origins of the Family*, p. 135.

24. Ibid., p. 137.

25. German, *Material Girls*, p. 86.

26. C. Wright and G. Jagger, 'End of century, end of family', in C. Wright and G. Jagger (eds.), *Changing Family Values*, London: Routledge, 1999, pp. 26 and 32.

27. German, *Material Girls*, p. 44.

28. Engels, *The Origins of the Family*, p. 139.

29. Ibid.

30. F. Butterfield, 'When the police shoot, who is counting?', *New York Times*, 29 April 2001.

31. D. Roediger, *The Wages of Whiteness: Race and The Making of the American Working Class*, London: Verso, 1999, p. 6.

32. C. Robinson, *Black Marxism: The Making of the Black Radical Tradition*, Chapel Hill, NC: University of North Carolina Press, 2000.

33. 'Address of the International Workingmen's Association to Abraham Lincoln', in *Karl Marx on America and the Civil War*, New York: McGraw-Hill, 1972, p. 237.

34. K. Marx, *Capital*, Volume 1, Harmondsworth: Penguin, 1976, p. 414.

35. K. Marx, 'Confidential communication', in K. Marx and F. Engels, *Ireland and the Irish Question,* Moscow: Progress Publishers, 1978, p. 255.
36. Ibid., p. 408.
37. A. Callinicos, *Race and Class,* London: Bookmarks, 1995.
38. H. Bhabha, *The Location of Culture,* London: Routledge, 1994, p. 67.
39. R. C. Lewontin, 'Confusions about human races', Social Science Research Council Web Forum, 7 June 2006.
40. R. Miles, *Capitalism and Unfree Labour: Anomaly or Necessity,* London: Tavistock, 1987, p. 7.
41. R. Miles, *Racism,* London: Routledge, 1989, p. 14.
42. L. Poliakov, *The History of Anti-Semitism,* Volume 2, London: Routledge, 1974, pp. 181–2.
43. Z. Bauman, *Modernity and the Holocaust,* Cambridge: Cambridge University Press, 1991, pp. 62–3.
44. E. Williams, *Capitalism and Slavery,* Richmond, NC: University of North Carolina Press, 1944, Chapter 3.
45. R. Blackburn, *The Making of the New World Slavery: From the Baroque to the Modern 1492–1800,* London: Verso, 1997, p. 542.
46. Declaration of Independence, www.archives.gov/exhibits/charters/declaration. html.
47. G. Fredrickson, *Racism: A Short History,* Princeton, NJ: Princeton University Press, 2003, p. 80.
48. L. P. Curtis, *Anglo-Saxons and Celts,* Bridgeport, CT: University of Bridgeport Press, 1968, p. 84.
49. E. Balibar, 'Racism and nationalism', in E. Balibar and I. Wallerstein (eds.), *Race, Nation, Class: Ambiguous Identities,* London: Verso, 1981, p. 43.
50. E. Weber, *Peasants into Frenchmen: The Modernization of Rural France 1880–1914,* London: Chatto and Windus, 1979, Chapter 18.
51. Marx to Meyer and Vogt, 19 April 1870, in K. Marx and F. Engels, *Selected Correspondence,* Moscow: Progress Publishers, 1965, pp. 236–7.
52. Quoted in Roediger, *The Wages of Whiteness,* p. 12.
53. Michael Reich, "The economics of racism', in R. C. Edwards, M. Reich and T. Weisskopf (eds.), *The Capitalist System,* Englewood Cliffs, NJ: Prentice-Hall, 1972, pp. 316 and 318.
54. B. Kelly, *Race, Class and Power in Alabama Coalfields 1908–21,* Champaign, IL: University of Illinois, 2001.

6   HOW WE ARE KEPT IN LINE

1. N. Machiavelli, *The Prince,* Ware, Herts: Wordsworth, 1993 p. 140.
2. A. Soboul, *The French Revolution,* London: New Left Books, 1974, p. 78.
3. B. de Holbach, *Good Sense,* Teddington: The Echo Library, 2006, p. 85.
4. K. Marx and F. Engels, *The German Ideology,* London: Lawrence & Wishart, 1970, p. 47.
5. Ibid., p. 64.
6. Ibid.
7. B. Bagdikian, *The New Media Monopoly,* Boston, MA: Beacon Press, 2004.
8. R. Greenslade, 'Their masters' voice', *Guardian,* 17 February 2003.

9. Quoted in J. Klaehn, 'A critical review of Herman and Chomsky's "Propaganda Model"', *European Journal of Communications*, Vol. 17, No. 2, 2002, pp. 147–82.

10. P. Nizan, *The Watchdogs: Philosophers of the Established Order*, New York: Monthly Review, 1971.

11. S. Bowles and H. Gintis, *Schooling in Capitalist America: Educational Reform and the Contradictions of Capitalist Life*, New York: Basic Books, 1976.

12. I. Meszaros, *The Power of Ideology*, Hemel Hempstead: Harvester, 1989, p. 167.

13. Ibid., p. 168.

14. S. Lukes, *Power: A Radical View*, Basingstoke: Palgrave Macmillan, 2005.

15. K. Marx, *A Contribution to the Critique of Political Economy*, Moscow: Progress 1970, p. 60.

16. K. Marx, *Grundrisse*, Harmondsworth: Penguin, 1973, p. 87.

17. H. Spencer, *Principles of Biology*, Volume 1, London: Williams & Norgate, 1864, p. 444.

18. R. Dawkins, *The Selfish Gene*, Oxford: Oxford University Press, 1976.

19. R. C. Lewontin, S. Rose and L. Kamin, *Not in Our Genes: Biology, Ideology and Human Nature*, New York: Pantheon, 1985.

20. Marx and Engels, *The German Ideology*, pp. 65–6.

21. J. Thompson, *Studies in the Theory of Ideology*, Cambridge: Polity Press, 1984.

22. V. Volosinov, *Marxism and the Philosophy of Language*, Cambridge, MA: Harvard University Press, 1973.

23. M. Friedman, *Capitalism and Freedom*, Chicago: University of Chicago Press, 1982.

24. A. France, *The Red Lily,* Denver, CO: Bibliolife, 2008, pp. 82–3.

25. K. Marx, *On the Jewish Question*, in *Early Writings*, Harmondsworth: Penguin, 1975, p. 229.

26. K. Marx, *Capital*, Volume 1, Harmondsworth: Penguin, 1976, pp. 168–9.

27. Ibid., p. 175.

28. K. Marx, *Capital*, Volume 3, Harmondsworth: Penguin 1981, p. 516.

29. Quoted in D. Harvey, 'The measure of a monster: Capital, class competition and finance', *Turbulence*, July 2008, pp. 29–32.

30. M. Lowy, *Georg Lukács: from Romanticism to Bolshevism*, London: New Left Books, 1979.

31. G. Lukács, *History and Class Consciousness*, London: Merlin, 1971, p. 93.

32. Ibid., p. 102.

33. Ibid., p. 135.

34. K. Marx and F. Engels, *The Holy Family*, in *Collected Works*, Volume 4, Moscow: Progress, 1975, p. 53.

35. For a wider discussion on hegemony, see P. Anderson, 'The antimonies of Antonio Gramsci', *New Left Review*, 100, November–December 1976, pp. 5–78.

36. Lukács, *History and Class Consciousness*, p. 172.

37. A. Gramsci, *Selections from the Prison Notebooks*, London: Lawrence & Wishart, 1971, p. 333.

38. R. Miliband, *The State in Capitalist Society*, London: Quartet, 1973, p. 47.

39. H. Draper, *Karl Marx's Theory of Revolution*, New York: Monthly Review Press, 1977, p. 245.

40. F. Engels, *The Origins of the Family, Private Property and the State*, London: Lawrence & Wishart, 1972, p. 229.

41. V. I. Lenin, *State and Revolution*, Dublin: Bookmarks, 2004, p. 11.
42. K. Marx, *Critique of Hegel's Doctrine of the State*, in *Early Writings*, p. 107.
43. R. Dahl, *Who Governs? Democracy and Power in an American City*, New Haven, CT: Yale University Press, 1981.
44. K. Marx and F. Engels, *The Communist Manifesto*, in Marx, *The Revolutions of 1848*, Harmondsworth; Penguin, 1973, p. 69.
45. M. Wang, *Japan between Asia and the West: Economic Power and Strategic Balance*, New York: East Gate, 2001, Chapter 2.
46. F. Engels, *The Condition of the Working Class of England in 1844*, Denver, CO: Bibliolife, 2008, p. 252.
47. Marx and Engels, *The German Ideology*, p. 80.
48. A. Roy, *The Greater Common Good*, Mumbai: India Book Distributor, 1999.
49. I. Journard, P. Kongsrud, Y. Narn and R. Price, 'Enhancing the effectiveness of public spending: Experience in OECD countries', *OECD Economic Studies*, No. 37, 2003, pp. 110-60.
50. Marx, *Capital*, Volume 1, p. 899.
51. Engels to the Spanish Federal Council of the International Workingman's Association, in Marx and Engels, *Selected Correspondence*, Moscow: Progress Publishers, 1965, p. 260.
52. 'MI5 put union leaders and protesters under surveillance during Cold War', *Guardian*, 6 October 2009.
53. A. Roy, 'People vs Empire', *In These Times*, 3 January 2005.
54. Quoted in P. Scannell and D. Cardiff, *A Social History of British Broadcasting, Volume 1 1922-39*, Oxford: Blackwell, 1991, p. 33.
55. K. Marx, *The Abolition of Landed Property: Memorandum for Robert Applegarth*, 3 December 1869, www.marxists.org/archive/marx/works/1869/12/03.htm.
56. 'The guys from government Sachs', *New York Times*, 17 October 2008.
57. N. Poulanzas, *Political Power and Social Classes*, London: Verso, 1978, Chapter 4.
58. K. Marx, *Class Struggles in France 1848-1850*, in Marx, *Surveys from Exile*, Harmondsworth: Penguin, 1973, p. 36.
59. K. Marx, 'Tories and Whigs', in Marx, *Surveys from Exile*, p. 258.
60. F. Engels, *Preface Addendum to The Peasant War in Germany*, www.marxists.org/archive/marx/works/1850/peasant-war-germany/ch0b.htm.
61. K. Marx, 'The attempt upon the life of Bonaparte', in Marx and Engels, *Collected Works*, Volume 15, p. 459.
62. Draper, *Karl Marx's Theory of Revolution*, p. 335.

7 HISTORICAL MATERIALISM

1. K. Marx and F. Engels, *The German Ideology*, London: Lawrence & Wishart, 1970, p. 57.
2. P. Anderson, *Arguments within English Marxism*, London: New Left Books, 1980, p. 22.
3. B. Pascal, *Pensées and Other Writings*, Oxford: Oxford University Press, 1995, p. 10.
4. R. Cobb, *The Police and the People: French Popular Protest 1789-1820*, Oxford: Clarendon Press, 1972, p. 200.

5. N. Bukharin, *Historical Materialism: A System of Sociology,* London: Allen & Unwin, 1925, p. 45.
6. T. Carlyle, *On Heroes, Hero Worship and the Heroic in History*, Pennsylvania: Penn State University Electronic Classics, 2001, p. 5.
7. M. Weber, *Economy and Society,* Volume 1, Berkeley, CA: University of California Press, 1978, pp. 242–4.
8. H. H. Gerth and C. W. Mills, *From Max Weber*, London: Routledge & Kegan Paul, 1948, p. 52.
9. R. Bendix, *Max Weber: An Intellectual Portrait,* London: Heinemann, 1960, p. 303.
10. J. Fest, *Hitler*, Orlando, FL: Harcourt, 1974, p. 4.
11. D. Hume, *An Inquiry Concerning Human Understanding*, Sioux Falls, SD: Nuvision Publications, 2008, p. 62.
12. Quoted in A. Callinicos, *Making History,* Cambridge: Polity Press, 1989, p. 26.
13. J. Molyneaux, *Is Human Nature a Barrier to Socialism?* London: Socialist Worker, 1993, p. 20.
14. K. Marx, *Capital*, Volume 1, Harmondsworth: Penguin, 1976, p. 290.
15. K. Marx, *Grundrisse,* Harmondsworth: Penguin, 1973, p. 84.
16. S. Hook, *From Hegel to Marx: Studies in Intellectual Development of Karl Marx*, New York: Colombia University Press, 1994, p. 277.
17. G. Cohen, *Karl Marx's Theory of History,* Oxford: Oxford University Press, 2000, p. 24.
18. Marx, *Capital*, Volume 1, p. 290.
19. Marx and Engels, *The German Ideology*, p. 48.
20. K. Marx, *Capital*, Volume 3, Harmondsworth, Penguin, 1981 p. 956.
21. G. W. F. Hegel, The *Phenomenology of Spirit*, Oxford: Oxford University Press, 1977, p. 11.
22. F. Engels, *Anti-Dühring*, Moscow: Progress Publishers, 1974, p. 164.
23. K. Marx and F. Engels, *The Holy Family*, in *Marx–Engels Collected Works*, Volume 4, Moscow: Progress Publishers, 1975, p. 79.
24. Ibid., p. 79.
25. Ibid., p. 93.
26. K. Marx, *A Contribution to the Critique of Political Economy*, Moscow: Progress Publishers, 1970, p. 20.
27. A. de Tocqueville, *Democracy in America*, London: Fontana 1994, Vol. 2, Chapter 5.
28. Marx, *Capital*, Volume 3, p. 791.
29. Engels to Starkenburg, 25 January 1894, in Marx and Engels, *Selected Correspondence*, p. 467.
30. F. Engels, *The Peasant War in Germany*, New York: International Publishers, 2000, p. 23.
31. C. Hill, *The World Turned Upside Down: Radical Ideas During the English Revolution*, Harmondsworth: Penguin, 1975, p. 112.
32. Ibid., p. 16.
33. J. Vogel, 'The tragedy of history', *New Left Review,* No. 220, November–December 1996, pp. 36–61.
34. Marx to Annenkov, 28 December 1846, in Marx and Engels, *Selected Correspondence*, p. 36.
35. C. Hill, 'The English civil war interpreted by Marx and Engels', *Science and Society*, Vol. 12, No. 1, 1948, pp. 130–56.

36. E. Pashukanis, *The General Theory of Law and Marxism*, New Brunswick, NJ: Transaction Publishers, 2003, p. 115.
37. Quoted in K. R. Srinivas, 'Intellectual property rights and bio commons – open source and beyond', *International Social Science Journal*, Vol. 58, No. 188, 2006, pp. 319–44.
38. M. Weber, *The Protestant Ethic,* New York: Charles Scribner's Sons, 1976, p. 5.
39. Quoted in C. Harman, *A People's History of the World*, London: Verso, 2008, p. 185.
40. J. Berger, *Ways of Seeing*, Harmondsworth: Penguin, 1972, p. 87.
41. K. Marx, *Capital*, Volume 2, Harmondsworth: Penguin, 1978, p. 120.
42. Marx, *Capital*, Volume 1, p. 443.
43. P. Anderson, *Lineages of the Absolutist State*, London: Verso, 1984, pp. 462–551.
44. O. Patterson, *Slavery and Social Death*, Harvard, MA: Harvard University Press, 1982, p. vii.
45. J. Dillery, 'Xenophon's *poroi* and Athenian imperialism', *Historia*, Vol. 42, 1993, pp. 1–11.
46. Cohen, *Karl Marx's Theory of History*, p. 231.
47. C. Harman, *Marxism and History*, London: Bookmarks, 1998.
48. Marx, Preface to a *Contribution to the Critique of Political Economy*, p. 21.
49. P. Blackledge, *Reflections on the Marxist Theory of History*, Manchester: Manchester University Press, 2006, p. 27.
50. Cohen, *Karl Marx's Theory of History*, p. 305.
51. Marx, *The Eighteenth Brumaire of Louis Bonaparte*, marxists.org.

8 CRASH: HOW THE SYSTEM IMPLODES

1. Actionaid, *The 20 Billion Dollar Question*, Johannesburg: Action Aid, 2010.
2. 'Opposition critical of Anglo bail out', *Irish Times*, 10 August 2010.
3. 'Bernanke, pro and con', *New York Times*, 3 December 2009.
4. Ibid.
5. Quoted in A. Callinicos, *Bonfire of Illusions: The Twin Crisis of the Liberal World*, Cambridge: Polity, 2010, p. 6.
6. Ibid., p. 7.
7. www.alternet.org/story/146883.
8. J. A. Aune, *Selling the Free Market: The Rhetoric of Economic Correctness*, New York: Guilford Press, 2001.
9. A. Shaikh, 'An introduction to the history of crisis theories', in *US Capitalism in Crisis*, New York: Union of Radical Political Economics, 1978, pp. 219–40.
10. Quoted in M. Dobb, *Political Economy and Capitalism*, London: Routledge, 1937, p. 42.
11. D. Ricardo, *On the Principles of Political Economy and Taxation*, London: John Murray, 1821, p. 339.
12. K. Marx, *Capital*, Volume 3, Harmondsworth: Penguin, 1981, pp. 351–2.
13. D. Harvey, *The Enigma of Capital*, London: Profile Books, 2010, p. 40.
14. Marx, *Capital*, Volume 1, p. 202.
15. K. Marx, *Capital*, Volume 1, New York: Cosimo Classics, 2007, pp. 127–8.

16. See C. Harman, *Zombie Capitalism*, London: Bookmarks, 2010, Chapter 3; and P. Maksakovsky, 'The general theory of the cycle', *Historical Materialism*, Vol. 10, No. 3, 2002, pp. 133–94.

17. Marx, *Capital*, Volume 1, pp. 227–8.

18. Marx, *Capital*, Volume 3, p. 365.

19. Ibid., p. 615.

20. R. Luxemburg, *The Accumulation of Capital*, New York: Monthly Review Press, 1968.

21. M. Itoh, *Value and Crisis,* London: Pluto Press, 1980.

22. M. Bleaney, *Underconsumption Theories: A History and Critical Analysis*, New York: International Publishers, 1976.

23. I. Mishel, J. Bernstein and S. Allegretto, *The State of Working America 2008/2009*, Ithaca, NY: Cornell University Press, 2009, Table 3.2.

24. M. Wolf, *Fixing Global Finance: How to Curb Financial Crises in the 21st Century*, New Haven, CT: Yale University Press, 2009, p. 32.

25. A. Shaikh, 'Economic crisis', in T. Bottomore (ed.), *A Dictionary of Marxist Thought*, Oxford: Basil Blackwell, 1983, p. 138.

26. K. Marx, *Grundrisse*, Harmondsworth: Penguin, 1973, p. 748.

27. Dobb, *Political Economy and Capitalism*, pp. 81–3.

28. Ibid., pp. 84–94.

29. A.Shaikh, 'The falling rate of profit', in Bottomore (ed.), *A Dictionary of Marxist Thought*, p. 159.

30. A. Shaikh, *The Current Economic Crisis: Causes and Implications*, Detroit: Against the Current, 1989, p. 3.

31. Marx, *Capital*, Volume 3, p. 331.

32. A. Shaikh, 'Explaining the global economic crisis', *Historical Materialism*, Vol. 5, No.1, 1999, pp. 3–34.

33. Marx, *Capital*, Volume 3, p. 331.

34. Harman, *Zombie Capitalism*, pp. 70–1.

35. Marx, *Capital*, Volume 3, p. 346.

36. Ibid.

37. S. Anderson and J. Cavanagh, *Field Guide to the Global Economy*, New York: Norton, 2005, p. 6.

38. L. Elliot and D. Atkinson, *The Age of Insecurity*, London: Verso, 1998, p. 102.

39. J. Gelinas, *Juggernaut Politics: Understanding Predatory Globalisation*, London: Zed, 2003, p. 37.

40. D. Harvey, *The Limits to Capital*, London: Verso, 2006.

41. Ibid., p. 270.

42. Marx, *Capital*, Volume 3, p. 597 (I have translated 'valorised' as 'expands itself').

43. E. Bernstein, *The Preconditions of Socialism*, Cambridge: Cambridge University Press, 2004, p. 88.

44. Marx, *Grundrisse*, p. 623.

45. Marx, *Capital,* Volume 3, p. 358.

46. A. Shaikh, 'Political economy and capitalism: Notes on Dobb's theory of crisis', *Cambridge Journal of Economics*, No. 2, 1978, pp. 233–51.

47. Dobb, *Political Economy and Capitalism*, pp. 121–2.

48. Marx, *Capital*, Volume 3, pp. 361–2.

9   UTOPIA OR REVOLUTION

1. D. Harvey, *The Enigma of Capital*, London: Profile Books, 2010, p. 6.
2. UN News Centre, 'Financial crisis to deepen extreme poverty, increase child mortality rates', 3 March 2010.
3. F. Fukuyama, *The End of History and the Last Man*, New York: Free Press, 1992, p. 46.
4. M. Fischer, *Capitalist Realism: Is There No Alternative?* London: Zero Books, 2009, p. 2.
5. J. Connolly, 'State monopoly versus socialism', *Workers Republic*, 10 June 1899.
6. F. Engels, *Socialism Utopian and Scientific*, New York: Cosimo, 2008, pp. 67–8.
7. T. More, *Utopia*, Bibliolife, 2008, p. 35.
8. Ibid., p. 108.
9. Quoted in F. Engels, *Socialism: Utopian and Scientific*, London: Bookmarks, 1993, p. 68.
10. C. Fourier, 'Degradation of women in civilization', in Susan Groag Bell and Karen M. Offen (eds.), *Women, the Family, and Freedom: The Debate in Documents, Volume One, 1750–1880*, Palo Alto, CA: Stanford University Press, 1983, pp. 40–1.
11. Ibid.
12. Engels, *Socialism: Utopian and Scientific*, p. 64.
13. K. Marx and F. Engels, *The Communist Manifesto*, in K. Marx, *The Revolutions of 1848*, Harmondsworth: Penguin, 1973, p. 95.
14. K. Marx, *Critique of the Gotha Programme*, in K. Marx, *The First International and After*, Harmondsworth: Penguin, 1974, p. 346.
15. K. Marx and F. Engels, *The German Ideology*, New York: Prometheus Books, 1998, p. 57.
16. Marx to F. Domela Neiuwenhuis, 22 February 1881, in K. Marx and F. Engels, *Selected Correspondence*, Moscow: Progress Publishers, 1965, p. 338.
17. K. Marx, *Capital*, Volume 3, Harmondsworth: Penguin, 1981, p. 568.
18. J. Holloway, *Changing the World without Taking Power: The Meaning of Revolution Today*, London: Pluto Press, 2003, pp. 19 and 20.
19. E. O. Wright, *Envisioning Real Utopias*, London: Verso, 2010.
20. R. Wilkinson and K. Pickett, *The Spirit Level: Why Equality is Better for Everyone*, London: Penguin, 2009, p. 262.
21. G. Tremlett, 'Basque co-op project protects itself with buffer of foreign workers', *Guardian*, 23 October 2001.
22. S. Kasmir, *The Myth of Mondragon: Cooperatives, Politics and Working Class Life in a Basque Town*, New York: New York State University Press, 1996, p. 162.
23. K. Marx, 'Critical notes on the King of Prussia and social reform', in *Early Writings*, Harmondsworth: Penguin, 1975, p. 420.
24. Marx and Engels, The Communist Manifesto, p. 98.
25. Marx to Kugelman, 12 April 1871, in Marx and Engels, *Selected Correspondence* p. 262.

26. K. Marx, *Moralising Criticism and Critical Morality: A Contribution to German Cultural History contra Karl Heinzen*, in *Marx–Engels Collected Works*, Volume 6, 1976, p. 312.

27. H. Draper, *Karl Marx's Theory of Revolution: The Politics of Social Classes*, New York: Monthly Review Press, 1978, p. 77.

28. K. Marx and F. Engels, *The German Ideology*, London: Lawrence & Wishart, 1974, p. 95.

29. F. Engels, 'The principles of communism', in K. Marx and F. Engels, *Manifesto of the Communist Party*, Moscow: Progress Publishers, 1977, p. 88.

30. V. Lenin, *Left Wing Communism – An Infantile Disorder*, in Lenin, *Selected Works*, Volume 3, Moscow: Progress Publishers, 1975, p. 351.

31. Ibid.

32. Ibid.

33. Engels to E. Bernstein, 27 August 1883, in Marx and Engels, *Selected Correspondence*, p. 364.

34. K. Marx, *The Eighteenth Brumaire of Louis Bonaparte*, in *Surveys from Exile*, Harmondsworth: Penguin, 1973, p. 150.

35. Marx, *Class Struggles in France*, in *Surveys from Exile*, pp. 46–7.

36. V. Lenin, *What is to be Done*, in *Selected Works*, Moscow: Progress Publishers, 1976, pp. 153–4.

37. K. Marx and F. Engels, 'Review *Les Conspirateurs*, par A. Chenu; ex-capitaine des gardes du citoyen Caussidière. Les sociétés secretes; la prefecture de police sous Caussidière; les corps-francs. *La naissance de la Republique en fevrier 1848* par Lucien de la Hodde', in *Marx–Engels Collected Works*, Volume 10, pp. 311–25.

38. F. Engels, 'The program of the Blanquist fugitives from the Paris Commune', *Der Volksstaat*, No.73, 26 June 1874, www.marxists.org.

10   AFTER THE REVOLUTION

1. F. Engels, 'On the 20th anniversary of the Paris Commune', Postscript to *The Civil War in France*, www. marxists.org.

2. K. Marx and F. Engels, *The Communist Manifesto*, in K. Marx, *The Revolutions of 1848*, Harmondsworth: Penguin, 1973, p. 86.

3. Ibid.

4. K. Marx, *The Class Struggles in France 1848–50*, in Marx, *Surveys from Exile*, Harmondsworth: Penguin, 1973, p. 123.

5. H. Draper, *Karl Marx's Theory of Revolution: Volume 3: The Dictatorship of the Proletariat*, New York: Monthly Review Press, 1986, p. 62.

6. Ibid., p. 269.

7. Marx to Kugelmann, 17 April 1871, in K. Marx and F. Engels, *Selected Correspondence*, Moscow: Progress Publishers, 1965, p. 264.

8. Engels, 'On the 20th anniversary of the Paris Commune'.

9. Ibid.

10. K. Marx, *The Civil War in France*, in Marx, *The First International and After*, Harmondsworth: Penguin, 1974, p. 209.

11. Ibid., p. 210.

12. C. Crouch, *Post Democracy*, Cambridge: Polity Press, 2004, p. 6.

13. S. Wolin, *Democracy Incorporated: Managed Democracy and the Specter of Inverted Totalitarianism*, Princeton, NJ: Princeton University Press, 2008.

14. P. Mair, 'Ruling the void: The hollowing of Western democracy', *New Left Review* No. 42, November–December 2006, pp. 25–51.
15. Consumer Education Foundation, *Sold Out: How Wall Street and Washington Betrayed America*, Washington: Essential Information, 2009.
16. Marx, *The Civil War in France*, p. 210.
17. Ibid.
18. Quoted in P. Anderson, 'The affinities of Norberto Bobbio', *New Left Review* Vol. 1, No. 170, July–August 1988, p. 25.
19. Ibid.
20. Marx, *The Civil War in France*, p. 209.
21. R. D. Storch, 'The plague of blue locusts: Police reform and popular resistance in northern England, 1840–1857', *International Review of Social History*, No. 20, 1975, pp. 61–90.
22. R. Reiner, *The Politics of the Police*, Brighton: Wheatsheaf, 1985, p. 51.
23. R. Quinney, *The Social Reality of Crime*, New Brunswick, NJ: Transaction Books, 2001, p. 114.
24. W. Westley, 'Violence and the police', *American Journal of Sociology*, No. 59, 1953, p. 35.
25. D. J. Smith and J. Gray, *Police and People in London*, London, PSI, 1983, p. 338.
26. R. Reiner, *The Blue Coated Worker*, Cambridge: Cambridge University Press, 1978; S. Holdaway, *Inside the British Police*, Oxford: Blackwell, 1983.
27. D. McBarnet, *Conviction: Law, The State and The Construction of Justice*, London: Macmillan, 1981.
28. Marx, *The Civil War in France*, p. 212.
29. J. Becker, 'Murdoch, ruler of a vast empire, reaches out for even more', *New York Times*, 25 June 2007.
30. Marx, *The Civil War in France,* p. 209.
31. Ibid., p. 210.
32. A. Pannekoek, *Workers Councils*, Oakland, CA: AK Press, 2003, p. 45.
33. Marx, *The Civil War in France,* p. 209.
34. L. Trotsky, *1905*, Harmondsworth: Penguin, 1971, p. 102.
35. Quoted in S. Cohen, 'Workers' councils: The red mole of revolution', in *The Commune*, 23 March 2010.
36. R. Michels, *Political Parties*, Ontario: Batoche Books, 2001, Chapter 2.
37. Marx, *The Civil War In France*, p. 213.
38. Ibid., p. 212.
39. Ibid., p. 213.

11   THE ECONOMICS OF SOCIALISM

1. J. Tapper, 'BP emails show disregard for "nightmare well"', ABC News website, 14 June 2010.
2. Engels to Otto von Boenigk, 21 August 1890, www.marxists.org/archive/marx/works/1890/letters/90_08_21.htm.
3. F. Engels, *Socialism: Utopian and Scientific*, London: Bookmarks, 1993, p. 100.
4. A. Etzioni, *Capital Corruption: The New Attack on American Democracy*, New Brunswick, NJ: Transaction Books, 1988, p. 25.
5. Quoted in D. Hall, *More Public Rescues for More Private Finance Failures*, London: Public Services International Research Unit, 2010, p. 5.

6. N. Klein, *No Logo*, London: Flamingo, 2001, p. 20.
7. World Watch Institute, *State of the World 2010*, Washington, DC: Earthscan, 2010, p. 11.
8. Ben H. Bagdikian, *The Media Monopoly*, Boston, MA: Beacon Press, 2000, p. 185.
9. B. Orbach, 'The durapolist puzzle: Monopoly power in durable goods market', *Yale Journal of Regulation*, No. 21, 2004, pp. 67–118.
10. V. Packard, *The Waste Makers*, New York: David McKay Co., 1960, p. 46.
11. The Corporation: Film Transcript, Part 1, darrellmoen.wordpress. com/2008/09/28/the-corporation-transcript-part-one.
12. K. Marx, 'The nationalisation of land', *The International Herald*, No. 11, 15 June 1872, www.marxists.org/archive/marx/works/1872/04/nationalisation-land.htm.
13. T. Cliff, 'Marxism and the collectivisation of agriculture', *International Socialism Journal*, No. 19, Winter 1964–65.
14. R. Dahl, *A Preface to Economic Democracy*, Berkeley, CA: University of California Press, 1985, p. 111.
15. K. Marx, *Capital*, Volume 1, Harmondsworth: Penguin, 1996, p. 482.
16. H. Braverman, *Labor and Monopoly Capital*, New York: Monthly Review Press, 1974, p. 67.
17. C. Hales, 'Management and empowerment programmes', *Work, Employment and Society*, Vol. 14, No. 3, pp. 501–19.
18. H. Cooke, 'Seagull management and the control of nursing work', *Work Employment and Society*, Vol. 20, No. 2, pp. 223–43.
19. K. Marx, *The Civil War in France*, in Marx, *The First International and After*, Harmondsworth: Penguin, 1974, p. 210.
20. K. Marx, *The Poverty of Philosophy*, New York: Prometheus Books, 1995, p. 190.
21. C. Goodrich, *The Frontier of Control: A Study of British Workshop Politics*, New York: Harcourt, Brace and Howe, 1921.
22. J. Monds, 'Workers' control and the historians: a new economism', *New Left Review*, No. 97, 1976, pp. 81–100.
23. M. Atzeni and P. Ghigliani, 'Labour process and decision-making in factories under workers' self-management: empirical evidence from Argentina', *Work, Employment and Society*, Vol. 21, No. 4, 2007, pp. 653–71; E. Toussaint, 'Venezuela. Nationalization, workers' control: achievements and limitations', Committee for Abolition of Third World Debt, 14 April 2010.
24. J. Reed, 'Soviets in action', *The Liberator*, October 1918.
25. M. Raptis, 'Self-management in the struggle for socialism', Paper at 10th Latin American Congress of Sociology, Santiago de Chile, August 1972.
26. T. Cliff, *State Capitalism in Russia*, London: Bookmarks, 1988, p. 140.
27. K. Marx, *Critique of the Gotha Programme*, in Marx, *The First International and After*, p. 346.
28. R. Dunayevskaya, *The Marxist-Humanist Theory of State Capitalism*, Chicago: News and Letter, 1992, p. 87.
29. M. Albert, *Parecon: Life After Capitalism*, London: Verso, 2003, p. 65.
30. F. Engels, *Anti-Dühring*, Moscow: Progress Publishers, 1978, p. 339.
31. Worldwatch Institute, *State of the World 2010*, Washington, DC: Earthscan, 2010, p. 4.

32. Quoted in J. B. Foster, *The Ecological Revolution*, New York: Monthly Review Press, 2009, p. 58.
33. Friends of the Earth, *A Dangerous Obsession: The Evidence against Carbon Trading and for Real Solutions to Avoid a Climate Crunch*, London: Friends of the Earth, 2009, p. 20.
34. Ibid., p. 32.
35. Bank of International Settlements, *OTC Derivatives Market Activity in the First Half of 2008*, Basel: BIS, 2008, p. 1.
36. P. Devine, *Democracy and Economic Planning*, Cambridge: Polity, 1988, p. 23.
37. G. Laird, *The Price of a Bargain: The Quest for Cheap and the Death of Globalization*, New York: Palgrave Macmillan, 2009, p. 121.
38. Ernst and Young, *Global Supply Chains: Balancing Cost Reduction and Performance Improvement*, New York: Ernst and Young, 2009.
39. Devine, *Democracy and Economic Planning*, p. 22.
40. L. Mishel, J. Bernstein and H. Shierholz, *The State of Working America 2008-2009*, Washington, DC: Economic Policy Institute, 2009, Figure 3AE, p. 220.
41. A. Nove, *The Economics of Feasible Socialism*, London: Allen & Unwin, 1983, p. 75.
42. A. Schand, *Free Market Morality: The Political Economy of the Austrian School*, New York: Routledge, 1990.
43. Nove, *The Economics of Feasible Socialism*, p. 43.

12 INTO THE BEYOND

1. K. Korsch, *Karl Marx*, New York: Russell and Russell, 1963, pp. 157 and 159.
2. S. Hook, *Towards the Understanding of Karl Marx*, New York: Prometheus Books, 2002, p. 314.
3. Ibid., p. 346.
4. K. Marx, *Grundrisse*, Harmondsworth: Penguin, 1973, p. 611.
5. F. Engels, *The Housing Question*, Moscow: Progress Publishers, 1970, pp. 24-5.
6. K. Marx, *The Critique of the Gotha Programme*, in Marx, *The First International and After*, Harmondsworth: Penguin, 1974 p. 347.
7. K. Marx, *Capital*, Volume 3, Harmondsworth: Penguin, 1981, p. 959.
8. P. Roberts, *The End of Food*, London: Bloomsbury, 2008, p. xvii.
9. K. Marx and F. Engels, *The German Ideology*, London: Lawrence & Wishart, 1974, p. 84.
10. F. Engels, *Anti-Dühring*, Moscow: Progress Publishers, 1947, pp. 340-1.
11. K. Marx and F. Engels, *The Communist Manifesto*, Marx, *The Revolutions of 1848*, Harmondsworth: Penguin, 1973, p. 84.
12. Ibid., p. 85.
13. A. Callinicos, *The Revenge of History*, Pennsylvania: Pennsylvania State University Press, 1991, pp. 130-1.
14. Marx, *Capital*, Volume 3, p. 959.
15. K. Marx, *Economic and Philosophic Manuscripts*, Moscow: Progress Publishers, 1977, p. 94.
16. Ibid., p. 95.

Guide to Further Reading

There is no substitute for reading Marx and Engels in the original and the best place to start is the *Communist Manifesto* and F. Engels, *Socialism: Utopian and Scientific* (London: Bookmarks, 1993). You might also get hold of *Marx's Political Writings* which was originally produced by Penguin and has now been reissued by Verso. This is a three-volume set: *The Revolutions of 1848*, *Surveys from Exile* and *The First International and After* (London: Verso, 2010). These contain many of the key texts, including *The Critique of the Gotha Programme* and the *Civil War in France* where Marx outlines elements of his alternative to capitalism. To appreciate these writings fully it would be useful to consult a good general history of France in the nineteenth century.

To get a deeper understanding of Marx's theory of historical materialism, read the short Preface to *A Contribution to a Critique of Political Economy*. You can access this and most of Marx and Engels' other articles and books on the excellent website www.marxists.org. You should then read the first part of *The German Ideology* (London: Lawrence & Wishart, 1974) in the excellent student edition edited by Chris Arthur. This contains other texts such as the short but cryptic *Theses on Feuerbach*.

Approaching Marx's economics can appear quite daunting, so start with Marx's *Wages, Prices and Profits* and *Wage Labour and Capital* which are published together (London: Bookmarks, 1996). You might then approach Volume 1 of *Capital* (Harmondsworth: Penguin,1976) and you could use as an accompaniment David Harvey's *Companion to Marx's Capital* (London: Verso, 2010) or download his lecture series on *Capital* from his website: davidharvey.org.

CHAPTER 1: REBEL WITH A CAUSE

Francis Wheen's *Karl Marx* (London: Fourth Estate, 1999) provides a lively and interesting account of Marx's life; while Werner Blumenberg's *Karl Marx* (London: New Left Books, 1972) is also useful. Alan Gilbert's *Marx's Politics* (Oxford: Martin Robertson, 1981) has a good overview of his political activity. One of the best discussions of Marx's relation to Hegel and the Young Hegelians can be found in Sidney Hook, *From Hegel to Marx* (New York: Colombia University Press, 1994).

CHAPTER 2: A FOR PROFIT SOCIETY

The clearest and most accessible introduction to Marx's economics can be found in Chris Harman, *Economics of the Madhouse* (London: Bookmarks, 1995). Part 1 of Paul Sweezy's, *The Theory of Capitalist Development* (New York: Monthly Review, 1970) provides a lucid summary of Marx's main economic concepts and D. Foley, *Understanding Capital: Marx's Economic Theory,* (Harvard, MA: Harvard University Press, 1986) is also useful. The shortest and most concise account can also be found in Joseph Choonara, *Unravelling Capitalism* (London: Bookmarks, 2009)

CHAPTER 3: ALIENATION

Read Ernest Mandel and George Novack's *The Marxist Theory of Alienation* (New York: Pathfinder, 1973) and then go on to Marx's own brilliant and profound *Economic and Philosophic Manuscripts* (Moscow: Progress Publishers, 1977). This can be quite difficult, but Bert Ollman's *Alienation: Marx's Conception of Man in Capitalist Society* (Cambridge: Cambridge University Press, 1976) will help. Once you are there, try Istvan Meszaros, *Marx's Theory of Alienation* (London: Merlin, 1972) for an insightful discussion.

CHAPTER 4: SOCIAL CLASS

Hal Draper's *Karl Marx's Theory of Revolution. Volume 2: The Politics of Social Classes* (New York: Monthly Review Press, 1978) provides an excellent overview; while Alex Callinicos and Chris Harman, *The Changing Working Class* (London: Bookmarks, 1987) is a good modern Marxist approach to social class.

CHAPTER 5: GENDER AND RACE

The classic Marxist text on gender is Friedrich Engels, *The Origin of the Family, Private Property and the State*, (London: Lawrence & Wishart, 1972). There is a very good introduction to this edition by Eleanor Burke Leacock and you will find an interesting updating of Engels' argument in Chris Harman, 'Engels and the origin of human society', *International Socialism Journal*, Vol. 2, No. 65, Winter 1994. The best introduction to a Marxist approach to racism can be found in Alex Callinicos, *Race and Class* (London: Bookmarks, 1995).

CHAPTER 6: HOW WE ARE KEPT IN LINE

Marx's account of ideology has been mangled by academics who try to mix his views with 'cultural studies' or 'discourse'. A good starting point is his own discussion in the *German Ideology* and you find an interesting but difficult update in Lukács essay on 'Reification and the consciousness of the proletariat', in his *History and Class Consciousness* (London: Merlin, 1971). Gramsci's views can be approached through Perry Anderson, 'The antimonies of Antonio Gramsci', *New Left Review*, No. 100, November–December 1976. The best account of the Marxist theory of the state is Lenin's *State and Revolution* (Dublin: Bookmarks, 2004).

CHAPTER 7: HISTORICAL MATERIALISM

P. Blackledge, *Reflections on the Marxist Theory of History*, (Manchester: Manchester University Press, 2006) provides an excellent overview of Marxist writings on historical interpretation. Chris Harman's *Marxism and History* (London: Bookmarks, 1998) provides a clear exposition; while G. A. Cohen, *Karl Marx's Theory of History* (Oxford: Oxford University Press, 2000) is the classic reference point for discussions on the subject.

CHAPTER 8: CRASH: HOW THE SYSTEM IMPLODES

David Harvey's *The Enigma of Capital* (London: Profile Books, 2010) is a good attempt to relate Marx's theory of capitalism to the current difficulties the system is experiencing; while his *The Limits to Capital* (London: Verso, 2006) is more difficult but does develop Marx's theories further. Chris Harman's *Zombie Capitalism* (London: Bookmarks, 2010) is a wonderful, comprehensive account of how Marxist theories of crises can be used to explain the current trajectory of the system.

CHAPTERS 9–12: THE ALTERNATIVE

Marx's vision of the alternative to capitalism was tarnished through its association with the old, 'communist' regimes that collapsed following the 1989 revolts. Tony Cliff's *State Capitalism in Russia* (London: Bookmarks, 1988) provides the definitive rebuttal of any connection. Ernest Mandel has written an excellent article, 'In defence of socialist planning', *New Left Review*, Vol. 1, No. 159, September–October 1986. Alex Callinicos has an interesting discussion on the original idea of communism in Part 4 of *The Revenge of History* (Pennsylvania: Pennsylvania State University Press, 1991). However, the alternative to capitalism will need to be constructed in practice before it can be adequately theorised.

Select Bibliography

WORKS BY MARX AND ENGELS

F. Engels, *Anti-Dühring*, Moscow: Progress, 1947.

F. Engels, *The Condition of the Working Class of England in 1844*, Denver: Bibliolife, 2008.

F. Engels, *The Housing Question*, Moscow: Progress Publishers, 1970.

F. Engels, *Ludwig Feuerbach and the End of Classical German Philosophy*, Moscow: Progress Publishers, 1946.

F. Engels, *The Origin of the Family, Private Property and the State*, London: Lawrence & Wishart, 1972.

F. Engels, *The Part Played by Labour in the Transition from Ape to Man*, Moscow: Progress Publishers, 1934.

F. Engels, *The Peasant War in Germany*, New York: International Publishers, 2000.

F. Engels, 'The principles of communism', in K. Marx and F. Engels, *Manifesto of the Communist Party*, Moscow: Progress Publishers, 1977.

F. Engels, *Socialism: Utopian and Scientific*, London: Bookmarks, 1993.

K. Marx, *Capital*, Volume 1, Harmondsworth: Penguin, 1976.

K. Marx, *Capital*, Volume 2, Harmondsworth: Penguin, 1978.

K. Marx, *Capital*, Volume 3, Harmondsworth, Penguin, 1981.

K. Marx, *The Civil War in France* in Marx, *The First International and After*, Harmondsworth: Penguin, 1974.

K. Marx, *Class Struggles in France 1848–1850* in K. Marx, *Surveys from Exile*, Harmondsworth: Penguin, 1973.

K. Marx, *A Contribution to the Critique of Political Economy*, Moscow: Progress Publishers, 1970.

K. Marx, *Critique of the Gotha Programme* in K. Marx, *The First International and After*, Harmondsworth: Penguin, 1974.

K. Marx, *Critique of Hegel's Doctrine of the State* in K. Marx, *Marx: Early Writings*, Harmondsworth: Penguin, 1975.

K. Marx, *The Economic and Philosophic Manuscripts*, Moscow: Progress Publishers, 1977.

K. Marx, *The Eighteenth Brumaire of Louis Bonaparte* in *Surveys from Exile*, Harmondsworth: Penguin, 1973.

K. Marx, *The German Ideology: Part One*, London: Lawrence & Wishart, 1974.

K. Marx, *Grundrisse*, Harmondworth: Penguin, 1973.

K. Marx, *On the Jewish Question* in *Early Writings*, Harmondsworth: Penguin, 1975.

K. Marx, *The Poverty of Philosophy*, New York: Prometheus Books, 1995.

K. Marx, *Pre-Capitalist Economic Formations*, New York: International Publishers, 1980.

K. Marx, *Theories of Surplus Value*, Parts 1–3, Moscow: Progress Publishers, 1978.

K. Marx and F. Engels, *The Communist Manifesto* in *The Revolutions of 1848*, Harmondsworth: Penguin, 1973.

K. Marx and F. Engels, *The Holy Family* in *Marx–Engels Collected Works*, Volume 4, Moscow: Progress Publishers, 1975.

K. Marx and F. Engels, *Selected Correspondence*, Moscow: Progress Publishers, 1965.

WORKS BY OTHER AUTHORS

M. Albert, *Parecon: Life after Capitalism*, London: Verso, 2003.

P. Anderson, 'The antimonies of Antonio Gramsci', *New Left Review*. No. 100, November–December 1976.

P. Anderson, *Arguments within English Marxism*, London: New Left Books, 1980.

P. Anderson, *Lineages of the Absolutist State*, London: Verso, 1984.

J. A. Aune, *Selling the Free Market: The Rhetoric of Economic Correctness*, New York: Guilford Press, 2001.

E. Balibar and I Wallerstein (eds.), *Race, Nation, Class: Ambiguous Identities*, London: Verso, 1981.

Z. Bauman, *Modernity and the Holocaust*, Cambridge: Cambridge University Press, 1991.

M. Beaud, *A History of Capitalism*, London: Macmillan, 1981.

J. Berger, *Ways of Seeing*, Harmondsworth: Penguin, 1972.

I. Berlin, *Karl Marx*, Oxford: Oxford University Press, 1996.

E. Bernstein, *The Preconditions of Socialism*, Cambridge: Cambridge University Press, 2004.

R. Blackburn, *The Making of the New World Slavery: From the Baroque to the Modern 1492–1800*, London: Verso, 1997.

P. Blackledge, *Reflections on the Marxist Theory of History*, Manchester: Manchester University Press, 2006.

M. Bleaney, *Underconsumption Theories: A History and Critical Analysis*, New York: International Publishers, 1976.

W. Blumenberg, *Karl Marx: An Illustrated History*, London: Verso, 1998.

H. Braverman, *Labour and Monopoly Capital*, New York: Monthly Review Press, 1974.

N. Bukharin, *Historical Materialism: A System of Sociology*, London: Allen & Unwin, 1925.

A. Callinicos, *Making History*, Cambridge: Polity Press, 1989.

A. Callinicos, *The Revenge of History*, Pennsylvania: Pennsylvania State University Press, 1991.

A. Callinicos, *Race and Class*, London: Bookmarks, 1995.

A. Callinicos, *The Revolutionary Ideas of Karl Marx*, London: Bookmarks, 2004.

A. Callinicos, *Bonfire of Illusions: The Twin Crisis of the Liberal World*, Cambridge: Polity, 2010.

J. Charlton, *The Chartists: The First National Workers Movement*, London: Pluto Press, 1997.

T. Cliff, 'Marxism and the collectivisation of agriculture' *International Socialism Journal* No. 19, Winter 1964–65.

T. Cliff, *State Capitalism in Russia*, London: Bookmarks, 1988.

T. Cliff and D. Gluckstein, *Marxism and Trade Union Struggle: The General Strike of 1926*, London: Bookmarks, 1986.

G. A. Cohen, 'Marx's dialectic of labour', *Philosophy and Social Affairs*, Vol. 3, No. 3, 1974, pp. 235–61.

G. Cohen, *Karl Marx's Theory of History*, Oxford: Oxford University Press, 2000.

R. Dahl, *A Preface to Economic Democracy*, Berkeley, CA: University of California Press, 1985.

P. Devine, *Democracy and Economic Planning*, Cambridge: Polity, 1988.

M. Dobb, *Political Economy and Capitalism*, London: Routledge, 1937.

H. Draper, *Karl Marx's Theory of Revolution: Volume 1: State and Bureaucracy*, New York: Monthly Review Press, 1977.

H. Draper, *Karl Marx's Theory of Revolution Volume 2: The Politics of Social Classes*, New York: Monthly Review Press, 1978.

H. Draper, *Karl Marx's Theory of Revolution: Volume 3: The Dictatorship of the Proletariat*, New York: Monthly Review Press, 1986.

H. Draper, *Karl Marx's Theory of Revolution. Volume. 4: Critique of Other Socialisms*, New York: Monthly Review, 1990.

R. Dunayevskaya, *The Marxist-Humanist Theory of State Capitalism*, Chicago: News and Letters, 1992.

L. Feuerbach, *The Essence of Christianity*, New York: Cosimo, 2008.

E. Fischer, *The Necessity of Art*, Harmondsworth: Penguin Books, 1978.

D. Foley, *Understanding Capital: Marx's Economic Theory*, Harvard, MA: Harvard University Press, 1986.

P. Foot, *The Vote: How it was Won and How it was Undermined*, London: Penguin-Viking, 2005.

J. B. Foster, *The Ecological Revolution*, New York: Monthly Review Press, 2009.

G. Fredrickson, *Racism: A Short History*, Princeton, NJ: Princeton University Press, 2003.

L. German, *Material Girls: Women, Men and Work*, London: Bookmarks, 2007.

A. Gilbert, *Marx's Politics: Communists and Citizens*, Oxford: Martin Robertson, 1981.

C. Goodrich, *The Frontier of Control: a Study of British Workshop Politics*, New York: Harcourt, Brace and Howe, 1921.

A. Gramsci, *Selections from the Prison Notebooks*, London: Lawrence & Wishart, 1971.

C. Harman, 'Engels and the origin of human society', *International Socialism Journal*, Vol. 2, No. 65, Winter 1994.

C. Harman, *Marxism and History*, London: Bookmarks, 1998.

C. Harman, *A People's History of the World*, London: Verso, 2008.

C. Harman, *Zombie Capitalism*, London: Bookmarks, 2010.

D. Harvey, *A Brief History of Neoliberalism*, Oxford: Oxford University Press, 2005.

D. Harvey, *The Limits to Capital*, London: Verso, 2006.

D. Harvey, *The Enigma of Capital*, London: Profile Books, 2010.

C. Hill, 'The English civil war interpreted by Marx and Engels', *Science and Society*, Vol. 12, No. 1, 1948, pp. 130–56.

C. Hill, *The World Turned Upside Down: Radical Ideas During the English Revolution*, Harmondsworth: Penguin, 1975.

J. Holloway, *Changing the World Without Taking Power: The Meaning of Revolution Today*, London: Pluto Press, 2003.

S. Hook, *From Hegel to Marx: Studies in the Intellectual Development of Karl Marx*, New York: Colombia University Press, 1994.

S. Hook, *Towards the Understanding of Karl Marx*, New York: Prometheus Books, 2002.

T. Hunt, *The Frock-coated Communist: The Revolutionary Life of Friedrich Engels*, London: Allen Lane, 2009.

M. Itoh, *Value and Crisis*, London: Pluto Press, 1980.

K. Korsch, *Karl Marx*, New York: Russell and Russell, 1963.

E. Leacock, *Myths of Male Dominance*, New York: Monthly Review Press, 1981.

V. Lenin, *Left Wing Communism – An Infantile Disorder* in V. Lenin, *Selected Works*, Volume 3, Moscow: Progress Publishers, 1975.

V. Lenin, *What is to be Done* in *Selected Works*, Volume 1, Moscow: Progress Publishers, 1976.

V. Lenin, *State and Revolution*, Dublin: Bookmarks, 2004.

P. Linebaugh, *The London Hanged: Crime and Civil Society in the Eighteenth Century*, London: Verso, 2003.

P. Lissagray, *The History of the Paris Commune*, London: New Park, 1976.

M. Lowy, *Georg Lukács: from Romanticism to Bolshevism*, London: New Left Books, 1979.

M. Lowy, *The Theory of Revolution in the Young Marx*, Chicago: Haymarket Books, 2005.

G. Lukács, *The Young Hegel*, London: Merlin, 1938

G. Lukács, *History and Class Consciousness*, London: Merlin, 1971.

S. Lukes, *Power: A Radical View*, Basingstoke: Palgrave Macmillan, 2005.

R. Luxemburg, *The Accumulation of Capital*, New York: Monthly Review Press, 1968.

P. Maksakovsky, 'The general theory of the cycle', *Historical Materialism* Vol. 10, No. 3, 2002, pp. 133–94.

E. Mandel, *The Formation of The Economic Thought of Karl Marx*, London: Verso, 1971.

H. Marcuse, *Reason and Revolution*, Oxford: Oxford University Press, 1941.

D. McClellan, *The Young Hegelians and Karl Marx*, London: Macmillan, 1969.

I. Meszaros, *Marx's Theory of Alienation*, London: Merlin Press, 1972.

I. Meszaros, *The Power of Ideology*, Hemel Hempstead: Harvester, 1989.

R. Miles, *Capitalism and Unfree Labour: Anomaly or Necessity*, London: Tavistock, 1987.

R. Miles, *Racism*, London: Routledge, 1989.

R. Miliband, *The State in Capitalist Society*, London: Quartet, 1973.

J. Molyneaux, *Is Human Nature a Barrier to Socialism?* London: Socialist Worker, 1993.

A. Nimtz, *Marx and Engels: Their Contribution to the Democratic Breakthrough*, New York: State University of New York Press, 2000.

A. Nove, *The Economics of Feasible Socialism*, London: Allen & Unwin, 1983.

B. Ollman, *Alienation: Marx's Conception of Man in Capitalist Society*, Cambridge: Cambridge University Press, 1976.

A. Pannekoek, *Workers' Councils*, Oakland, CA: AK Press, 2003.

E. Pashukanis, *The General Theory of Law and Marxism*, New Brunswick, NJ: Transaction Publishers, 2003.

O. Patterson, *Slavery and Social Death*, Harvard, MA: Harvard University Press, 1982.

L. Poliakov, *The History of Anti-Semitism*, Volume 2, London: Routledge, 1974.

N. Poulanzas, *Classes in Contemporary Capitalism*, London: New Left Books, 1975.

N. Poulanzas, *Political Power and Social Classes*, London: Verso, 1978.

S. S. Prawer, *Karl Marx and World Literature*, Oxford: Clarendon Press, 1976.

C. Robinson, *Black Marxism: The Making of the Black Radical Tradition*, Chapel Hill, NC: University of North Carolina Press, 2000.

D. Roediger, *The Wages of Whiteness: Race and The Making of the American Working Class*, London: Verso, 1999.

M. Rubel, *Marx: Life and Works*, London, Macmillan, 1980.

A. Shaikh, 'An introduction to the history of crisis theories', in *US Capitalism in Crisis*, New York: Union of Radical Political Economics, 1978, pp. 219–40.

A. Shaikh, 'Political economy and capitalism: Notes on Dobb's theory of crisis', *Cambridge Journal of Economics*, No. 2, 1978, pp. 233–51.

A. Shaikh, *The Current Economic Crisis: Causes and Implications*, Detroit: Against the Current, 1989.

A. Shaikh, 'Explaining the global economic crisis', *Historical Materialism*, Vol. 5, No. 1, 1999.

A. Soboul, *The French Revolution*, London: New Left Books, 1974.

G. E. M. de Ste Croix, *The Class Struggle in the Ancient World*, London: Duckworth, 1983.

P. Sweezy, *The Theory of Capitalist Development*, New York: Monthly Review, 1970.

C. Taylor, *Hegel*, Cambridge: Cambridge University Press, 1975.

E. P. Thompson, 'Time, work discipline and Industrial capitalism', *Past and Present*, Vol. 38, No. 1, 1967, pp. 56–97.

A. de Tocqueville, *Democracy in America*, London: Fontana, 1994.

R. Wilkinson and K. Pickett, *The Spirit Level: Why Equality is Better for Everyone*, London: Penguin, 2009.

E. Williams, *Capitalism and Slavery*, Richmond, NC: University of North Carolina Press, 1944.

R. Williams, *Keywords: A Vocabulary of Culture and Society*, London: Fontana, 1983.

E. O. Wright, *Class, Crisis and the State*, London: Verso, 1978.

E. O. Wright, *Envisioning Real Utopias*, London: Verso, 2010.

Index

Printed in Great Britain
by Amazon